POLICY PARADIGMS, TRANSNATIONALISM, AND DOMESTIC POLITICS

This collection of essays explores the relationship between transnationalism and domestic policy paradigms, enquiring into the circumstances under which the activities and ideas of transnational actors affect domestic policy paradigm development. The contributors examine the role of different types of transnational actors in policy paradigm construction and changes; they also investigate how domestic factors facilitate or impede the impact of transnational actors and refine our conceptual understanding of policy paradigms and our theories of processes of paradigm development and change.

The volume offers case studies of paradigm development in diverse policy domains, including recognition of same-sex unions, early childhood education and care, risk regulation of genetically modified organisms, and refugee and immigration policy. These case studies shed light on the roles of formal international organizations such as the OECD and the European Union, as well as informal international networks of state actors, transnational epistemic communities, and networks of private sector actors. Spanning the United States, Canada, and Europe, the case studies also provide insights into paradigm development in a variety of institutional and cultural domestic settings.

GRACE SKOGSTAD is a professor in the Department of Political Science at the University of Toronto.

Studies in Comparative Political Economy and Public Policy

Editors: MICHAEL HOWLETT, DAVID LAYCOCK, STEPHEN MCBRIDE, Simon Fraser University.

Studies in Comparative Political Economy and Public Policy is designed to showcase innovative approaches to political economy and public policy from a comparative perspective. While originating in Canada, the series will provide attractive offerings to a wide international audience, featuring studies with local, subnational, cross-national, and international empirical bases and theoretical frameworks.

Editorial Advisory Board

Jeffrey Ayres, St Michael's College, Vermont
Neil Bradford, University of Western Ontario
Janine Brodie, University of Alberta
William Carroll, University of Victoria
William Coleman, McMaster University
Rodney Haddow, University of Toronto
Jane Jenson, Université de Montréal
Laura Macdonald, Carleton University
Riane Mahon, Carleton University
Michael Mintrom, University of Auckland
Grace Skogstad, University of Toronto
Leah Vosko, York University
Kent Weaver, Brookings Institute
Linda White, University of Toronto
Robert Young, University of Western Ontario

For a list of books published in the series, see page 257.

Policy Paradigms, Transnationalism, and Domestic Politics

Edited by Grace Skogstad

UNIVERSITY OF TORONTO PRESS
Toronto Buffalo London

© University of Toronto Press 2011
Toronto Buffalo London
utorontopress.com

ISBN 978-1-4426-4369-7 (cloth)
ISBN 978-1-4426-1220-4 (paper)

Library and Archives Canada Cataloguing in Publication

Policy paradigms, transnationalism, and domestic politics / edited by
Grace Skogstad.

Includes bibliographical references.
ISBN 978-1-4426-4369-7 (bound).   ISBN 978-1-4426-1220-4 (pbk.)

1. International organization.   2. International agencies.   3. Political
planning – Canada.   4. Policy sciences.   I. Skogstad, Grace, 1948–

JZ4850.P64 2011   341.2   C2011-904007-7

Cover illustration: iStock.com/dem10

University of Toronto Press acknowledges the financial assistance to its
publishing program of the Canada Council for the Arts and the Ontario
Arts Council.

University of Toronto Press acknowledges the financial support for its
publishing activities of the Government of Canada through the Canada
Book Fund.

Canada Council   Conseil des Arts
for the Arts   du Canada

ONTARIO ARTS COUNCIL
CONSEIL DES ARTS DE L'ONTARIO

Contents

Acknowledgments

This book had its origins in a one-day workshop at the School of Public Policy and Governance at the University of Toronto in April 2008. This workshop was part of a seminar series organized by me and my colleague Steven Bernstein on the theme of Internationalization and Public Policy. The 2008 workshop, exploring how developments in the international political economy were impacting public policy paradigm change, provided the occasion for the authors who appear in this book to meet and present early versions of their chapters. Funding for the workshop was provided by several academic units at the University of Toronto, and I would like to thank those units and their heads: David Cameron, chair of the Department of Political Science; Mark Stabile, director of the School of Public Policy and Governance; Janice Stein, director of the Munk Centre for International Studies (now the Munk School of Global Affairs); and Louis Pauly, director of the Centre for International Studies. Several others also helped launch the project by participating in the workshop and/or acting as official discussants for the workshop papers: Steven Bernstein, Martin Hering, Katerina Linos, Willem Maas, Ito Peng, and Carolyn Tuohy. Special thanks are owed to Peter Hall, whose 1993 article in *Comparative Politics*, 'Policy Paradigms, Social Learning, and the State,' was an important touchstone for the workshop. Peter attended the workshop, and his reflections, 'What have we learned about paradigm change?' at the day's end stimulated thinking about policy paradigms and their development in a context of transnationalism.

This is also the occasion to thank other individuals who have helped to bring this book to fruition. Celine Mulhern, then completing her PhD in political science, was invaluable in organizing the workshop.

Jenn Wallner, David Houle, and Matthieu Mondou have been very able research assistants for the project. At the University of Toronto Press, Daniel Quinlan, Cathy Frost, and Anne Laughlin have been very helpful editors. I thank them, as well as the anonymous reviewers whose thoughtful comments have improved the manuscript. Finally, I am enormously grateful to my fellow contributors to this book and thank them for their patience and goodwill during the inevitable delays of peer review and publication.

Grace Skogstad

Abbreviations

AcSEC	Accounting Standards Executive Committee
AICPA	American Institute of Certified Public Accountants
AIP	Agreement in Principle
APEC	Asia-Pacific Economic Cooperation
BVH	Bundesverband Homosexualitaet (Federal Association of Homosexuality)
CAP	Canada Assistance Plan
CAP	Common Agricultural Policy
CAPC	Community Action Program for Children
CCED	Child care expense deduction
CDU	Christian Democratic Union
CIAR/CIFAR	Canadian Institute for Advanced Research
CNC	Conseil national de la comptabilité
CSU	Christian Social Union
ECDA	Federal-Provincial-Territorial Early Childhood Agreement
ECD	Early Childhood Development
ECE	Early Childhood Education
ECEC	Early Childhood Education and Care
ECJ	European Court of Justice
ECtHR	European Court of Human Rights
EFSA	European Food Safety Authority
EITF	Emerging Issues Task Force
ELCC	Early learning and child care
EMS	European Monetary System
EMU	European Monetary Union
EC	European Community

EP	European Parliament
EU	European Union
FAS	Financial Accounting Standards
FASB	Financial Accounting Standards Board
FDP	Freie Demokratische Partei (Free Democratic Party)
FMVSS	Federal Motor Vehicle Safety Standards
GAAP	Generally Accepted Accounting Principles
GGN	Global government network
GMO	Genetically modified organism
GTRs	Global Technical Regulations
IAS	International Accounting Standards
IASC	International Accounting Standards Committee
IASB	International Accounting Standards Board
IFRS	International Financial Reporting Standards
IGC	Inter-Governmental Consultation on Asylum, Refugee and Migration Policies
ILGA	International Lesbian and Gay Association
IO	International organization
IOM	International Organization for Migration
IR	International relations
IRPA	Immigrant and Refugee Protection Act
JASIC	Japan Automobile Standards Internationalization Center
LGBT	Lesbian, Gay, Bisexual, and Transgender
LMO	Living modified organism
LPartG	Lebenspartnerschaftsgesetz
LSVD	Lesben- und Schwulenverband in Deutschland (Lesbian and Gay Federation in Germany)
MEP	Member of the European Parliament
MFA	Multilateral Framework on Early Learning and Child Care Agreement
NGO	Non-governmental organization
NHTSA	National Highway and Transport Safety Administration
PCAOB	Public Company Accounting Oversight Board
PISA	Programme for International Student Assessment (OECD)
RCPs	Regional consultative processes
RP	Registered partnership
SEC	Securities and Exchange Commission

SPS	Sanitary and Phytosanitary [Agreement]
SPD	Social Democratic Party
SSU	Same-sex union
STC	Safe Third Country
SVD	Schwulenverband in Deutschland (Gay Federation in Germany)
TIMSS	Trends in International Mathematics and Science Study (US Department of Education)
UNECE	United Nations Economic Commission for Europe
UNHCR	United Nations High Commissioner for Refugees
WP.29	Working Party 29 (UNECE)
WTO	World Trade Organization

POLICY PARADIGMS, TRANSNATIONALISM,
AND DOMESTIC POLITICS

1 Introduction: Policy Paradigms, Transnationalism, and Domestic Politics

GRACE SKOGSTAD AND VIVIEN A. SCHMIDT

Two literatures in the social sciences are reshaping our accounts of public policy development. Both are concerned with the role of ideas in the generation, continuity, and change of 'policy paradigms.' One highlights the role of ideas in policy making in national institutional contexts and has been the purview largely of political scientists in comparative politics and political economy. The other points to the diffusion of policy ideas in transnational contexts and is more the domain of international relations scholars. These two literatures rarely speak to one another, given differences in focus as well as in disciplinary field. Yet they could gain much from greater interchange about the questions that both confront involving how to account for the nature, processes, scope, and timing of ideational change. This book proposes just such an exchange of ideas about the role of ideas in transformative policy change.

Students of comparative political economy who have taken the 'ideational turn' in the social sciences (Blyth 1997; see also Béland and Cox 2010) generally focus on the policy paradigms (Hall 1993), programmatic ideas, frames, and discourses (Campbell 2002; Schmidt 2008) that serve to generate new kinds of public action on the basis of new principles and norms. They tend to consider how such ideas become embedded in political discourses, collective identities, and institutions (Berman 2001), acting as 'cognitive locks' that create 'an intellectual path dependency in policy making' (Blyth 2001, 4). But especially more recently, they also explore how (other) ideas – both their substance and the discourse around them – can break these 'cognitive locks' in order to reorient public policies on the basis of new principles of necessary and appropriate courses of action (Blyth 2002; Cox 2001; Schmidt

2008; Hay 2006). Explaining both these developments – how and why interpretive frameworks get locked into public policy ideas and actions and how, why, and when they are later unlocked – in national institutional contexts is a major puzzle and preoccupation of these political scientists.

For their part, international relations scholars who have taken the 'constructivist' turn in the social sciences (Finnemore 1996; Ruggie 1998; Checkel 1999) point to specific sets of ideas that have diffused spatially, such as norms of human rights (Keck and Sikkink 1998), cultural beliefs about the authority of science (Drori et al. 2003), ideas about appropriate and effective policy instruments (Busch, Jörgens, and Tews 2005), and policy paradigms of economic and political liberalism (Simmons and Elkins 2004; Simmons, Dobbin, and Garrett 2006; Eising 2002; Swank 2006; Weyland 2005; Orenstein 2008). They explore the active role of a diverse group of transnational actors in ideational and policy diffusion processes that includes international organizations, transgovernmental networks of state actors, epistemic communities, networks of private authority, and advocacy networks (Keohane and Nye 1974; Haas 1992; Finnemore and Sikkink 1998; Cutler, Haufler, and Porter 1999; Barnett and Finnemore 2004; Slaughter 2004; Miller 2007; Orenstein 2008). An ancillary, sociological, literature argues that a world culture of universalistic models of appropriate state behaviour and epistemic understandings of how the world works has been constructed and diffused globally, and that transnational state and non-state actors have played a major role in this development (Meyer, Ramirez, and Soysal 1992; Boli and Thomas 1997; Meyer et al. 1997a).

Does the literature on policy diffusion in the transnational context give us purchase on why ideas can get locked in and also why they can become 'unlocked' in the national context? Does the literature on national policy paradigms give us insight into why ideas may not diffuse as expected in the international arena? There are no simple answers to these questions. Even while there is a growing literature that suggests that policy ideas diffuse transnationally, especially from international institutions to developing countries, empirical studies often point to the domestic limits to the diffusion of ideas and the influence of transnational actors as ideational entrepreneurs. Sectoral policy paradigms, particularly those that entail redistributive outcomes, vary considerably across countries. Transnational actors' ideas and global norms often fail to penetrate domestic policy making, being obstructed by domestic political, institutional, and cultural factors (Cortell and Davis, 1996, 2000; Risse-Kappen 1995; Checkel 1999; Legro 1997; Kollman 2007). Moreover, where transnational norms are not rejected, they are likely to be localized, rather than adopted wholesale (Acharya 2004). By the same token, however, national policy paradigms are far from impervious to transnational ideas and norms. As perceptions of what is appropriate or even necessary shift in the international arena, strategic national policy actors reinterpret and articulate those ideas in ways that resonate with national publics (Hay 2001; Schmidt 2002a). The relationship between transnationalism and domestic policy paradigms thus is complicated and not readily revealed by studies that show broad patterns over time of countries adopting seemingly similar institutions and policies (e.g., Simmons and Elkins 2004; Meyer et al. 1997a, b). As students of public policy are only too aware, similar organizational forms and public polices can function quite differently and have different meanings in different contexts.

This edited collection sets itself the task of helping to elucidate the relationship between domestic policy paradigms and transnationalism. As used here, transnationalism entails two phenomena: first, the regularized interactions of state and non-state actors across and beyond national borders with the intent to shape political and social outcomes; and second, the existence and influence of transcendent cultural frames and principles that constitute part of the global order (Boli and Thomas 1997; Meyer et al. 1997a). The collection inquires into the circumstances under which the ideas of transnational actors and their norm-, rule-, and knowledge-making activities affect policy paradigm development. The focus is mainly on domestic policy paradigms, but some attention is also given to transnational policy paradigm development. The book seeks to bridge the theoretical perspectives of comparative politics scholars who, as noted earlier, have overwhelmingly focused on the domestic dynamics and agents of paradigm change (Hall 1993; Blyth 2002; Schmidt 2002a) with those of international relations scholars who have addressed the construction and diffusion of international norms and knowledge/epistemes.

The book has three objectives. The first is to refine our conceptual understanding of policy paradigms and our theories of processes of paradigm development and change. The second is to examine the role and dynamics of different types of transnational actors and transnational ideas in policy paradigm construction and change in Europe and North America. And the third, closely related, objective is to uncover further how domestic factors – institutional, cultural, and discursive – interact with transnational actors and their ideas to affect domestic and transnational policy paradigm development.

To accomplish these three goals, the book presents a series of case studies that examine the activities of a variety of transnational political actors in different policy domains in both North America and Europe. Several chapters explore the interrelationship between international and domestic norms and epistemes, examining how, as well as when, shifting international ideas regarding appropriate standards of behaviour (norms) and/or knowledge about cause-effect relationships affect domestic policy paradigm development. Informing the individual case studies is a body of diverse literature that provides neither a single conceptualization of policy paradigms nor a uniform theory of how, when, and why policy paradigms change. Exactly how the processes by which transnational and domestic ideas and actors interact in policy paradigm development and change remains speculative and has been as much a matter of inductive generalization from empirical investigation as of deductive theorizing. The remainder of this Introduction reviews literature on paradigm change and describes how the book's chapters, individually and collectively, are positioned to provide some early answers to the questions at the core of this book.

Policy Paradigms and Other Ideas

What are policy paradigms and why are they worthy of investigation? An answer to this question is found in agreement among scholars of comparative politics that 'normal' policy making is guided by more or less coherent interpretive frameworks that consist of beliefs about how the world works and should work in a policy domain. Hall (1993), drawing on Thomas Kuhn's (1970) seminal work in the philosophy of science, described these interpretive frameworks as policy paradigms (see also Majone 1989; Schmidt 2002a, 222–5). Kuhn argued that the scientific community is dominated by one 'paradigm,' which bundles together certain theories, objectives, instruments, ideals, goals, and methods. Although he observed that 'fully elaborated' policy paradigms did not exist in all policy fields – in some fields the ideas affecting policy might be more loosely webbed (Hall 1993, 291) – Hall did argue for a single 'policy paradigm' in macroeconomic policy. He defined its constituent elements to be consensual beliefs about the problems to be addressed in that policy domain, the goals of public policies, and the appropriate means or policy instruments to realize them. This set of ideas structures policy making by virtue of being 'embedded in the very terminology through which policymakers communicate about their work, and it is influential precisely because so much of it is taken for granted and unamenable to scrutiny as a whole' (279).

Other scholars use different terms to capture the same theme of the importance for policy making of delimiting ideas/beliefs. For example, Schön and Rein (1994, 23) emphasize the importance of a (policy) frame or structure of tacit 'beliefs, perceptions and appreciations' to determine 'what counts as a fact and what arguments are taken to be compelling and relevant.' Bleich (2002, 1063), also preferring the term 'frame,' defines it in terms analogous to a policy paradigm: 'a set of cognitive and moral maps that orients an actor within a policy sphere,' that helps 'actors identify problems and specify and prioritize their interests and goals,' and points 'toward causal and normative judgements about effective and appropriate policies in ways that tend to propel policy down a particular path and to reinforce it once on that path.' The concept of *référentiel*, or frame of reference, as used by French social scientists (Jobert and Muller 1987; Jobert 1989; Muller 1995; Surel 1995), similarly posits that policy makers in a given policy domain adhere to a common intellectual framework that entails shared values and norms about desirable goals, 'algorithms' or theories of causal relations, and images of society and the sector. Much as in a Kuhnian/Hall paradigm, this référentiel provides the shared intellectual framework for finding solutions to policy problems (Jobert 1992: 17; Muller 1995). Whatever the term – policy paradigm, frame, or frame of reference – the significant point is that policy outcomes in a given policy domain will normally be consistent with the prevalent dominant ideas about politically feasible, practical, and desirable policies.

How do policy paradigms differ from other types of ideas? This question is discussed more fully by Vivien Schmidt in chapter 2, where, consistent with Campbell (1998, 2002), she situates policy paradigms within a broader set of ideas that, if understood as 'public philosophies' or 'world views' (*Weltanshauung*), transcend policy domains and are, arguably, at a deeper level of ideas than sectoral policy paradigms. Policy paradigms can also be distinguished from the 'programmatic ideas' that are specific to the choice and calibration of policy instruments and can be conceived as causal ideas about how to realize policy goals or solve policy problems (Weir 1992; Campbell 2002). The distinction between policy paradigms and 'policy regimes' (Wilson 2000; Esping-Anderson

1993) or 'regulatory regimes' (Moran and Prosser 1994; Harris and Milkis 1996) is perhaps less obvious. 'Regimes' denotes not only the shared ideational framework of policy actors but also the structural arrangements within which ideas are embedded. Insofar as the essence of a policy paradigm is that it endures over time in the templates that guide political actors' approaches to public policies as well as in extant public policies, some scholars argue that the organizational structures within which a paradigm is institutionalized are a constitutive element of the paradigm itself (Carson, Burns, and Calvo 2009). Still, analytically at least, it is useful to distinguish the ideational component of a policy regime (the policy paradigm) from the structures of rules and power relationships within which policy making proceeds, since doing so allows us to reflect on how the ideational and the institutional – as well as the material – elements of policy domains relate to and reinforce one another.

How do policy paradigms differ from the ideational concepts to which international relations scholars ascribe causal force: international regimes, norms, and epistemes? International regimes, as defined by Krasner (1983a, 1), are 'principles, norms, rules, and decision-making procedures around which actor expectations converge in a given issue-area.' Fortified and given authority by international institutions and rules, ideas within international regimes are by definition virtually assured of having an impact on domestic policy making, as the examples of 'embedded liberalism' in the post-war period (Ruggie 1982) and the neoliberal 'Washington consensus' in the late twentieth century (Gore 2000) illustrate. International regimes are thus an important dimension of transnationalism, and theorizing about their independent capacity to shape domestic politics, as noted later in this Introduction, can help us to understand policy paradigm development (Krasner 1983b). Several contributions to this text do examine how the constitutive elements of international regimes (norms and epistemes) affect policy paradigm development.

Both comparative politics and international relations scholars have studied norms and epistemes, and these concepts thus provide a bridge between domestic policy paradigms and transnational actors and their interactions. Norms concern appropriate standards of behaviour or desirable actions that are shared by members of a social entity (Campbell 2002; Finnemore 1996). Norms are more specific ideas than policy paradigms. While a norm of universal human rights, for example, may be one constituent idea in a social policy or citizenship paradigm, the paradigm will comprise not only other norms (about how things ought to work) but also cognitive ideas about how the world works (i.e., what is) (Finnemore and Sikkink 1998, 891). Whereas norms are ideas about what ought to be, epistemes are ideas about what constitutes knowledge and, by extension, what kinds of expertise are legitimate and relevant in the construction of such knowledge (Carson, Burns, and Calvo 2009, 24). Policy paradigms include both normative and cognitive ideas.

If, in summary of the discussion to this point, there is (rough) agreement that it is useful to define the overarching ideas – about important policy problems and goals and suitable means and actors for addressing and achieving them – that normally guide domestic policy making in a given policy domain, and to distinguish these paradigms from other types of ideas, consensus stops here. Among the points of debate are, first, the degree of internal coherence that can be expected of sectoral policy paradigms and, second, whether one paradigm is likely to dominate in a given policy domain (with respect to refugee, immigration, and childcare policy, for example) or whether competing paradigms exist in tension with one another even while one is hegemonic. Hall (1993) argued that a single, coherent paradigm of macroeconomic policy dominated during the period that he investigated (1970 to late 1980s). Against this view, others suggest that competing ideational frameworks are likely to coexist even while one dominates temporally (Schmidt 2002b, 220–5) and the dominant paradigm itself can be controversial (Jobert 1992, 221). The case for competing belief systems is made most explicitly by Sabatier (1987, 1993) and his co-author, Jenkins-Smith (Sabatier and Jenkins-Smith 1993). Although they accept the premise of a dominant paradigm – or belief system, to use their language – they argue that it will be opposed by minority belief systems. The advocacy coalitions that support these minority belief systems wait in the wings, invoking different cognitive ideas and appealing to alternative sets of normative values in the polity to contest the validity of the dominant paradigm. Likewise, analysts who eschew the term 'policy paradigm' for other terms – frame, référentiel – are likely to stress that sectoral interpretive frameworks are more heterogeneous and ambiguous than scientific paradigms (Jobert 1989; Surel 2000).

As discussed further below, assumptions about whether there exists a single, coherent paradigm in a policy sector or whether the dominant paradigm is likely to be neither internally consistent nor without rivals have implications for theories of paradigm change. Presumably paradigms that are neither internally consistent nor unrivalled will be more vulnerable to change.

How Do Paradigms Develop and Change?

Scholars have documented how extant policy ideas become embedded in ways of thinking about policy, in political and economic institutions, and in public policies themselves (Berger 1996; Keohane and Milner 1996; Skogstad 1998; Weiss 1998; Bernstein and Cashore 2000; Scharpf and Schmidt 2000; Schmidt 2002a; Kahler and Lake 2003; Campbell 2004). Moreover, as Tony Porter argues in his chapter in this book, paradigms are likely to be enmeshed with the material world and inscribed in technologies and built environments. If policy paradigms are ideationally and materially inscribed, how are their ideas unlocked? Addressing this question is at the heart of developing a theory of policy paradigm development and requires seeking answers to questions such as the following. Under what circumstances – when and how – are new policy paradigms constructed and adopted? How does paradigm change unfold? Is it a relatively abrupt transition to a new paradigm? Or does it occur more slowly, via incremental adjustments that add up to system-shifting changes over time? How do we know when paradigm change has occurred, especially when it is the result of incremental changes over time and the possibility exists for putative paradigm-shifting developments to be reversed in the short term? When paradigms do change, what does the replacement paradigm look like? Are its constitutive ideas incommensurable with those of the paradigm it has replaced? Alternatively, are replacement paradigms more likely to be hybrids that retain vestiges of ideas in the old paradigm?

In the search for answers to these questions, it is helpful to distinguish two models of *how* paradigm development proceeds. One model, documented by Hall (1993), adopts Kuhnian logic to posit paradigm change as an episodic rupture with the past. A second, favoured by social scientists, describes paradigm change as an evolutionary process. We begin with Hall (1993) and other scholars who point to 'anomalous outcomes,' policy failures, and crises as the initial triggers for paradigm change. For Hall, paradigm change begins with anomalies: events that do not fit with paradigmatic assumptions about how the world works and the failure of policies predicated on this paradigm to solve the problems brought on by those events. In his case of macroeconomic policy, the anomalous events were developments that contradicted Keynesian assumptions about how economies work. When these anomalies could not be corrected with incremental reforms, the normal equilibrium was punctured, and the precondition existed for another, alternative and incommensurable paradigm (monetarism) to displace Keynesianism.

Whereas Hall and others define anomalies and subsequent policy failures to correct them as the trigger for paradigm change, other social scientists demarcate a crisis, or another 'stressor,' such as demographic changes or shifts in modes of production (Wilson 2000), as a precipitating event. Crises precipitated by events become the 'critical moments' in which 'collective memories' are made or changed, as in the case of Swedish collective bargaining institutions in the 1930s (Rothstein 2005, chap. 8); the 'critical junctures' when public debates serve to reframe how countries 'come to terms with the past,' as in Germany and Austria in the 1980s with regard to the Nazi period (Art 2006); and the times of 'great transformations,' when ideas serve to recast political economic policies, as occurred during the 'disembedding' of liberalism in the United States and Sweden beginning in the 1980s (Blyth 2002). Still, what constitutes a crisis and who defines it is not self-evident and, as discussed further below, is usually a matter of discursive construction. Those who get to interpret the crisis to policy makers and to specify models to tame it can be expected to have an important impact on policy paradigm developments (Abdelal, Blyth, and Parsons 2010, 234).

As a model of paradigm development and change, the Kuhn/Hall model is a highly systemic view of paradigms, in which in response to crisis the system as a whole undergoes revolutionary change to another system. This model has been critiqued by both philosophers of science and social scientists. Philosophers of science criticized Kuhn's paradigm approach as too simplistic in its view of progress through incommensurable system change. They argued that ideational change occurs via systemically overlapping 'research programmes' (Lakatos 1971), historically developed 'research traditions' (Laudan 1977), or evolving 'disciplinary enterprises' (Toulmin 1972), where certain elements in a program, tradition, or enterprise change while others, whether the goals, problems, procedures, methods, concepts, or even ideals, continue (Schmidt 1986, 1988). In Surel's words (2000, 508), 'Far from making a clean slate of the past, a new societal paradigm must in effect be composed of previous cognitive and normative structures;' new paradigms are 're-translations' and 'new hierarchical rankings' of the elements of earlier paradigms. In like vein, others describe paradigm development as entailing reconfigurations of previous cognitive and normative structures through processes of 'bricolage' or 'assemblage' (Douglas 1986; Seitz 1961) – a view advanced by Tony Porter in his chapter in this book – or combinations of new and old ideas in new 'translations' (Campbell 2004, 163). Investigation of policy paradigm change across six different policy domains in the European Union lends support to the view that a replacement paradigm is likely to be 'a reordering' of its guiding principles and underlying assumptions, rather than incommensurate with antecedent principles/assumptions – and indeed, 'presented as a means for protecting the achieved goals of the earlier paradigm' (Carson, Burns, and Calvo 2009, 360).

As an alternative to the Kuhn/Hall model of an episodic shift to an incommensurable paradigm, a second model views paradigm change as an evolutionary process, the result of cumulative reforms that may take a decade or more (Sabatier 1993). Seemingly small changes over time, which appear not to have visible or immediate impacts in the basic characteristics and goals of a policy paradigm can nonetheless add up to a change in its basic philosophy (Hinrichs and Kangas 2003; Howlett and Cashore 2009). Here, the very use of the term 'paradigm' to describe such change is sometimes contested, 'ideational' change being the preferred substitute term. In such a view, rather than focusing on how an all-encompassing system of ideas shifts radically in response to crisis, theories of paradigm development are better directed towards demonstrating how and why an agreed set of loosely interrelated ideas changes slowly over time. Paradigm shift, in this view, is more a metaphor for major ideational change than it is a specification of a crisis-driven revolutionary moment of change.

Evolutionary models of paradigm change draw on a host of historical institutionalist concepts to explain processes of change. They include 'layering,' 'conversion,' 'reactive sequences,' and 'policy drift.' Change via layering comes with the addition of new elements to an existing institution (Thelen 2002; 2004, 35). Change via conversion occurs with the adoption of new goals that alter the institutional role or core objectives of an institution (Thelen 2002, 229). Change via reactive sequences takes place when each event in a chain of temporally ordered and causally connected events is both a reaction to antecedent events and a cause of subsequent events (Mahoney 2000, 509, 526). And change via drift results from the failure of policy makers to deal with social and economic change, so that while the institution (paradigm) remains, its impact is no longer the same (Hacker 2004).

The first concept, layering, is used by Kay (2007) to explain the emergence of a new synthetic paradigm of 'universalism plus choice' in Australian health care. Kay argues that layering/adding a public health insurance scheme to a private health insurance plan produced tensions that had to be, and were, accommodated in a new paradigm. Unlike the paradigms described by Kuhn or Hall, synthetic paradigms, says Kay (2007, 584), are not 'necessarily consistent or cogent,' as the Australian public and private systems coexist without either being dominant. Palier (2005) also uses the concept of layering, arguing that the incremental layering of new policies on top of old ones effected a paradigm change in France's welfare state policy. Daugbjerg (2009) explains the evolution of the European Union's Common Agricultural Policy (CAP) to be the outcome of reactive sequences: the feedback effects of *incremental* policy adjustments over time resulted in substantial change to the CAP: 'Each step in the reform sequence was made possible by previous events which decreased the distance to other policy options which earlier in the reform sequence would have been politically unrealistic.' Béland (2007) says all of layering, conversion, and policy drift help to account for changes over time in 'the meaning and status' of American social security, that is, its evolution from a family protection paradigm that emphasized redistribution to a financial paradigm that emphasizes privatization. Finally, without explicitly using these terms, processes of conversion (adding new policy goals to old ones) and reactive sequences (cumulative policy feedback effects from changes to policy instruments and their settings) have been used to explain agricultural policy change in the European Union (Garzon 2006) and North America and Australia (Coleman, Skogstad, and Atkinson 1997).

An evolutionary model that views policy paradigm change to be the result of incremental adjustments to an ideational framework over time raises some important questions of its own. How do we demarcate the moment at which a new paradigm can be said to be in place – that is, when steps towards it have congealed to the point that they are no longer reversible? This moment may be unclear, as vestiges of the old paradigm linger in the replacement paradigm. This dilemma leads some scholars to argue that paradigm change is complete only when the replacement paradigm is institutionalized, that is, when its normative and epistemic claims are inscribed in (new) public policies, (revised) organizational structures, and/or accorded legitimacy by those who previously opposed it (Carson, Burns, and Calvo 2009, 21; Wilson 2000).

Whether paradigm development adheres to a punctuated equilibrium or an incremental/evolutionary model, it is the work of political actors – and is therefore highly contingent. Evolutionary/incremental models of paradigm change tend to focus their accounts on political actors endogenous to the policy subsystem and the cumulative impacts on interpretive frameworks that result from the negotiations, subterfuge strategies, and/or opportunistic behaviours of these actors (Coleman, Skogstad, and Atkinson 1996; Mahoney and Thelen 2010). By contrast, episodic models of paradigm change, as abrupt ruptures with the past, usually turn to actors exogenous to the policy subsystem to explain transformative ideational change. Thus, Hall (1993), for example, argued that the transition from Keynesianism to monetarism necessitated a shift in the locus of authority that saw the installation of new political decision makers wedded to the new paradigm.

Theorizing about which political actors matter and why for policy paradigm development is closely linked to the relative importance ascribed to puzzling, persuasion, and powering dynamics in 'unlocking' the policy ideas that constitute policy-making cognitive and normative templates, and in thereby providing a key that opens the door to other templates (Blyth 2007; Mandelkern and Shalev 2010). Puzzling accounts emphasize the importance of an alternative paradigm to provide guidance in contexts of uncertainty. They often stress the role of knowledge elites in constructing and legitimating alternative policy paradigms; those who hold power or aspire to power learn from these experts about how to proceed, for example, by adopting different understandings of policy problems and solutions. Such knowledge elites appear to be particularly influential when cognitive/epistemic beliefs (about how the world works) are under challenge and/or destabilized.

For their part, persuasion accounts stress the capacity of political actors to use discourses, arguments, and framing strategies to delegitimize an existing paradigm and/or present an alternative paradigm in a way that resonates (Schmidt 2001, 2002b, 2008; Bhatia and Coleman 2003). Stories or narratives, metaphors that rely on shared cultural understandings and memories, and other images are invoked to make sense of complicated situations and articulate what could be and why the 'could' should be (Hajer 1993, 2003; Rein and Schön 1993; Roe 1994; Schlesinger and Lau 2000; Fischer 2003, chap 8;). Some persuasion accounts focus on inter-elite persuasion and argue that persuasion is an important dynamic in ideational change in situations of uncertainty (crisis) (Blyth 2007). Others who emphasize the importance of persuasion focus on

the need to convince a broader array of political actors of the meaning of events and the need for change. Moreover, just who needs to be
persuaded varies across institutional contexts, so that there is a need
to tailor persuasive discourses to the political actors whose consent is
needed for change (Schmidt 2002b, chap. 2). In this more polity-wide
persuasive exercise, the media are likely to play an influential role in
disseminating and popularizing replacement paradigms (Wilson 2000;
Hall 1993).

Where persuasion dynamics are viewed as vital to paradigm transformation, what matters above all are discursively strategic political actors
and their capacity to exploit contextual developments, particularly contexts of uncertainty, to create a 'crisis narrative' that creates an opening
for new understandings of public policy (Hay 2004, 505; Blyth 2007).
Such narratives around a 'crisis' may be *cognitive/epistemic* and highlight how causal assumptions about the way the world works are no
longer sustained by events, as Hall (1993) seems to suggest was the case
with macroeconomic policy paradigm change. Alternatively, the crisis
narrative may be a *normative* one, which undermines the values embedded in existing public policies, as Cox (2001) suggests made possible
welfare reform in Denmark when reformers established new collective
understandings of the purpose of the welfare state and new grounds
for evaluating the legitimacy of policy proposals. In the absence of a
crisis but in a context of shifting norms, discourses that can tap into the
altered normative context may be a successful strategy for paradigm
reform. Lindval (2006), for example, argues that shifting norms about
the purpose of political authority (i.e., the state) in the Swedish political
culture precipitated paradigm change in Swedish economic policy over
the 1970s and 1990s.

Compared with puzzling and persuasion accounts, powering accounts
highlight the conditioning effects of the political resources of political
actors on persuasion and puzzling dynamics and ultimately paradigm
development. Besides expertise (as mentioned above), resources of social
and political capital (the latter entailing links to veto-holding political
actors) are important to the success of persuasion efforts (Mandelkern and
Shalev 2010). Even when policy makers recognize that their paradigm
no longer solves the problems they confront and are therefore willing
to adopt a new paradigm, reformers may be impeded by institutionally embedded veto players. Paradigm change may then depend upon
a shift in the institutional venue of policy making to bring new actors
with new ideas into positions of authoritative decision making (Hall

1993; Howlett 1994; Howlett and Ramesh 2002; Wilson 2000; Walsh 2006). Failing a new site of policy making, a transition in political power that ushers into office a new coalition sympathetic to an alternative paradigm is likely necessary for paradigm change (Hall 1993; Coleman and Perl 1999; Hay 2001; Howlett and Ramesh 2002). Even then, a transition in the governing coalition before the paradigm change can be institutionalized can result in its stalling and even being reversed over time (Patashnik 2003; Skogstad 2008).

Many accounts of paradigm development attribute causal force to powering, puzzling, and persuasion dynamics in tandem. For example, Hall (1993) finds both puzzling and powering to be reinforcing causal mechanisms in the United Kingdom's macro-economic policy paradigm change. Mandelkern and Shalev (2010), who argue that persuasion depends upon political resources, merge puzzling, powering, and persuasion dynamics to explain why radical economic ideas were taken up in Israel at one time when similar ideas had earlier failed. Other accounts that stress the importance of puzzling and persuasion to transformative change are not unmindful of the structures of power within which policy developments unfold (Schmidt 2001, 2002b, 2008; Blyth, 2007). At issue in this book is not only how dynamics of puzzling, powering, and persuasion interact to make paradigm change more or less likely, but also how these dynamics and policy paradigm developments are affected by processes of transnationalism.

Transnationalism and Paradigm Development and Change

Since the 1970s students of comparative politics and international relations have theorized and investigated the impact of the international political economy on domestic politics, including how economic and political relations across states affect domestic political structures and the interests of domestic political actors (Gourevitch 1978) as well as domestic paths of political development (Skocpol 1979). Early attention to the influence of non-state transnational actors in the domestic and international political economies (Keohane and Nye 1977) has grown considerably, as scholars theorize the implications for domestic politics and policy development of a diverse group of transnational actors (cf. Dolowitz and Marsh 2000; Holzinger and Knill 2005; Knill 2005; and Stone 2004). Some are bottom up: civil society advocacy groups (Keck and Sikkink 1998), private actors (Cutler, Haufler, and Porter 1999), and epistemic communities (Haas 1992). Other transnational actors are top down; they are networks of state actors (Slaughter 2004) and formal international organizations, such as the OECD (Mahon and McBride 2008), the World Bank (Stone 2003; Orenstein 2008), and the European Union (Risse-Kappen 1995).

What, if any, are the implications for policy paradigm development of the interactions of such transnational state and non-state actors and the diffusion of policy ideas across and beyond national boundaries – phenomena described here as transnationalism (Djelic and Sahlin-Andersson 2006, 3; Orenstein and Schmitz 2006)? Do these activities, whose intent is to shape political and social outcomes at home and abroad – including by constructing and diffusing policy ideas and even having a role in their implementation – have transformative effects on the interpretive frameworks that guide sectoral policy making? A growing literature suggests that they do – under certain conditions.

First, transnational actors are the sources of (new) *norms* or standards of appropriate behaviour for domestic policy making (Finnemore and Sikkink 1998; Keck and Sikkink 1998; Risse and Sikkink 1999; Checkel 1999; Weaver 2010; Best 2010). Norm entrepreneurs – operating in international organizations, non-governmental organizations, and advocacy networks – transform a standard of appropriate behaviour in one or more countries into an international standard. They do so through processes of framing and socialization and succeed when state actors adopt these standards of behaviour, because they have come to believe in their appropriateness, seek to maintain or enhance their state's international status and legitimacy, and/or want to bolster their individual standing and self-esteem (Finnemore and Sikkink 1998, 895).

Second, and more broadly, transnational actors engage in *knowledge-making* and *knowledge-remaking* activities. These activities entail 'setting international knowledge standards'; 'bringing into being new ontological frameworks, classifications, and mappings that frame the conceptual underpinnings of global deliberation'; and 'constructing new deliberative spaces in which claimants acquire standing through claims to knowledge and expertise' (Miller 2007, 328). This epistemic role is played by international organizations, such as the European Union (Borzel and Risse 2000; Toller 2004; Dimitrova and Rhinard 2005), the United Nations (Barnett and Finnemore 2004), the World Bank (Stone 2003; Orenstein 2008), and the OECD (Mahon and McBride 2008; Dostal 2004; Djelic and Sahlin-Andersson 2006). It is also played by transnational epistemic communities: networks 'of professionals, with recognized expertise and competence in a particular domain and an authoritative claim to policy-relevant knowledge within that domain or issue-area' (Haas 1992, 3). Transgovernmental networks of state officials – more specifically, judges, regulators, parliamentarians – are yet other transnational actors whose roles in constructing, legitimating, and diffusing knowledge across states have been shown to have an impact on domestic policy development (Keohane and Nye 1974; Raustiala 2002; Slaughter 2004; Newman 2008; Levi-Faur 2005). These state actors, operating at a level below national actors, use their expertise and delegated authority to (re)define and (re)frame the domestic policy agendas of their own and other countries. By virtue of processes of learning and socialization within transnational networks, state actors not only transmit but also represent in domestic policy making the shared ideas of their fellow network members (Slaughter 2004). Finally, private actors, on their own or in conjunction with public actors, are also important transnational knowledge makers, particularly in technically complex policy areas where they often have a monopoly on policy-relevant information (Cutler, Haufler, and Porter 1999; Porter 2005).

A major question under investigation in this book is the circumstances under which transnational agents affect domestic policy paradigm development by virtue of their activities in constructing and diffusing norms and epistemes – the constitutive ideas of policy paradigms. While this question has increasingly been posed in the context of developing countries (cf. Hall 2003; Weyland 2004, 2005; Chwieroth 2007; Orenstein 2008; Best 2010; Weaver 2010), here the focus is on North America and Europe. By virtue of its institutional architecture and other features, the European Union is often cited as especially prone to the dynamics of transnational politics and the diffusion of policy ideas and interpretive templates (cf. Risse-Kappen 1995; Coleman and Perl 1999; Kaiser 2009). A substantial literature documents the role of transnational epistemic communities and advocacy groups in shaping EU discourse and policy ideas, especially under conditions of issue complexity (Verdun 1992; Kälberer 2003; Zito 2001; Zippel 2004), while another literature documents the prevalence of transnational networks of governmental officials, which often include private actors (e.g., Eberlein and Grande 2005; Eberlein and Newman 2008). Comparative case studies that include not only European countries but also Canada and the United States thus allow the opportunity to submit to plausibility probes (Eckstein 1975) some propositions that have emerged in this literature. Among the latter are claims that the role and impact of transnational actors in domestic paradigm development are likely to be affected by the following three factors: the attributes of transnational political actors, the features of the policy domain, and the attributes of the domestic target polity.

First, some transnational actors possess resources – of legal, expert, and moral authority – that make them more effective agents in constructing, legitimating, and diffusing (alternative) policy ideas and policy paradigms. Transgovernmental institutions that have been delegated legal authority usually enjoy sufficient legitimacy also to be able to bind their members to standards of behaviour. This authority can also extend to issuing non-binding standards and benchmarks of good behaviour that can be picked up by state and non-state actors. Some transnational actors – notably, international institutions, the World Bank, for example (Stone 2003; Orenstein 2008) – derive their capacity to construct and diffuse policy ideas and paradigms from their superior expertise and material resources of expertise. Others leverage their institutional authority into even greater authority (Barnett and Finnemore 2004; Mahon and McBride 2008) by acting as a 'hub' for other transnational actors, including transnational epistemic communities and transnational civil society groups. They often promote such non-state actors when they need the latter's expertise and legitimacy to bolster their own (on the behaviour of EU institutions in this regard, see Kaiser 2009).

Besides their resources of information, the influence of non-state transnational actors on paradigm development will often depend on their normative legitimacy (Keck and Sikkink 1998) as well as their internal coherence around epistemes and norms. The latter – internal cohesion on policy ideas – is as important to the influence of transnational political actors as it is to domestic epistemic actors (Mandelkern and Shalev 2010). Chwieroth (2007) argues that neoliberal economists were successful in persuading developing countries to liberalize controls over international capital markets in no small measure because their ideational coherence made it easier for politicians to resist societal demands to rebuff such ideas. International organizations that are internally divided over norms or that inscribe contradictory norms in their standards of behaviour are less likely to be able to diffuse their ideas and have them implemented (Bukovansky 2010; Weaver 2010). Finally, transnational actors are likely to be more influential in promoting their policy ideas across jurisdictions when they are not countered by other equally well-mobilized and resourced coalitions (Orenstein 2008).

Second, some policy domains are more fertile territory for transnational political actors than are others. Policy domains that are defined as 'technical' are theorized to be such a domain. Newman's (2008) study of the role of transgovernmental networks in the diffusion of the European data privacy directive lead him to conclude that transgovernmental actors are influential in technical policy matters. This argument is also made with respect to transnational epistemic communities, whose influence is hypothesized to be greatest in situations of complexity and uncertainty, especially so when these experts are cohesive in their knowledge (Haas 1992). By contrast, some domestic policy domains are likely to be simply 'inhospitable territory,' says Weyland (2005), who cites redistributive policies where the fact of domestic winners and losers from change will ensure that any changes to them involve societal actors and debate. Indeed, social policies are often embedded in corporatist institutional frameworks, so that any changes to them will be a matter of negotiation across domestic state and non-state actors (Swank 2002). Using another policy domain – agriculture – Coleman, Skogstad, and Atkinson (1996) argue that paradigmatic changes in policy issues with a low level of public visibility are also likely to be a matter of domestic societal group-state actor bargaining and learning.

Third, it is ultimately characteristics of the domestic polity and domestic political actors that affect the influence of transnational actors on domestic paradigm development. Blyth (2007, 764) stresses the importance of 'locally generated ideas regarding what is possible and what was deemed legitimate' in explaining why American responses to the Great Depression differed from those in France, Sweden, and Germany. Orenstein (2008, 59), making a strong case for the influence of transnational actors, nonetheless states that they lack the formal power to enact their policy ideas and 'necessarily act in partnership with domestic actors,' who do determine final outcomes of efforts to construct and implement paradigms. The most important of these domestic actors are those who exercise a veto over policy paradigm change. Still, across domestic polities, there will be both differing rationales for domestic political actors – both those who are veto players and those who are not – to adopt alternative norms and epistemes, including those in good standing elsewhere, and different opportunities/constraints for these same political actors to implement and institutionalize these alternative policy ideas.

Policy ideas and paradigms diffuse under dynamics of emulation, learning, competition, and coercion (Simmons and Elkins 2004; Elkins, Guzman, and Simmons 2006; Lee and Strang 2006; Dobbin, Simmons, and Garrett 2007; Weyland 2004, 2005). The last of these, coercion, occurs when states are forced to adopt certain policies as a condition of organizational membership, to procure funding by an international body, or are under pressure from a coercive foreign country. While coercion has been found to be an important mechanism for the diffusion of ideas from international organizations to developing countries (see, e.g., Sharman 2008), it is not expected to be consequential in the well-established democracies in North America and Europe. Emulation (also labelled 'mimicry') occurs when political actors adopt the policy ideas of transnational actors because of who the transnational actor is – for example, because the adoptee has an affinity with the latter or sees it as trustworthy and/or able to affect its status. Learning occurs when political actors change their policy ideas (and take on alternative ideas) as a result of acquiring new information about the merits of policy goals or ways to achieve them (Bennett and Howlett 1992; Zito and Schout 2009). And dynamics of competition affect the diffusion of policy ideas when they are perceived to position the recipient of these ideas favourably vis-à-vis competitors.

Emulation and learning dynamics are supported by empirical patterns of diffusion of policies and paradigms across countries that share cultural attributes and geography (Simmons and Elkins 2004; Dobbin, Simmons, and Garrett 2007, 462). Paradigms that have been shown to be successful in economically and politically powerful states can be attractive to decision makers when they promise to resolve existing problems (Hansen and King 2001; McNamara 1998; Weyland 2005). Emulation and learning dynamics obviously are not exclusive to state actors, but also apply to non-state domestic actors who can draw on foreign policy models and norms in order to delegitimize existing domestic policy models/norms and present alternatives to them (Bernstein and Cashore 2000; Pralle 2003; Princen 2007). Competitiveness concerns arising from processes of market integration are also evident when distinctive policy paradigms undermine the efficiency of businesses and create trade tensions with partners, thus giving private and public actors *incentives* to harmonize local economic and regulatory policy paradigms with those of competitors (Vogel 1995; Simmons and Elkins 2004; Meseguer 2005; Dobbin, Simmons, and Garrett 2007). The discourse of competitiveness can be a potent ideational weapon for policy makers whose goal is to replace statist paradigms with neoliberal ones (Hay 2001; Hay and Rosamond, 2002). In contexts of policy interdependence, these dynamics – competition, emulation and learning – can work in concert to diffuse policy ideas, as Cao (2010) suggests has occurred with respect to capital taxation policy changes.

Attention to how domestic factors 'mediate, refract, and filter' the impact of foreign policy models and international norms and epistemes (Risse-Kappen 1995, 293) also directs attention to local cultural (such as religious) norms, local institutions/structures of decision making, and the discursive (sense-making) strategies and interactions of domestic political actors. Norms of transnational actors that 'match' or resonate with domestic norms (Cortell and Davis 1996, 2000; Kollman 2007) or that can be utilized by strategic domestic entrepreneurs to achieve prior goals (Checkel 1999) are more likely to be diffused into the domestic arena and have policy impacts than those that lack these characteristics. When the cultural match is imperfect, the international norms can nonetheless be rendered acceptable by 'localization,' that is, building congruence between them and local beliefs and practices by retaining some characteristics of the pre-existing local normative order (Acharya 2004, 241). Because a frame that resonates in one context cannot be guaranteed to do so in another (Blyth 2007), Acharya highlights the fact that framing (using language that names, interprets, and dramatizes issues) often requires making a global norm appear local and associating it with a pre-existing local norm and cognitions. These reframing efforts, he cautions, are not always possible. Nor do local actors necessarily have the incentives and abilities to localize foreign norms.

Among the features of the domestic institutional framework considered most consequential for transformative ideational change is the number of veto players. Systems with multiple veto players, such as the EU multi-level governance system, present opportunities as well as obstacles to transformative ideational change (cf. Bulmer and Padgett 2004). On the one hand, they provide opportunities for strategic political actors to advance paradigm change through venue shifting, that is, shifting policy debates to a more receptive arena (Pralle 2003). This opportunity, suggests Princen (2007), favours challengers of the status quo over its defenders. On the other hand, multi-level governance systems normally have multiple veto players and joint decision-making rules that require paradigmatic changes to be agreed to by many players. In these cases, new ideas have to achieve a consensus to be actionable or at the very least must offer a balance of positive and negative policy outcomes to have a chance of succeeding, as in the cases of liberalizing welfare reform in Switzerland and Germany (Bonoli 2001; Häusermann 2008). By contrast, political systems in which political authority is concentrated in a single set of actors appear to offer better prospects for paradigm change when incumbent political actors are persuaded of its necessity. However, even they are likely to have difficulty imposing paradigm change when the public has not been 'converted' to the new sets of ideas (Schmidt 2002b, chap. 2). The discursive strategies and interactions of transnational and domestic political actors are thus a key factor both in de-legitimating extant policy models and legitimating alternative policy models and ideas (cf. Hall 2003; Sharman 2008). The significance of discursive interactions is treated more fully by Vivien Schmidt in the next chapter of this volume.

Design and Methods of the Study

The authors of the chapters that follow engage with the debates described above regarding how best to conceptualize paradigms and to demarcate paradigm shifts; whether processes of paradigm development are episodic ruptures of substituting one paradigm for another, incommensurable paradigm or whether paradigm change is a more evolutionary process of incremental change in which new ideas are layered on old; the role of various transnational state and non-state actors in policy paradigm development; and how domestic factors interact with transnational actors and transnationalism processes to affect paradigm development and change. They adopt similar qualitative methodologies to probe more deeply into how paradigms develop: in-depth case studies that rely on close analyses of government documents and other public records, media accounts, as well as information gained in interviews. Such methods facilitate tracing the processes by which the ideas and beliefs of actors influence policy making. They avoid thereby the limitation of large-N diffusion studies, which, while they can demonstrate broad trends of diffusion of ideas and paradigms across countries over time, are unable to do little more than speculate on the reasons why paradigms develop as they do.

The findings of these chapters and their insights for theories of policy paradigms and policy paradigm development await fuller discussion in the concluding chapter of this book. Here, it will suffice to describe their focus. In chapter 2, Vivien Schmidt continues the theoretical discussion begun here about how best to conceptualize policy paradigms and paradigm change. She attributes causal force to discursive interactions – 'what is said' and 'to whom, where, and why' (Schmidt 2001, 2002b, 2008) – and highlights the significance of communicative and coordinative discursive interactions in facilitating transformative political economic change in western European countries in recent decades.

Subsequent chapters examine the role of different transnational political actors in policy paradigm development. In chapter 3, Tony Porter examines the efforts of transnational private actors and international (transgovernmental) institutions to develop policy paradigms that harmonize American and EU standards in two areas: vehicle safety and accounting. His comparative case studies lead Porter to argue that we should understand policy paradigms as entanglements of ideational and material factors. Chapter 4, by Grace Skogstad, also examines transnational policy paradigm development. She argues that transnational actors, including advocacy groups and international organizations in the form of both the EU and the World Trade Organization, have importantly shaped the epistemic beliefs that are at the core of the EU's paradigm with respect to risk regulation of genetically modified organisms (GMOs) but also have contributed to its controversy. Kelly Kollman in chapter 5 also focuses on paradigm development in Europe, investigating the role of EU institutions and a transnational advocacy movement in changing Germany's family policy to one that recognizes same-sex unions. Her case concludes that a new paradigm may need to incorporate old ideas to gain traction.

Three chapters deal with paradigm development in North America. In chapter 6, Phil Triadafilopoulos investigates the impact of the norms of the international human rights movement in the post-World War II period on the transition of immigration policy paradigms in Canada and the United States from racially based to non-racist paradigms. Sandy Irvine, in chapter 7, provides an account of change in the Canadian refugee paradigm in the late twentieth century that attributes causal influence to a transgovernmental network of bureaucratic officials that served as a mechanism of socialization of Canadian bureaucrats. Transnational epistemic actors and international organizations figure prominently in Linda White's account in chapter 8 of arrested development towards an early childhood education and care (ECEC) policy paradigm in Canada.

REFERENCES

Abdelal, Rawi, Mark Blyth, and Craig Parsons, eds. 2010a. *Constructing the International Economy*. Ithaca: Cornell University Press.
– 2010b. Re-constructing IPE: Some Conclusions Drawn from a Crisis. In Abdelal, Blyth, and Parsons, *Constructing the International Economy*.

Acharya, Amitav. 2004. How Ideas Spread: Whose Norms Matter? Norm Localization and Institutional Change in Asian Regionalism. *International Organization* 58:239–75.

Art, D. 2006. *The Politics of the Nazi Past in Germany and Austria.* New York: Cambridge University Press.

Barnett, Michael, and Martha Finnemore. 2004. *Rules for the World.* Ithaca: Cornell University Press.

Béland, Daniel. 2007. Ideas and Institutional Change in Social Security: Conversion, Layering and Policy Drift. *Social Science Quarterly* 88 (1):20–38.

– and Robert Henry Cox. 2010. *Ideas and Politics in Social Science Research.* New York: Oxford University Press.

Bennett, Colin, and Michael Howlett. 1992. The lessons of learning: reconciling theories of policy learning and policy change. *Policy Sciences* 25 (3): 275–94.

Berger, Suzanne. 1996. Introduction. In *National Diversity and Global Capitalism,* edited by S. Berger and R. Dore. Ithaca: Cornell University Press.

Berman, Sheri. 2001. Review Article: Ideas, Norms, and Culture in Political Analysis. *Comparative Politics* 33 (2):231–50.

Bernstein, Steven, and Benjamin Cashore. 2000. Globalization, Four Paths of Internationalization and Domestic Policy Change: The Case of Eco-Forestry in British Columbia, Canada. *Canadian Journal of Political Science* 33:67–99.

Best, Jacqueline. 2010. Bringing Power Back In: The IMF's Constructivist Strategy. In Abdelal, Blyth, and Parsons, *Constructing the International Economy.* Ithaca: Cornell University Press.

Bhatia, Vandna, and William D. Coleman. 2003. Ideas and Discourse: Reform and Resistance in the Canadian and German Health Systems. *Canadian Journal of Political Science* 36(4):715–39.

Bleich, Erik. 2002. Integrating Ideas into Policy-Making Analysis: Frames and Race Policies in Britain and France. *Comparative Political Studies* 35:1054–76.

Blyth, Mark M. 1997. Any More Bright Ideas? The Ideational Turn in Comparative Political Economy. *Comparative Politics* 29 (2):229–50.

– 2001. The Transformation of the Swedish Model: Economic Ideas, Distributional Conflict, and Institutional Change. *World Politics* 54:1–26.

– 2002. *Great Transformations: Economic Ideas and Institutional Change in the Twentieth Century.* New York: Cambridge University Press.

– 2007. Powering, Puzzling, or Persuading? The Mechanisms of Building Institutional Orders. *International Studies Quarterly* 51:761–77.

Boli, John, and George M. Thomas. 1997. World Culture in the World Polity: A Century of International Non-Governmental Organization. *American Sociological Review* 62 (2):171–90.

Bonoli, Giuliano. 2001. Political Institutions, Veto Points, and the Process of Welfare State Adaptation. In *The New Politics of the Welfare State*, edited by P. Pierson. New York: Oxford University Press.

Borzel, T.A., and T. Risse. 2000. When Europe Hits Home: Europeanization and Domestic Change. *European Integration Online Papers* 4 (15).

Bukovansky, Mlada. 2010. Institutionalized Hypocrisy and the Politics of Agricultural Trade. In Abdelal, Blyth, and Parsons, *Constructing the International Economy*.

Bulmer, Simon, and Stephen Padgett. 2004. Policy Transfer in the European Union: An Institutionalist Perspective. *British Journal of Political Science* 35 (1):103–26.

Busch, Per-Olof, Helge Jörgens, and Kerstin Tews. 2005. The Global Diffusion of Regulatory Instruments: The Making of a New International Environmental Regime. *Annals of the American Academy of Political and Social Science* 598 (1):146–67.

Campbell, John L. 1998. Institutional Analysis and the Role of Ideas in Political Economy. *Theory and Society* 27:377–409.

– 2002. Ideas, Politics and Public Policy. *Annual Review of Sociology* 28:21–38.

– 2004. *Institutional Change and Globalization*. Princeton: Princeton University Press.

Carson, Marcus, Tom R. Burns, and Dolores Calvo. 2009. *Paradigms in Public Policy: Theory and Practice of Paradigm Shifts in the EU*. Frankfurt: Peter Lang.

Cao, Xun. 2010. Networks as Channels of Policy Diffusion: Explaining Worldwide Changes in Capital Taxation, 1998–2006. *International Studies Quarterly* 54(3): 823–51.

Checkel, Jeffrey T. 1999. Norms, Institutions, and National Identity in Contemporary Europe. *International Studies Quarterly* 43:83–114.

Chwieroth, Jeffrey M. 2007. Neoliberal Economists and Capital Account Liberalization in Emerging Markets. *International Organization* 61 (2):443–63.

Coleman, William D., and Anthony Perl. 1999. Internationalized Policy Environments and Policy Network Analysis. *Political Studies* 47:691–709.

Coleman, W.D., Grace Skogstad, and M.M. Atkinson. 1996. Paradigm Shifts and Policy Networks: Cumulative Change in Agriculture. *Journal of Public Policy* 16 (3):273–301.

Cortell, A., and J. Davis. 1996. How Do International Institutions Matter? The Domestic Impact of International Rules and Norms. *International Studies Quarterly* 40 (4):451–78.

– 2000. Understanding the Domestic Impact of International Norms: A Research Agenda. *International Studies Review* 2 (1):65–87.

Cox, Robert Henry. 2001. The Social Construction of an Imperative: Why Welfare Reform Happened in Denmark and the Netherlands, but Not in Germany. *World Politics* 53:463–98.

Cutler, A. Claire, Virginia Haufler, and Tony Porter, eds. 1999. *Private Authority and International Affairs.* Albany: SUNY Press.

Daugbjerg, Carsten. 2009. Sequencing in Public Policy: The Evolution of the CAP over a Decade. *Journal of European Public Policy* 16 (3):395–411.

Dimitrova, A.L., and M. Rhinard. 2005. The Power of Norms in the Transposition of EU Directives. *European Integration Online Papers.* 9 (16).

Djelic, Marie-Laure, and Kerstin Sahlin-Andersson, eds. 2006. *Transnational Governance: Institutional Dynamics of Regulation.* New York: Cambridge University Press.

Dobbin, Frank, Beth Simmons, and Geoffrey Garrett. 2007. The Global Diffusion of Public Policies: Social Construction, Coercion, Competition or Learning? *Annual Review of Sociology* 33:449–72.

Dolowitz, David P., and David Marsh. 2000. Learning from Abroad: the Role of Policy Transfer in Contemporary Policy-Making. *Governance* 13 (1):5–24.

Dostal, Jörg Michael. 2004. Campaigning on Expertise: How the OECD Framed Welfare and Labour Market Policies – and Why Success Could Trigger Failure. *Journal of European Public Policy* 11 (3):440–60.

Douglas, Mary. 1986. *How Institutions Think.* Syracuse, NY: Syracuse University Press.

Drori, S. Gili, John W. Meyer, Francisco O. Ramirez, and Evan Schofer. 2003. *Science in the Modern World Polity: Institutionalization and Globalization.* Stanford: Stanford University Press.

Eberlein, Bukhard, and Edgar Grande. 2005. Beyond Delegation: Transnational Regulatory Regimes and the EU Regulatory State. *Journal of European Public Policy* 12 (1):89–112.

Eberlein, Burkhard, and Abraham L. Newman. 2008. Escaping the International Governance Dilemma? Incorporated Transgovernmental Networks in the European Union. *Governance* 21 (1):25–52.

Eckstein, Harry. 1975. Case Study and Theory in Political Science. In *Handbook of Political Science.*, edited by F.I. Greenstein and N.W. Polsby. Reading, MA: Addison-Wesley.

Eising, Rainer. 2002. Policy Learning in Embedded Negotiations: Explaining EU Electricity Liberalization. *International Organization* 56 (1):85–120.

Elkins, Zachary, Andrew T. Guzman, and Beth A. Simmons. 2006. Competing for Capital: The Diffusion of Bilateral Investment Treaties, 1960–2000. *International Organization* 60 (4): 811–46.

Esping-Anderson, G. 1993. *The Three Worlds of Welfare Capitalism.* Princeton: Princeton University Press.

Finnemore, Martha. 1996. Norms, culture, and world politics: insights from sociology's institutionalism. *International Organization* 50 (2):325–47.

– and Kathryn Sikkink. 1998. International Norm Dynamics and Political Change. *International Organization* 52 (4):887–917.

Fischer, Frank. 2003. *Reframing Public Policy: Discursive Politics and Deliberative Practices.* Oxford: Oxford University Press.

Garzon, Isabelle. 2006. *Reforming the Common Agricultural Policy: History of a Paradigm Change.* New York: Palgrave Macmillan.

Gore, Charles. 2000. The Rise and Fall of the Washington Consensus as a Paradigm for Developing Countries. *World Development* 28 (5):789–804.

Gourevitch, Peter. 1978. The Second Image Reversed: The International Sources of Domestic Politics. *International Organization* 32 (4):881–911.

Haas, Peter M. 1992. Introduction: Epistemic Communities and International Policy Coordination. *International Organization* 46:1–35.

Hacker, Jacob S. 2004. Privatizing Risk without Privatizing the Welfare State: The Hidden Politics of Social Policy Retrenchment in the United States. *American Political Science Review* 98 (2):243–60.

Hajer, Maarten A. 1993. Discourse Coalitions and the Institutionalization of Practice: The Case of Acid Rain in Great Britain. In *The Argumentative Turn in Policy Analysis and Planning,* edited by F. Fischer and J. Forester. Durham, NC: Duke University Press.

– 2003. A Frame in the Fields: Policymaking and the Reinvention of Politics. In *Deliberative Policy Analysis: Understanding Governance in the Network Society,* edited by M.A. Hajer and H. Wagenaar. Cambridge: Cambridge University Press.

Hall, Peter A. 1993. Policy Paradigms, Social Learning, and the State: The Case of Economic Policymaking in Britain. *Comparative Politics* 25:175–96.

Hall, Rodney Bruce. 2003. The Discursive Demolition of the Asian Development Model. *International Studies Quarterly* 47:71–99.

Hansen, Randall, and Desmond King. 2001. Eugenic Ideas, Political Interests, and Policy Variance: Immigration and Sterilization Policy in Britain and the United States. *World Politics* 53:237–63.

Harris, Richard A., and Sidney M. Milkis. 1996. *The Politics of Regulatory Change: A Tale of Two Agencies.* New York: Oxford University Press.

Häusermann, Silja. 2008. What Explains the 'Unfreezing' of Continental European Welfare States? The Socio-Structural Basis of the New Politics of Pension Reforms. Paper read at the American Political Science Association Annual Meetings, Boston, MA, 28–31 August.

Hay, Colin. 2001. The Crisis of Keynesianism and the Rise of Neoliberalism in Britain: An Ideational Institutionalist Approach. In *The Rise of Neoliberalism and Institutional Analysis*, edited by J.L. Campbell and O.K. Pedersen. Princeton: Princeton University Press.

– 2004. The Normalizing Role of Rationalist Assumptions in the Institutional Embedding of Neoliberalism. *Economy and Society* 33 (4):500–27.

– 2006. Constructivist Institutionalism. In *The Oxford Handbook of Political Institutions*, edited by R.A.W. Rhodes, S.A. Binder, and B.A. Rockman. Oxford: Oxford University Press.

– and Ben Rosamond. 2002. Globalization, European Integration and the Discursive Construction of Economic Imperatives. *Journal of European Public Policy* 9:147–67.

Hinrichs, Karl, and Olli Kangas. 2003. When Is a Change Big Enough to Be a System Shift? Small System-Shifting Changes in German and Finnish Pension Policies. *Social Policy & Administration* 37 (6):573–91.

Holzinger, Katharina, and Christopher Knill. 2005. Causes and Conditions of Cross-National Policy Convergence. *Journal of European Public Policy* 12 (5):775–96.

Howlett, Michael. 1994. Policy Paradigms and Policy Change: Lessons from the Old and New Canadian Policies towards Aboriginal Peoples. *Policy Studies Journal* 22 (4):631–49.

– and Benjamin Cashore. 2009. The Dependent Variable Problem in the Study of Policy Change: Understanding Policy Change as a Methodological Problem. *Journal of Comparative Policy Analysis* 11 (1):33–46.

– and M. Ramesh. 2002. The Policy Effects of Internationalization: A Subsystem Adjustment Analysis of Policy Change. *Journal of Comparative Policy Analysis: Research and Practice* 4:31–50.

Jobert, B. 1989. The Normative Frameworks of Public Policy. *Political Studies* 37:376–86.

– 1992. Représentations sociales, controverses et débats dans la conduite des politiques publiques. *Revue française de science politique* 42 (2):219–34.

– and P. Muller. 1987. *L'état en action*. Paris: Les Presses Universitaires de France.

Kahler, Miles, and David A. Lake. 2003. Globalization and Governance. In *Governance in a Global Economy*, edited by M. Kahler and D.A. Lake. Princeton: Princeton University Press.

Kaiser, Wolfram. 2009. Bringing History Back In to the Study of Transnational Networks in European Integration. *Journal of Public Policy* 29 (2):223–39.

Kälberer, M. 2003. Knowledge, Power and Monetary Bargaining: Central Bankers and the Creation of Monetary Union in Europe. *Journal of European Public Policy* 10 (3):365–79.

Kay, Adrian. 2007. Tense Layering and Synthetic Policy Paradigms: The Politics of Health Insurance in Australia. *Australian Journal of Political Science* 42 (4):579–91.

Keck, M.E., and K. Sikkink. 1998. *Activists Beyond Borders: Advocacy Networks in International Politics.* Ithaca: Cornell University Press.

Keohane, Robert O., and Helen V. Milner. 1996. *Internationalization and Domestic Politics.* Cambridge and New York: Cambridge University Press.

Keohane, Robert O., and Joseph S. Nye. 1974. Transgovernmental Relations and International Organizations. *World Politics* 27 (1):39–62.

– eds. 1977. *Transnational Relations and World Politics.* Cambridge, MA: Harvard University Press.

Knill, Christoph. 2005. Introduction: Cross-National Policy Convergence: Concepts, Approaches and Explanatory Factors. *Journal of European Public Policy* 12 (5):764–74.

Kollman, Kelly. 2007. Same-Sex Unions: The Globalization of an Idea. *International Studies Quarterly* 51:329–57.

Krasner, Stephen D. 1983a. Structural Causes and Regime Consequences: Regimes as Intervening Variables. In *International Regimes,* edited by S.D. Krasner. Ithaca: Cornell University Press.

– 1983b. Regimes and the Limits of Realism. In *International Regimes,* edited by S.D. Krasner. Ithaca: Cornell University Press.

Kuhn, Thomas. 1970. *The Structure of Scientific Revolutions.* 2nd ed. Chicago: University Chicago Press.

Lakatos, I. 1971. Methodology of Scientific Research Programmes. In *Criticism and the Growth of Knowledge,* edited by I. Lakatos and A. Musgrave. Cambridge: Cambridge University Press.

Laudan, Larry. 1977. *Progress and Its Problems.* Berkeley: University of California Press.

Lee, Chang Kil, and David Strang. 2006. The International Diffusion of Public-Sector Downsizing: Network Emulation and Theory-Driven Learning. *International Organization* 60 (4):883–909.

Legro, Jeffrey W. 1997. Which Norms Matter? Revisiting the 'Failure' of Internationalism. *International Organization* 51:31–63.

Levi-Faur, David. 2005. 'Agents of Knowledge' and the Convergence on a 'New World Order': A Review Article. *Journal of European Public Policy* 13 (5):954–65.

Lindvall, Johannes. 2006. The Politics of Purpose: Swedish Economic Policy after the Golden Age. *Comparative Politics* 38 (3):253–72.

Mahon, Rianne, and Stephen McBride. 2008. *The OECD and Transnational Governance.* Vancouver: UBC Press.

Mahoney, James. 2000. Path Dependency in Historical Sociology. *Theory and Society* 29(4):507–48.

– and Kathleen Thelen. 2010. A Theory of Gradual Institutional Change. In *Explaining Institutional Change: Ambiguity, Agency and Power,* edited by James Mahoney and Kathleen Thelen. Cambridge: Cambridge University Press.

Majone, G. 1989. *Evidence, Argument, and Persuasion in the Policy Process.* New Haven: Yale University Press.

Mandelkern, Ronen, and Michael Shalev. 2010. Power and the Ascendance of New Economic Policy Ideas: Lessons from the 1980s Crisis in Israel. *World Politics* 62 (3):459–95.

McNamara, Kathleen. 1998. *The Currency of Ideas: Monetary Politics in the European Union.* Ithaca: Cornell University Press.

Meseguer, C. 2005. What Role for Learning? The Diffusion of Privatisation in OECD and Latin American Countries. *Journal of Public Policy* 24: 299–325.

Meyer, John, Francisco O. Ramirez, and Yasmine N. Soysal. 1992. 'World Expansion of Mass Education, 1870–1980.' *Sociology of Education* 65(2): 128–49.

– John Boli, George M. Thomas, and Francisco O. Ramirez. 1997a. World Society and the Nation State. *American Journal of Sociology* 103 (1):144–81.

– D. Frank, A. Hironaka, E. Schofer, and N.B. Tuma. 1997b. The Structuring of a World Environmental Regime, 1870–1990. *International Organization* 51:623–51.

Miller, Clark A. 2007. Democratization, International Knowledge Institutions, and Global Governance. *Governance* 20 (2):325–57.

Moran, M., and T. Prosser. 1994. *Privatization and Regulatory Change in Europe.* Buckingham, UK: Open University Press.

Muller, Pierre. 1995. Les politiques publiques comme construction d'un rapport au monde. In *La construction du sens dans les politiques publiques. Débats autour de la notion de référentiel,* edited by A. Faure, G. Pollet, and P. Warin. Paris: Harmattan.

Newman, A.L. 2008. Building Transnational Civil Liberties: Transgovernmental Entrepreneurs and the European Data Privacy Directive. *International Organization* 62 (1):103–30.

Orenstein, Mitchell A. 2008. *Privatizing Pensions: The Transnational Campaign for Social Security Reform.* Princeton: Princeton University Press.

– and Hans Peter Schmitz. 2006. Review Article: The New Transnationalism and Comparative Politics. *Comparative Politics* 38:479–500

Palier, Bruno. 2005. Ambiguous Agreement, Cumulative Change: French Social Policy in the 1990s. In *Beyond Continuity: Institutional Change in Advanced Political Economies,* edited by W. Streeck and K. Thelen. Oxford: Oxford University Press.

Patashnik, Eric. 2003. After the Public Interest Prevails: The Political Sustainability of Policy Reform. *Governance* 16 (2):203–34.

Phillips, Deborah, and Kathleen McCartney. 2005. The Disconnect between Research and Policy on Child Care. In *Developmental Psychology and Social Change: Research, History, and Policy,* edited by D.B. Pillemer and S.H. White. New York: Cambridge University Press.

Pierson, Paul. 2000. Not Just What but When: Timing and Sequence in Political Processes. *Studies in American Political Development* 14:72–92.

Porter, Tony. 2005. The Private Production of Public Goods: Private and Public Norms in Global Governance. In *Complex Sovereignty: Reconstituting Political Authority in the Twenty-first Century,* edited by E. Grande and L.W. Pauly. Toronto: University of Toronto Press.

Pralle, Sarah B. 2003. Venue Shopping, Political Strategy, and Policy Change: The Internationalization of Canadian Forest Advocacy. *Journal of Public Policy* 23 (3):233–60.

Princen, Sebastiaan. 2007. Advocacy Coalitions and the Internationalization of Public Health Policies. *Journal of Public Policy* 27 (1):13–33.

Raustiala, Kal. 2002. The Architecture of International Cooperation: Transgovernmental Networks and the Future of International Law. *Virginia Journal of International Law* 43 (1):1–92.

Rein, Martin, and Donald Schön. 1993. Reframing Policy Discourse. In *The Argumentative Turn in Policy Analysis and Planning,* edited by F. Fischer and J. Forester. Durham, NC: Duke University Press.

Risse, Thomas, and Kathryn Sikkink. 1999. The Socialization of International Human Rights into Domestic Practices: Introduction. In *The Power of Human Rights: International Norms and Domestic Change,* edited by T. Risse, S. Ropp, and K. Sikkink. Cambridge: Cambridge University Press.

Risse-Kappen, Thomas. 1995. Bringing Transnational Relations Back In: Introduction. In *Bringing Transnational Relations Back In: Non-State Actors, Domestic Structures and International Institutions,* edited by T. Risse-Kappen. Cambridge: Cambridge University Press.

Roe, E. 1994. *Narrative Policy Analysis: Theory and Practice.* Durham, NC: Duke University Press.

Rothstein, Bo. 2005. *Social Traps and the Problem of Trust.* Cambridge: Cambridge University Press.

Ruggie, John. 1982. International Regimes, Transactions and Change: Embedded Liberalism in the Postwar Economic Order. *International Organization* 36:195–231.

– 1998. What Makes the World Hang Together? Neo-Utilitarianism and the Social Constructivist Challenge. *International Organization* 52 (4):855–85.

Sabatier, Paul A. 1987. Knowledge, Policy-Oriented Learning and Policy Change: An Advocacy Coalition Framework. *Knowledge: Creation, Diffusion, Utilization* 8 (4):649–92.

– 1993. Policy Change over a Decade or More. In Sabatier and Jenkins-Smith, *Policy Change and Learning*.

– and H.C. Jenkins-Smith, eds. 1993. *Policy Change and Learning: An Advocacy Coalition Approach*. Boulder, CO: Westview Press.

Scharpf, Fritz W. 2000. Economic Changes, Vulnerabilities, and Institutional Capabilities. In Scharpf and Schmidt, *Welfare and Work in the Open Economy*. Vol. 1: *From Vulnerability to Competitiveness*.

– and Vivien A. Schmidt, eds. 2000. *Welfare and Work in the Open Economy*. 2 vols. Oxford: Oxford University Press.

Schlesinger, Mark, and Richard R. Lau. 2000. The Meaning and Measure of Policy Metaphors. *American Political Science Review* 94 (3):611–26.

Schmidt, Vivien A. 1986. Four Approaches to Scientific Rationality. *Methodology and Science* 19 (3):207–32.

– 1988. The Historical Approach to Philosophy of Science: Toulmin in Perspective. *Metaphilosophy* 19:223–36.

– 2001. The Politics of Economic Adjustment in France and Britain: When Does Discourse Matter? *European Journal of Public Policy* 8:247–64.

– 2002a. Does Discourse Matter in the Politics of Welfare State Adjustment? *Comparative Political Studies* 35 (2):168–93.

– 2002b. *The Futures of European Capitalism*. Oxford: Oxford University Press.

– 2008. Discursive Institutionalism: The Explanatory Power of Ideas and Discourse. *Annual Review of Political Science* 11:303–26.

Schön, Donald A., and Martin Rein. 1994. *Frame Reflection: Toward the Resolution of Intractable Policy Controversies*. New York: Basic Books.

Seitz, William C. 1961. *The Art of Assemblage*. New York: Museum of Modern Art.

Sharman, J.C. 2008. Power and Discourse in Policy Diffusion: Anti-Money Laundering in Developing States. *International Studies Quarterly*, 52:635–56.

Simmons, Beth A., and Zachary Elkins. 2004. The Globalization of Liberalization: Policy Diffusion in the International Political Economy. *American Political Science Review* 98 (1):171–189.

– Frank Dobbin, and Geoffrey Garrett. 2006. Introduction: The International Diffusion of Liberalism. *International Organization* 60:781–810.

Skocpol, Theda. 1979. *States and Social Revolutions: A Comparative Analysis of France, Russia and China*. Cambridge: Cambridge University Press.

Skogstad, Grace 1998. Ideas, Paradigms and Institutions: Agricultural Exceptionalism in the European Union and the United States. *Governance* 11:463–90.

– 2008. *Internationalization and Canadian Agriculture: Policy and Governing Paradigms*. Toronto: University of Toronto Press.

Slaughter, Anne-Marie. 2004. *A New World Order*. Princeton: Princeton University Press.

Stone, Diane. 2003. The 'Knowledge Bank' and the Global Development Network. *Global Governance* 9:43–61.

– 2004. Transfer Agents and Global Networks in the 'Transnationalization' of Policy. *Journal of European Public Policy* 11 (3):545–66.

Surel, Y. 1995. Les politiques publiques comme paradigmes. In *La construction du sens dans les politiques publiques. Débats autour de la notion de référentiel*, edited by A. Faure, G. Pollet, and P. Warin. Paris: Harmattan.

– 2000. The Role of Cognitive and Normative Frames in Policy-Making. *Journal of European Public Policy* 7:495–512.

Swank, Duane. 2002. *Global Capital, Political Institutions, and Policy Change in Developed Welfare States*. Cambridge: Cambridge University Press.

– 2006. Tax Policy in an Era of Internationalization: Explaining the Spread of Neoliberalism. *International Organization* 60:847–82.

Thelen, Kathleen. 2002. How Institutions Evolve: Insights from Comparative Historical Analysis. In *Comparative Historical Analysis in the Social Sciences*, edited by J. Mahoney and D. Rueschemeyer. New York: Cambridge University Press.

– 2004. *How Institutions Evolve: The Political Economy of Skills in Germany, Britain, the United States, and Japan*. Cambridge: Cambridge University Press.

Toller, A.E. 2004. The Europeanization of Public Policies – Understanding Idiosyncratic Mechanisms and Contingent Results. *European Integration Online Papers* 8 (9).

Toulmin, Stephen. 1972. *Human Understanding*. Princeton: Princeton University Press.

Verdun, Amy. 1992. The Role of the Delors Committee in Creating the EMU: An Epistemic Community. *Journal of European Public Policy* 6 (2):308–28.

Vogel, David. 1995. *Trading Up: Consumer and Environmental Regulation in a Global Economy*. Cambridge, MA: Harvard University Press.

Walsh, James I. 2006. Policy Failure and Policy Change: British Security Policy after the Cold War. *Comparative Political Studies* 39 (4):490–518.

Weaver, Catherine. 2010. The Meaning of Development: Constructing the World Bank's Good Governance Agenda. In Abdelal, Blyth, and Parsons, *Constructing the International Economy*.

Weir, Margaret. 1992. Ideas and the Politics of Bounded Innovation. In *Structuring Politics: Historical Institutionalism in Comparative Politics*, edited by S. Steinmo, K. Thelen, and F. Longstreth. Cambridge: Cambridge University Press.

Weiss, Linda. 1998. *The Myth of the Powerless State*. Cambridge: Polity Press.

Weyland, Kurt. 2005. Theories of Policy Diffusion: Lessons from Latin American Pension Reform. *World Politics* 57:262–95.

– ed. 2004. *Learning from Foreign Models in Latin American Policy Reform.* Baltimore: Johns Hopkins University Press.

Wilson, Carter A. 2000. Policy Regimes and Policy Change. *Journal of Public Policy* 20 (3):247–74.

Zippel, Kathryn. 2004. Transnational Advocacy Networks and Policy Cycles in the European Union: The Case of Sexual Harassment. *Social Politics* 11 (1):57–85.

Zito, A. 2001. Epistemic Communities, Collective Entrepreneurship and European Integration *Journal of European Integration* 8 (4): 585–603.

– and Adrian Schout. 2009. Learning Theory Reconsidered: EU Integration Theories and Learning. *Journal of European Public Policy* 16 (8):1103–23

2 Ideas and Discourse in Transformational Political Economic Change in Europe

VIVIEN A. SCHMIDT

The introduction to this book has addressed a number of theoretical questions regarding how we define what constitutes a paradigm shift and the criteria by which to determine how, when, and why, as well as by whom, paradigms change. It shows that the very notion of a paradigm shift, although instinctively clear, can be problematic. Developed first as a concept in the philosophy of science applied to scientific communities alone, its usage in social science is complicated by the fact that it applies simultaneously to social scientific communities and to society, and that it involves not only cognitive ideas about 'what is' but also normative ideas about 'what is appropriate' in the view of social agents as well as social scientists. The sources of paradigm change are also in question. Is change exogenous, a result of external economic 'shocks' that diminish its problem-solving ability? Or is it endogenous as a result of diminishing explanatory reach? Alternatively, is it exogenous as a result of the intrusion of transnational ideas into national contexts or endogenous as a consequence of national agents' ideational change? Moreover, the timing of paradigm change remains open, as either revolutionary in response to a critical juncture or evolutionary because it is incremental. Finally, the processes by which paradigm change occurs are empirically rich but often under-theorized in the comparative politics literature, while in the international relations literature the highly theorized mechanisms of change such as learning, mimesis, and diffusion do not always work 'all the way down' to the national level. In short, why, when, how, and where paradigm change occurs could still benefit from further specification.

In this chapter, I look more deeply into how we may explain transformational political economic change, whether seen as occurring at critical junctures or more incrementally over time. In so doing, I shift from a focus on paradigm theory per se to an approach that I call 'discursive institutionalism,' to contrast with the three older neo-institutionalisms most prevalent in comparative politics and political economy that are concerned mainly with rationalist interests, path-dependent institutions, or cultural frames (Schmidt 2008, 2010). As such, discursive institutionalism could be seen as an umbrella concept that serves to encompass a wide range of the approaches to paradigm change discussed in the introductory chapter, including not only the 'ideational turn' that most characterizes comparative politics but also the agent-centred 'normative' turn found in international relations.

Discursive institutionalism is an analytic framework concerned with the substantive content of ideas and the interactive processes of discourse in institutional context. The ideas it elucidates may be cognitive or normative and are at different levels of generality, including policy, programs, and philosophy. The discursive interactions may occur among policy actors engaged in a 'coordinative' discourse of policy construction and/or among political actors and the public engaged in a 'communicative' discourse of deliberation, contestation, and legitimization of the policies developed in the coordinative discourse (see Schmidt 2002, chap. 5; 2006, chap. 5). The directional arrows of these discursive interactions may come not only from the top down through the influence of the ideas of supranational or national actors but also from the bottom up through the ideas and discourse of local, national, and/or international 'civil society' and social movement activists. The institutional context, moreover, can be understood in two ways: first, in terms of the meaning context in which agents' discursive interactions proceed following nationally situated logics of communication; second, in terms of the formalized as well as informal (historical/cultural) institutions that inform their ideas and discursive interactions (Schmidt 2008, 2010). Agents' ideas, discourse, and actions in any institutional context, however, must also be seen as responses to the material (and not so material) realities that affect them – including material events and pressures, the unintended consequences of their own actions, the actions of others, and the ideas and discourse that seek to make sense of all such realities. It is in this perspective that we consider the impact of globalization and Europeanization, as supranational economic, institutional, and ideational pressures for change that have led to economic adjustment and institutional adaptation in national varieties of capitalism and welfare states.

In what follows, I use discursive institutionalism to explore in greater detail the theoretical issues related to time and the timing of paradigm change, the ideational content of paradigm change, and the discursive processes of paradigm change in an institutional context. I illustrate the theoretical arguments with empirical examples of the major political economic transformations European countries have undergone since the 1980s in response to the pressures of globalization and Europeanization. The countries considered in particular detail include ones that fit into each of the three main 'varieties of capitalism' in Western Europe: Britain and Ireland as 'liberal market economies' characterized by market-driven, competitive inter-firm relations; Germany and Sweden as 'coordinated market economies' with non-market managed, corporatist business-labour interactions (Hall and Soskice 2001); and France and Italy as 'state-influenced market economies' in which the 'influencing' state plays a greater role, for better or worse, in hierarchically organized business and labour relations by contrast with the liberal or enabling state of the two other varieties (Schmidt 2002, 2009). As we shall see, the role of ideas and discourse helps explain differing trajectories in policy reforms over time both within and between varieties of capitalism (see also Schmidt 2009).

Time and the Timing of Paradigm Change

The concept of paradigm change leaves us with a number of theoretical questions. They can be summed up as follows: How do we know a paradigm shift when we see one? Is paradigm change limited to its original Kuhnian definition as a rapid and revolutionary process of ideational conversion, or can it also potentially be a slow and incremental process of ideational evolution? What are the criteria by which we determine which ideas represent paradigm changes and how, when, and why do paradigms change?

As we saw in the Introduction, large numbers of social scientists have embraced the use of paradigm theory to explain ideational change, in particular in the policy sphere. Among them, Peter Hall (1993) produced one of the most influential analyses of ideational progress through the identification of three orders of change in paradigms: from minor 'first-order' renewal of policy instruments to middling 'second-order' recasting of policy instruments and objectives to paradigmatic 'third-order' replacement of instruments, objectives, and core ideas. The first two orders of change suggest evolutionary development within a paradigm, while the third order of change is revolutionary, since it would replace one paradigm with another (see Schmidt 2002, 222–5). Hall (1993) argued that a paradigm shift occurred in the case of Britain in the late 1970s and early 1980s, where revolutionary third-order change was involved in the replacement of the paradigm of Keynesianism with monetarism in the country's macroeconomic policy by the government of Margaret Thatcher. We could take this further by suggesting that beginning in the late 1990s, evolutionary second-order change could be seen in the recasting of the neoliberal social policy paradigm, when the Blair government's ideas of the 'third way' reversed Thatcherite social policy instruments and objectives but not the core neoliberal ideas, as its policies moved from punishing the poor by denying them benefits to providing opportunities while instituting workfare (Schmidt 2000; 2002, chap. 6).

However, with regard to revolutionary change, we still need to pinpoint the moment of change. As it turns out, a 'switching point' or critical juncture may appear so only in hindsight, when we look back at a process that is much more gradual or incremental. For example, if we were to go beyond the policy-specific macroeconomic paradigm identified by Hall (1993), which does have a clear transformational moment with the imposition of monetarism in 1979, to consider the shift from the more general post-war paradigm that mixed Tory paternalism and Labour 'socialism' to Thatcher's neoliberal paradigm, it is much more difficult to pinpoint a single critical moment. Do we say that the shift came when Thatcher and those around her changed their ideas about how to reform the economy prior to the election? Or at the moment that Thatcher won election in 1979? Or when she instituted monetarism that same year? Or when she began privatizations of major industries and council housing in 1984? Or when the public seemingly accepted the new ideas and values with regard to capitalism but not the welfare state (as evidenced in public opinion polls by the mid- to late 1980s (Taylor-Gooby 1991)? Or when the Labour Party became New Labour, having adopted the core neoliberal ideas of the Thatcherite paradigm, even as it recast the objectives in terms of the discourse of the 'third way'?

In addition to difficulties in determining exactly when paradigm shifts occur are those related to why and how they occur. Kuhn's (1970) explanation of change in science is a highly systemic one. The paradigm starts from an original core idea with great potential, develops through 'normal science' until it generates more and more anomalies unexplainable within the system, such that a crisis ensues along with the search for a new 'paradigm.' The new paradigmatic core idea, once found, produces a revolution in scientific world view through the adoption and development by the scientific community of a new, incommensurable paradigm. The paradigm shift itself is abrupt, as all elements in the system change, including goals, objectives, instruments, and core ideas. The conversion process itself is radical and incommensurable, much like Kuhn's image of the duck-rabbit: in the first instance, an image looks like a duck; in the next, the same image looks like a rabbit, with no way of switching back.

But is this what major ideational change looks like in social science and society? Kuhn (1970, 163–4) himself doubted that 'paradigmatic science' explained change in the social sciences, because social scientists' concerns were generated exogenously by problems in society, rather than endogenously by problems generated by the science alone. As Alfred O. Hirschman (1989) put it, ideational change in social science and society often results from external processes and events that create a receptive environment for new ideas. But there is no automatic correlation between ideas-opening events such as economic crises and the advent of new ideas. Even what constitutes a crisis is socially constructed, since it involves subjective perceptions of the actors involved even more than any seemingly 'objective' material conditions related, say, to rising unemployment and plummeting business production and labour productivity along with consumers' buying power. Thus, for example, although globalization pressures beginning with the two oil shocks certainly count as external events that precipitated national macroeconomic crises, ideational crisis and 'paradigm shift' from neo-Keynesianism to monetarism occurred at different times in different countries: early in the UK (in 1979), later in France (1983), and even later in Sweden (early 1990s). This said, crisis need not bring in a new paradigm if the existing one is robust enough and flexible enough for renewal or recasting, as in the macroeconomic shift to harder monetary policy (from an already hard one) in Germany, even earlier than anywhere else (in 1974) (see Scharpf 2000).

Moreover, what happens over time with regard to a new paradigm is more complicated than the situation Kuhn described for science. This is because once the policy ideas of the paradigm are put into action, there are many possible disconnects between words and deeds, for example, disconnects between the ideas embedded in the policy program as originally articulated and the actions taken in the name of the program, which may be very different from that intended, not to mention the unexpected and unintended consequences of those actions (see Schmidt 2002, 225–30). Here, in fact, we might usefully borrow concepts from historical institutionalist approaches (e.g., Streeck and Thelen 2005) to consider the problem of 'drift' as the ideas attached to the original program seem to fade, as new ideas are 'layered' onto the old to generate new kinds of actions under the aegis of the policy program, and as new ideas serve to reinterpret the program or even to convert actors to other programs.

In short, a paradigm's development over time may involve incremental change rather than abrupt conversions of all components in an ideational system. This is not to suggest that moments of 'great transformation' do not exist, that is, periods of uncertainty in which ideas may be used as 'weapons' to recast countries' long-standing political economic policies, as in the case of the embedding of liberalism in the US and Sweden in the 1930s and their dis-embedding, beginning in the 1970s (Blyth 2002). It is, rather, to insist that paradigmatic change also can occur slowly over time, as in the case of the slow shifts across the twentieth century in social democrats' 'programmatic beliefs,' as they sought to find workable and equitable democratic solutions to the economic challenges of globalizing capitalism (Berman 2006).

But it also leaves open the possibility that revolutionary change in ideas can occur not just without an abrupt conversion process but also without any clear idea behind the change. This prospect, of course, challenges the whole Kuhnian notion of paradigm change, in which one big idea is assumed to replace another big idea in crisis. Take the case of the reform of social policy in France. This sector underwent a largely unnoticed 'third-order revolutionary change' in its welfare state policy on pensions without any abrupt shift in policy ideas or any clear set of ideas about what to do, let alone any persuasive political discourse of legitimization. As Palier (2005) explains, pension reforms resulted from an incremental process of 'layering' new policies on top of the old, spurred by ambiguous agreements following the diagnosis of failure and the elaboration of alternatives to past policies. Institutional change, in consequence, was the construction of French policy actors inventing new 'recipes' for social policy to 'layer' onto the old – although we might instead see that as 'drift' from the perspective of the original paradigm of French welfare. But such change, whether seen as layering or drift, did not entail coming up with a new 'paradigm' containing some overarching core idea or frame of reference for reform.

This development also raises questions about the extent to which any single overarching paradigm, or even a single 'frame of reference' (Jobert 1989; Muller 1995), is dominant at any one time or over time. In the social sciences and society, there is rarely only one predominant paradigm, since there are ordinarily other minority (opposition) programs waiting in the wings, contesting the validity of the dominant program, invoking different cognitive ideas, and appealing to alternative sets of normative values in the polity (Schmidt 2002, 220–5). Moreover, ideational paradigms in social science and society never entirely expire; they wait to be resurrected when new events call for new explanations, which are rarely entirely new but are, rather, renewals of old but now again relevant ideas of the past, whether liberal ideas about how markets should work or Marxian ideas about capitalist exploitation (Dryzek and Leonard 1988). In addition, there are often many different, even conflicting, ideas embedded in any given policy program, since any program is the result of conflicts as well as compromises among actors who bring different ideas to the table. Paradigms, after all, are not simply ideas floating above the fray. They are the product of policy as well as political discussion, deliberation, and contestation about principles as well as interests, and they represent the outcomes of policy negotiation, electoral bargaining, and political compromise.

Explaining paradigm change in public action is a much more complicated proposition than ideas borrowed from the philosophy of science are able to handle. In the end, then, although the concept of paradigm shift may serve nicely as a metaphor for radical ideational change, it offers little guidance as to how, why, or even when the shift takes place, and it cannot account for incremental change. Moreover, it fails to specify closely enough the process of ideational change: how old ideas fail and new ideas come to the fore, the reasons for ideational change – that is, why certain ideas rather than others are taken up – and the timing of ideational change, since paradigm theory's emphasis on abrupt shifts in ideational systems rules out not only evolutionary change but also revolutionary change in ideas that is not abrupt.

This is not to suggest that we throw the baby out with the bathwater and get rid of the notion of paradigm change altogether. Rather, it suggests that we need a more elaborate methodological approach to the question, with wider empirical investigations, to get at the ways in which 'paradigm' changes (read major ideational shifts) seem to occur. And this is where discursive institutionalism can help, in particular as it suggests a deeper exploration of the substantive content of ideas and the interactive processes of discourse in the explanation of paradigm change in given institutional contexts.

Ideational Content of Paradigm Change

Paradigm change can be understood in terms of shifts in ideas at different levels of generality, including policy, program, and philosophical ideas, as well as in terms of different types of ideas, whether cognitive or normative. Setting out the differences helps us understand the different ways in which paradigms may be defined as well as differences in the pace of ideational shifts. Policy ideas may change much more quickly than programmatic ideas, and both much more quickly than the philosophical ideas underpinning them. Similarly, the cognitive ideas justifying the policy and program may change more quickly than their normative philosophical legitimization.

Levels of Ideas: Policy, Programmatic, Philosophical

One of the problems with the term 'paradigm' is that it does not specify the level of ideas to which it applies. Take the paradigm of 'Keynesianism.' Do we define it primarily intellectually, as an overarching transnational constellation of ideas about governing the economy above and beyond the countries in which it has been applied, the many forms it has taken in different countries constituting different policy ideas about the paradigm itself? Or do we define it in terms of its empirical application, as the particular policy ideas of different European countries on how to implement (or not) neo-Keynesianism in the post-war years? Clearly, the Keynesian 'paradigm' can be both, but choosing one or the other leads to very different kinds of studies. If we choose to define an applied paradigm of Keynesian ideas, we would identify a French, a British, and a Swedish variant of the Keynesian paradigm and none at all for Germany (except for its brief flirtation with Keynesianism in the late 1960s) in order to focus on the significant differences in the timing of change in states' radical shift from neo-Keynesian to monetarist paradigms. This is the preferred approach of scholars of comparative politics. If we instead define 'paradigm' as an intellectual constellation of Keynesian ideas, we are likely to concentrate instead on the processes of diffusion of a single set of ideas across countries and time, seeing little change in the overarching paradigm itself. This is the preferred approach of international relations and international political economy scholars.

A further question deals with understanding the ways any given sectoral policy paradigm fits into more general paradigms, say, about how to govern the economy. Thus, whereas the Keynesian macroeconomic paradigm tends to fit within a more 'liberal' political philosophical paradigm (read intellectual constellation of ideas) of how the state should steer the economy, with greater interventionism and, arguably, higher inflation and debt, monetarism has commonly been seen as part of a larger neoliberal paradigm, in which the agenda was the retreat of the state, deregulation of business, increased flexibility of labour markets, and rationalization (even privatization) of the welfare state. The 2008 economic crisis, with the seeming return of Keynesian macroeconomic management and greater state interventionism and proposals (but little action as yet) for re-regulation of the financial markets, raises the question of whether the policies undertaken constitute a real paradigm shift, or just a set of stop-gap measures that suspend, but do not replace, the neoliberal political philosophical paradigm in crisis. And it leads us to ask whether this is another moment of 'great transformation,' one of layering, or one of drift in the midst of crisis.

Note that we just shifted from discussing paradigms in terms of policy and programmatic ideas to discussing them in terms of philosophical ideas. Such philosophical ideas are arguably longer lasting and harder to change than programmatic ideas such as Keynesianism or monetarism, whether they are called 'public philosophies' (Campbell 2004), 'world views,' *Weltanshauung*, or 'deep core' beliefs that underlie policy programs (Sabatier and Jenkins-Smith 1993). These 'big' ideas generally stay deep in the background, hidden from view by the policy and programmatic ideas in the foreground, and they are rarely contested except at moments of deep crisis (see Campbell 2004, 93–4). The experience of Germany across the post-war period illustrates the ways in which a country may shift its policy programs without affecting its basic public philosophy. We have already seen that German policy actors had little need to change their macroeconomic policy program, even though it is important to note that the stricter recasting of the monetarist policy paradigm, beginning in the mid-1970s, required significant reorientation by business and labour. This is in contrast to the battle of ideas over microeconomic and social policy that began in the mid-1990s, as labour resisted business leaders' push for greater business liberalization and labour market flexibility as well as the government's push for pension reform, beginning in the early 2000s. In both arenas, however, almost no policy actors questioned the deeper philosophical ideas about the nature and purpose of the 'social market economy' and Germany's coordinated, non-market, managed approach to the political economy. All the discourse was about how to develop new policies and programs that would not undermine the underlying philosophical approach to economic management. Whether the policy makers succeeded in not undermining the social market economy is another, highly contested, issue (see Streeck 2009).

This discussion, then, brings us to the question of how to consider programmatic and philosophical ideas that last over the long term: thus, continuity, not just change. Should it be described in terms of the historical institutionalist notion of 'path-dependence,' which suggests little alteration in the core ideas over time (e.g., Pierson 2004, 39)? Or could we find less deterministic and more dynamic ways of thinking about continuity that, as already discussed, may involve extensive change and incremental development?

A better way to think about such 'continuity through change' would be in terms of Merrien's (1997) concept of 'imprints of the past' (*l'empreinte des origines*), with which he seeks to explain the influence of the foundational principles of welfare states on their subsequent trajectories. He shows that such principles leave imprints that may frame future development, but that this in no way determines the path of development, given that social institutions tend to be infused with new ideas as well as reformed via new practices over time. Another way to think about such continuity through change would be Rothstein's (2005,168–98) use of the concept of 'collective memories' to explain the long-term survival of Sweden's peaceful and collaborative industrial relations system, which was established at critical junctures but nonetheless changed over time with changes in institutional performance. Its origins, he shows, stem from two 'critical moments.' The first was in the early 1930s, when, in response to a violent strike in which five people were killed, the social partners engaged in greater cooperation, while the prime minister even-handedly condemned the violence of the military as he chided the strikers. The second was in the late 1930s, when agreements on collective bargaining institutions were struck; this event became the basis for a collective memory, serving to remind all parties to the discussions that cooperation was both possible and desirable. This collective memory, Rothstein argues, continues to underpin ideas about the collective bargaining system today, even though the system has changed greatly, in particular since the employers pulled out of the national central system in the early 1980s but continue to participate in sectoral bargaining.

Types of Ideas: Cognitive and Normative

Ideas not only emerge at different levels that may help explain their pace of change. They also emerge as different types. Cognitive ideas generally are embedded in discourse focused on justifying a policy or program, by satisfying policy makers as to the robustness of the solutions provided – which is where most scholars who build on the philosophy of science tend to focus (e.g., Hall 1993; Majone 1989). Normative ideas, by contrast, tend to be embedded in discourse focused on legitimating the program, by satisfying policy makers and citizens alike that those solutions also serve the underlying values or public philosophies of the polity, whether long-standing or newly emerging ones. Policy and programmatic ideas can fail where the cognitive discourse justifying a particular program collides with deep-seated normative commitments, for example, when monetarist policies to stabilize budgets clash with commitments to sustain a generous welfare state. This was the long-standing problem for French government attempts to reform work and welfare policy, as their cognitive arguments about the necessity of reform clashed with their constant – and poorly supported – normative claims to protect 'social solidarity' (Schmidt 2000; 2002, 274–87).

Comparative political economists of advanced welfare states tend to highlight the importance of cognitive ideas in the explanation of the successful negotiation of social policy reform. In countries such as Switzerland, Germany, and France, such ideas served to balance perceptions of positive and negative interest-based effects (e.g., Bonoli and Mach 2000; Häuserman 2008). But normative ideas also matter, since we cannot explain the successes – or failures – of welfare state reform efforts without considering the role of discourses about the normative legitimacy of reform, not just its cognitive necessity. In the UK, contrast Prime Minister Thatcher's difficulty in instituting welfare reform with Blair's success, despite similar political institutional capability to impose reform. Thatcher's difficulty was due not just to unpopular neoliberal policies but also in no small measure to a normative discourse that sought to legitimate those policies by distinguishing the 'worthy poor' from the 'feckless and the idle.' This discourse failed to resonate with a public that remained concerned about the poor and valued the universal benefits of the national health service (Taylor-Gooby 1991). Blair's success was due largely to his 'third way' discourse. It legitimated neoliberal policies that went far beyond Thatcher's wildest dreams, such as workfare, mainly because it appealed to values of equality and compassion by promising 'to promote opportunity instead of dependence' through positive actions (i.e., workfare) rather than to negative values that focused on limiting benefits and services. Blair offered 'not a hand out but a hand up,' 'not a hammock but a trampoline' (Schmidt 2000; 2002, chap. 6). In France, similarly, contrast Prime Minister Juppé's dismal failure to impose public sector pension reform without any normative legitimizing discourse in 1995, which resulted in paralyzing strikes, with President Sarkozy's success twelve years later. Sarkozy legitimated eliminating special privileges for public sector workers – in particular those railroad employees who could retire at age fifty – by normative arguments that referred to long-standing republican principles of equality, violated in a context in which all private and many public sector employees could not retire before age sixty or older (Schmidt 2002, chap. 6; 2007).

Paying attention to the substantive content of ideas, in terms of both level and type, helps show the complexities of ideational paradigm change. But we are still missing any theoretical conception of the dynamics of change, that is, not just when ideas change but why they change, which involves questions about the processes by which agents may change their ideas not simply in response to crisis but more gradually over time. Answering these questions requires that we understand discourse not just as the representation of ideas but also as an interactive process of the conveying and exchanging of ideas.

Discursive Processes of Paradigm Change

While the criteria by which we explain paradigm change may be ideational – involving different 'orders' of evolutionary or revolutionary change in cognitive and normative ideas at different levels of generality – the processes of change are discursive, involving not just what social agents say but also to whom, when, how, and why they say it in both policy and political spheres.

Discursive Interactions in Theory

Besides problems in identifying when or why paradigms may be in crisis are others related to who decides that the paradigm is failing or succeeding. Whereas in Kuhnian science, scientists alone judge paradigm success or failure, in society this is judged not only by social scientists but also by citizens. The subjectivity of social science and the reflexive nature of social action, as Peter Winch (1958) argued long ago, make problematic any direct borrowing from the philosophy of science for the social sciences, just as much as it does for any direct modelling of social scientific methods on scientific ones. As Fritz Machlup (1969) suggested, if 'molecules could talk,' they might have a set of ideas about what it is they do very different from those suggested by scientists. Molecules can't talk, but men and women can, and therefore taking account of how they discuss, deliberate, dissent, and legitimate their ideas in the process of deciding to take collective action is an integral part of any account of ideational change.

Ideas do not 'float freely' (Risse-Kappen 1994). Ideas cannot be discussed without pointing to the agents who, as the 'carriers' of ideas and articulators of the discourse, serve as drivers of change. Focusing on 'sentient' (i.e., thinking, speaking, acting) agents is important, because it emphasizes the fact that 'who is speaking to whom about what, where, and why,' or the interactive processes of discourse, make a difference (Schmidt 2008). As sociolinguistics shows (e.g., Ager 1991), we need to consider more than the source of ideas, or who is articulating the ideas in what context with what objective in mind aimed at which audience, including the meaning context for the speaker. We also need to consider the 'speech act' itself: the message, how it is delivered, in what medium or format, and what is said as well as what is not said but nonetheless is tacitly understood. And we have to consider the receptor, or the audience, in terms of who they are, what they are expecting, what their capacity is for understanding the message, and how they respond, which itself can constitute a kind of agency.

For political scientists, complicating matters is the fact that the way the communicative process works in terms of sources, message, and audience depends upon the part of the public sphere in which agents are situated: the policy sphere or the political sphere. Whereas the policy sphere is characterized mainly by a 'coordinative' discourse among policy actors engaged in creating, deliberating, arguing, bargaining, and reaching agreement on ideas, the political sphere is characterized by a 'communicative' discourse between political actors and the public engaged in presenting, contesting, deliberating, and legitimating those ideas (see Schmidt 2002, chap. 5; 2006, chap. 5; 2008).

The agents in the coordinative discourse are generally the actors involved in the policy process, including 'policy makers' or government officials, policy consultants, experts, lobbyists, business and union leaders, and others. They generate policy ideas in different ways with different degrees and kinds of influence, whether as members of 'epistemic communities' of loosely connected individuals who share cognitive and normative ideas about a common policy enterprise (Haas 1992), as in the development of the euro (Verdun 2000); as members of 'advocacy coalitions' of more closely connected individuals who share ideas and access to policy making, as in water policy in California (Sabatier and Jenkins-Smith 1993); or as members of 'discourse coalitions' of policy actors who share ideas across extended periods of time, as in the rise of ordo-liberalism in Germany (Lehmbruch 2001). Alternatively, they themselves may be policy 'entrepreneurs' (Kingdon 1984) or 'mediators' (Jobert 1989; Muller 1995), who serve as catalysts for change as they articulate the ideas of the various discursive communities.

In the communicative discourse, not only do the agents of change consist of the usual suspects: political leaders, elected officials, party members, policy makers, spin doctors, and the like, who act as 'political entrepreneurs' as they attempt to form mass public opinion (Zaller 1992), engage the public in debates about the policies they favour (Mutz, Sniderman, and Brody 1996), and win elections. They also include the media, interest groups acting in the specialized 'policy forums' of organized interests (e.g., Rein and Schön 1994), public intellectuals, opinion makers, social movements, and even ordinary people through their 'everyday talk,' which can play an important role not just in the forum of 'opinion-formation' but also in that of 'will-formation' (Mansbridge 2009). In other words, all manner of discursive publics engaged in 'communicative action' (Habermas 1989) may be involved, communication going not only from the top down but also from the bottom up.

It is important to note that, in addition to any formalized, elite processes of coordinative consultation and whatever the elite-led processes of communicative deliberation, the public has a wide range of ways of deliberating about and responding to elite-produced policies. The media, for instance, are often key in framing the terms of the communicative discourse, creating narratives and images that become determinant of interpretations of a given set of events. For example, the Barings Bank debacle was personalized in terms of a 'rogue trader' as opposed to being generalized as a deeper criticism of the internationalized banking system or of top bankers' negligence (Hudson and Martin 2010). Here, we could also mention Martha Stewart as the poster child for the early 2000s financial crisis or Bernie Madoff for the 2008 crisis.

Social movements are also significant forces in a 'bottom-up' communicative discourse, as scholars who focus on 'contentious politics' demonstrate the ways in which leaders, social movement activists, along with everyday actors spur change through ideas that contest the status quo, conveyed by discourse that persuades others to join in protest, which in turn generates debate (e.g., Aminzade et al. 2001). In fact, new ideas can appear from anywhere to generate transformative public debates. Rothstein (2005), for example, tells the story of how a novel written in Finland in the 1950s that created an understanding of the actions of the 'reds' during the bloody civil war in the early part of the twentieth century enabled the Finns finally to heal their long-standing wounds. The novel spurred public debates and discussions in which the Finnish public came to reconsider the past and to reconcile themselves to it.

Not to be neglected, however, are the 'everyday practices' of ordinary people, even in cases where ideas are unarticulated and change is individual, subtle, and slow, taking shape from the everyday actions of the general public rather than from elite ideas and discourse. As Seabrooke (2007) argues, leaders need legitimacy from the general public. Public views are felt not only at the ballot box or in the street but through the 'everyday practices' of ordinary people whose unspoken discourse in actions make clear that they no longer see the established rules as legitimate. When this unspoken discourse is then picked up by the media and reformist political leaders, it can lead to significant reform. Thus, in a study of the changes in macroeconomic policy in Britain in the interwar years culminating in the 'Great Revelation' of Keynesian economic policy, Seabrooke (2006) shows that the drivers of domestic institutional change in the face of international economic crisis were not government elites but the mass public, whose everyday discourses delegitimizing government policy served as the impulse for those elites to close the 'legitimacy gap' by experimenting with and then instituting more acceptable policies.

The importance of taking account of the everyday actions of ordinary people in its turn brings us back to the need to explain the 'governors' responses to the governed.' This requirement may be met when policy makers seek to institute reforms to remedy the 'drift' by conveying ideas about how they will solve the problem and engaging in communicative discourse that serves to legitimate their proposed solution. It may also explain why scholars in the public policy sphere were first to use ideas and discourse (e.g., Kingdon 1984; Baumgartner and Jones 1993) as a way to account for new laws or rules being brought in to solve problems.

Discursive Interactions in Practice

Discursive interactions, thus, may be bottom up as well as top down, where ideas are generated not only by actors in the coordinative discourse of the policy sphere but also by those in the communicative discourse of the political sphere, which includes the everyday actions of the general public as well as the articulated ideas of a wide range of political and public actors. Only by considering empirical cases can we see exactly how complex these processes of interactive construction and communication of ideas may be.

To begin, the spheres of coordinative policy construction and communicative policy legitimization are always interconnected. The most successful discursive interactions, the ones most likely to produce paradigm change, are therefore not only those in which both coordinative and communicative discourses are well developed but also those that develop similar ideas, such that ideas constructed in the policy sphere are then translated in the political sphere into language accessible and persuasive for the general public. Ideational change can be more difficult where only the coordinative or the communicative discourse is present. And it can go very wrong where what is said in the policy sphere behind closed doors contradicts what is said in the political sphere, especially if this discrepancy is found out and communicated, say, by the media (see Schmidt 2006, chap. 5).

In the case of the neoliberal paradigm shift in the UK beginning in the late 1970s, for example, the coordinative and communicative discourses were fully mutually reinforcing. The ground was prepared even before Thatcher's election, when the neoliberal ideas tied to monetary policy change developed in a coordinative discourse consisting of a small group of the 'converted' from the Conservative party, financial elites, and the financial press (Hall 1993). Thatcher herself, however, was the political entrepreneur who put these ideas into more accessible language through a communicative discourse to the general public that spoke to the cognitive necessity of reform because of 'TINA' – there is no alternative – as well as to its normative appropriateness because of the country's past economically liberal values (Schmidt 2000; 2002, chap. 6). Not only did this communicative discourse serve to legitimate radical monetary policy reform. It also helped Conservative leaders subsequently to convert the electorate to further policy ideas that radically altered the economy through reduced public spending and privatization of major industries and of council housing (Prasad 2006).

Rothstein's (2005) case of Sweden in the 1930s, moreover, points to how the collective memory of the successful coordinative discourse framed by the prime minister's cooperation-oriented communicative discourse in the early 1930s framed the late 1930s coordinative discourse on collective bargaining institutions. In the case of France, interestingly, the two spheres are often united, as political leaders are at one and the same time policy and political entrepreneurs as they forge agreements in the coordinative sphere on a new ideational 'master frame,' which they then legitimate in the communicative sphere. An example is Giscard d'Estaing's role in the creation of the European Monetary System (EMS). It set the path for France to shift from Keynesianism to monetarism (McNamara 1998, 123–6; Parsons 2003, 175–8).

The two spheres of discursive interaction need not be equally important for ideational change, however, since the agents of change may generate ideas in one sphere of discursive interaction rather than another at different times. In political economic policy making, for example, Tiberghien (2007) demonstrates that the post-war *dirigiste* or developmental states of France, Japan, and Korea have become 'entrepreneurial states' as the political economic agents of change shifted from being bureaucratic policy entrepreneurs in the coordinative policy sphere to political entrepreneurs in the communicative political sphere. Here, they harnessed the tools and the discourse of the previous system to create a new set of policies for innovation and modernization. For France, specifically, Tiberghien (2007, chap. 4) shows that starting in the mid-1980s major transformations of macroeconomic policy and industry were the top-down constructions of political leaders with new ideas about how to revitalize the economy. In particular, during the period from 1997 to 2002 Socialist Finance Minister Dominique Strauss-Kahn was the core political entrepreneur, whose ideas about privatization and the role of the state in the economy were transformative. Tiberghien also reinforces the point, made earlier for the French social policy arena, about the problems political leaders have had in normatively legitimating their reforms, especially given public resistance to globalization (see also Gordon and Meunier 2001; Schmidt 2002, 2007).

In the French social policy arena, by contrast, the centre of play moved in the opposite direction, from the communicative to the coordinative, as Palier (2005) shows, with reforms that political leaders had difficulty legitimating to the general public successfully brokered nevertheless with the social partners. This was the case with Prime Minister Balladur's reform of private sector pensions in 1993, to which the social partners agreed on the basis of an 'ambiguous consensus' that mixed positive and negative benefits (Palier 2006; Häusermann 2008). Consensus occurred despite the general absence of any communicative discourse with the public about reforms that were floated as 'trial balloons,' to be quickly withdrawn in the case of negative response (Levy 2000). It was also the case for Prime Minister Raffarin's public sector pension reforms a decade later, in 2003. Another four years were to pass before President Sarkozy's success on special pension regimes, which, by contrast, was largely due to his communicative discourse about republican equality (as noted above). The power of the communicative discourse was such that the union leaders themselves acknowledged that there was little they could do to counter it in their own communicative discourse to the public, and they therefore sought to recoup their losses through side payments in exchange for labour peace in the behind-closed-door coordinative negotiations (Schmidt 2009).

In Germany, a more complicated dynamics was operative. Reform was the product of a mix of policy and political entrepreneurship, although the discursive interactions in the coordinative sphere tended to be the key to success (the following case discussion expands on Schmidt 2009, 536–7). In the 1990s most reform efforts were stymied by a stalemated coordinative discourse characterized by diverging ideas pitting management against the unions. Management increasingly favoured neoliberal reforms to promote labour market flexibility and rationalize pensions; the unions resisted such reforms, blaming European Monetary Union and macroeconomic policy for the lack of economic growth (Schmidt 2002; Kinderman 2005). In the early 2000s, however, the stalemate was overcome with the Hartz IV reforms. The ground for the Hartz IV reforms was prepared by a communicative discourse in which neoliberal ideas were brought in from the outside, first by business and then by political leaders, as noted earlier. But reform success cannot be attributed to Schröder's acting as a political entrepreneur, since his communicative discourse failed to persuade the public either of the necessity or the appropriateness of the reforms (Bosenecker 2008). Schröder provided no normative arguments legitimating the merger of unemployment compensation and means-tested social assistance into a single system: a development that violated the public's basic beliefs about the appropriateness of an insurance-based system. His persistence in the face of plummeting popularity ratings and public discontent nevertheless earned him some grudging respect while it allowed time for the coordinative discourse with the social partners to succeed. These deliberations were led by ministers in Schröder's government who acted as 'ideational leaders' with regard to reforms of pensions, unemployment insurance, and health care, by 'framing' the terms of the discussion (Stiller 2007).

But this is only half the story, since success takes all parties to be persuaded by the ideas in any kind of discursive interaction, in particular in the coordinative discourse. Persuasion of all parties is needed, especially where agreement is based on ambiguity, different parties having different ideas about how the deal serves their interests and values (Bonoli and Mach 2000; Palier 2005; Häusermann 2008). If we were to stop with the ideational leadership of government ministers, we could make it appear as if success in German social policy reform were due to a top-down discursive process in which the 'right' ideas were developed and conveyed by political leaders. Häusermann's (2008) critique of the 'framing' thesis demonstrates that for Germany, as much as for France, success depends upon the structure of the reform coalition of political parties and corporate actors representing groups with very different interests, as well as on a package of reforms that allow a compromise appeal to interests by balancing positive and negative effects. Häusermann's critique stops just as it gets interesting, however, leaving us to ask how (or whether) the government ministers' discourse served to help reframe the social partners' ideas about social policy reform in such as way to lead them to reconceptualize their own ideas about their interests as these had been conceived up until the reform. Another question would be about the discursive interactions themselves. Did government ministers act more as ideational leaders or as 'brokers' of ideas, the flow of ideas coming not from top down – from ministers to the unions, political parties, and business associations – but from top to top, through a kind of participatory empowerment among all of these groups in the negotiations and deliberations (e.g., Fung and Wright 2003)? Such a process of arriving at common agreement on ideas could alternatively be described as one that involves 'common knowledge creation' through reasoned argument about cause and effect, as Culpepper (2008) suggests in the cases of the creation of social pacts in Ireland and Italy, also discussed below.

We still have a problem, however, because this discussion remains focused primarily on the discourse of elites, whether in a top-to-top coordinative discourse or in a top-down communicative discourse. Yet both top-to-top and top-down discourses often need to be understood within the context of a wider sharing of ideas originating in the bottom-up communications of the public. In the case of welfare reform in Sweden in the 1990s, for example, although the ideas emerged from a coordinative discourse that was highly restricted, consisting of an epistemic community of specialized politicians and policy experts alone because the famous concertation among business, labour, and government no longer worked for such macro-level reforms (Marier 2008), it was followed by a more open communicative discourse. The welfare reform ideas were subjected to a kind of decentralized deliberative process in which social-democratic politicians sought to build legitimacy for such reforms by holding meetings in local communities, listening to responses, and changing their proposals accordingly (Schmidt 2003, 141).

Deliberative processes, whether in the coordinative or communicative spheres, tend to mix up the top-down, top-to-top, and bottom-up kinds of distinction that we have so far used. Ireland offers a fascinating case of how one country managed to create a deliberative coordinative discourse among not just the social partners but also civil society. In so doing, it had a radical paradigm shift in its approach to labour relations – a highly unusual reform for a liberal market economy. This shift was a response to major economic meltdown at a 'critical juncture' in 1986–7. Although Irish leaders' ideas and communicative discourse were similar to those of Thatcher with regard to the necessity of neoliberal reforms in macro- and microeconomic policy, their approach to the labour markets was entirely different. Thatcher engaged in no coordinative discourse with labour as she radically decentralized the labour markets, crushing the unions and then instituting legislation to keep them down, claiming that they were the problem. By contrast, Irish leaders enlisted the collaboration of unions through social pacts. At the same time as they engaged in an elaborate coordinative discourse with a wide range of groups, they developed an elaborate communicative discourse to the general public in which they presented globalization as a non-negotiable constraint in order to ensure wage restraint and to reinforce the corporatist cooperation between labour, management, and government (Hay and Smith 2005). The coordinative discourse brought in a wide range of stakeholders in an elaborate process that has sometimes been termed 'deliberative democracy,' involving a 'four-room' negotiating procedure consisting of a main room comprising the main employer and trade union associations; a business room of those not involved in pay negotiations, such as the Chamber of Commerce and Small Firms Association; a farming room; and a community room representing the voluntary and community sector; bilaterals were held between the different rooms, coordinated by the Prime Minister's Office (Teague 2006).

Finally, even Italy, notable for its inability to institute any kind of serious economic or social policy reforms in the 1980s was able to engage in major macroeconomic and social policy reforms in the 1990s by mustering both a successful corporatist coordinative discourse with labour and a communicative discourse with the general public. Italian leaders' communicative discourse invoked the EU as a *vincolo esterno* – the external constraint or, better, 'opportunity'; appealed to national pride in making the sacrifices required to ensure that Italy joined the European Monetary Union from the start; cast the EU tax as the 'price of the last ticket to Europe' (Radaelli 2002, 225–6); and legitimated the pension reform necessitated by joining EMU through appeal to social equity. The *vincolo esterno* would end unfairness and corruption as well as give *'piu ai figli, meno ai padri,'* more to the sons, less to the fathers, so as to ensure intergenerational solidarity (Ferrera and Gualmini 2004; Schmidt 2000). This communicative discourse was accompanied by an equally effective coordinative discourse among highly placed policy actors. They crafted the successful macroeconomic discourse based on sound monetary policy that pushed state and societal actors alike to accept the austerity budgets, the one-off EU tax, and the labour and pension reforms necessary to enable the country to accede to the European Monetary Union. But reforms were also spurred by a coordinative discourse with the unions. In 1995, for example, the discourse engaged not just national union leaders with business and government in tripartite discussions, but also the entire union rank and file in deliberations culminating in a referendum that ensured that opposing union members would accept the 'procedural justice' of the vote and therefore not stage wildcat strikes, as they had in the past (Regini and Regalia 1997; Locke and Baccaro 1999). Berlusconi, by contrast, both in his short tenure in 1994 and his longer ones from 2001 to 2006 and after 2008, adopted a different strategy. He used a communicative discourse to the general public to accuse all of the left, and by extension the unions, of being communists, and he had little productive coordinative discourse. As a result, his attempts to impose policies failed time and again in the face of union strikes.

Institutional Context

Institutional context also matters for paradigm change. But institutional context can be understood in two ways: first and foremost in terms of the meaning-based structures of understanding or discursive patterns of communication of sentient agents but also in terms of the formal or informal institutions that are the focus of other institutionalist approaches, as external structures of constraint. The latter institutions can serve as background information for discursive institutionalists. For example, to explain nationally situated logics of communication, such as the prevalence of the communicative discourse in some polities, it can be useful to turn to historical institutionalism. This approach can help explain, for example, why political systems organized in 'simple' polities where power is concentrated in the executive by way of majoritarian electoral processes in unitary states, as it is in France and the UK, tend to have a more elaborate communicative discourse with the public, since leaders who make decisions with little consultation in the coordinative sphere with the relevant policy actors need to do their utmost to legitimate their decisions to the general public in order to win it over, or else face protest in the street (mainly in France) and electoral sanctions (Schmidt 2006, chap. 5). Similarly, moreover, we could turn to sociological institutionalism, to the cultural frames and norms regarding what can or cannot appropriately be communicated in public to explain why certain topics are not broached, for instance, in Thailand, where, in the debate over political modernization, the role of the monarchy cannot be questioned.[1] Here, though, we might add a rational choice institutionalist focus on incentive structures, since one can also be thrown in jail for criticism of the monarchy.

However, the institutional context may be more purely discursive according to the 'forum' within which the discourse proceeds, following a particular logic of communication. Thus, for example, Toulmin (1958) shows that in any given 'forum of argumentation' or discourse the procedural rules create a common set of understandings, even when speakers lack trust or consensus, as in the adversarial arguments that take place in a courtroom. Moreover, in international negotiations where the rules are not pre-established and the 'forum' is an ad hoc creation dependent upon the players and the circumstances, pre-negotiations are the context within which the rules of discursive interaction are set, even though the actual process involves other kinds of discursive interactions outside the negotiating context, such as occurs among domestic constituencies and other international actors (Stein 1989). Here we could also mention differences as understood by the *référentiel* school, between the forums in which deliberation is more open by contrast with the arenas in which bargaining is the focus.

The last example of institutional context switches the definition of institutions from formal or informal institutions that serve mainly as static external constraints on action to more internal institutions or rules of meaning and communication that tend by definition to be much more dynamic. This is because these kinds of institutions or rules are in a constant process of (re) creation, as constructs as well as structures. The dynamics, however, originates not only from sentient agents' 'background ideational abilities' – what Searle (1995) calls 'background abilities,' Bourdieu calls '*habitus*' (1990), and psychology terms 'cognitive dissonance' (Harmon-Jones and Mills 1999) – that is, their capacity to think beyond their structures of meaning as much as within them, creating new rules as well as following old ones. It also results from agents' 'foreground discursive abilities' to communicate about their rationale for creating new rules, for following old rules, or for critiquing the old rules even as they follow them (Schmidt 2008). This is at the heart of Habermas's (1989) 'communicative action' and the wide range of approaches to 'deliberative democracy' (e.g., Dryzek 2000). While agents' background ideational abilities underpin their ability to make sense in a given meaning context, that is, to 'get it right' in terms of a given institutional setting, their foreground discursive abilities are key to explaining change because they refer to agents' ability to communicate and deliberate about their institutions and to persuade others to take action collectively to change them.

Paradigm change generally occurs within given institutional contexts and can be assumed to alter the institutions that make up that context. But what do we mean by change in institutions here? Most certainly it would entail a change in agents' structures of meaning, that is, what agents think in terms of a given policy, program, and/or philosophy. Remaining open is whether paradigm change also alters the external structures of constraint, that is, the rationalist incentive structures, historical institutions, and cultural frames. But this question is empirical, – whether a shift in ideas leads to change in formal and informal institutions – and the answer requires a focus on the discursive interactions among agents and whether these interactions lead to actions that produce 'revolutionary' or even evolutionary change in the rules.

Conclusion

Paradigm change thus can best be understood as a metaphor for a transformational shift in policy and/or political ideas 'in action.' It is a conversion and/or reinterpretation of 'what is to be done' that has led to major alteration and/or innovation in 'what is done.' Discursive institutionalism deepens the theory of paradigm change by showing that, whatever the timing of change, to understand it we need to examine not just the ideational shift but also the complex processes of discursive interactions. Doing so entails considering both the coordinative and communicative discourses in top-down, top-to-top, and bottom-up directions in given institutional contexts. For political economic change in Europe, a focus on discursive interactions shows that paradigm change, in terms of rapid, revolutionary alterations in ideas, did occur. However, there were also many more incremental changes in ideas, with slower processes of layering and drift that could also be seen to have produced conversion. In assessing the nature and scope of paradigm change, much depends upon the time span one is looking at, as well as the level and type of ideas considered.

NOTE

1 My thanks to an anonymous reviewer for this example.

REFERENCES

Ager, Dennis. 1991. *Sociolinguistics and Contemporary French*. Cambridge: Cambridge University Press.

Aminzade, Ronald R., Jack A. Goldstone, Doug McAdam, Elizabeth J. Perry, William H. Sewell, Jr, Sidney Tarry, and Charles Tilly. 2001. *Silence and Voice in the Study of Contentious Politics*. New York: Cambridge University Press.

Baumgartner, Frank R., and Bryan D. Jones. 1993. *Agendas and Instability in American Politics*. Chicago: University of Chicago Press.

Berman, S. 2006. *The Primacy of Politics: Social Democracy and the Making of Europe's Twentieth Century*. New York: Cambridge University Press.

Blyth, Mark. 2002. *Great Transformations: Economic Ideas and Institutional Change in the Twentieth Century*. New York: Cambridge University Press.

Bonoli, Giuliano, and André Mach. 2000. Switzerland: Adjustment Politics within Institutional Constraints. In Scharpf and Schmidt, *Welfare and Work in the Open Economy*. Vol. 2: *Diverse Responses to Common Challenges in Twelve Countries*.

Bosenecker, Aaron. 2008. The Power of Defining Work and Welfare: Politics and Discourse in European Welfare Reform. Paper read at the 6th International Conference of the Council for European Studies, 6–8 March Chicago.

Bourdieu, Pierre. 1990. *In Other Words: Essays Towards a Reflexive Sociology.* Translated by Matthew Adamson. Stanford: Stanford University Press.

Campbell, John L. 2004. *Institutional Change and Globalization.* Princeton: Princeton University Press.

Culpepper, Pepper. 2008. The Politics of Common Knowledge: Ideas and Institutional Change in Wage Bargaining. *International Organization* 62:1–33.

Dryzek, John. 2000. *Deliberative Democracy and Beyond.* Oxford: Oxford University Press.

– and Stephen T. Leonard. 1988. History and Discipline in Political Science. *American Political Science Review* 82 (4):1245–60.

Ferrera, Maurizio, and Elisabetta Gualmini. 2004. *Rescued by Europe? Social and Labour Market Reforms in Italy from Maastricht to Berlusconi.* Amsterdam: Amsterdam University Press.

Fung, Archon, and E.O. Wright. 2003. Countervailing Power in Empowered Participatory Governance. In *Deepening Democracy,* edited by A. Fung and E.O. Wright. New York: Verso.

Gordon, Philip, and Sophie Meunier. 2001. *The French Challenge: Adapting to Globalization.* Washington, DC: Brookings Institution Press.

Haas, Peter M. 1992. Introduction: Epistemic Communities and International Policy Coordination. *International Organization* 46:1–35.

Habermas, Jürgen. 1989. *The Structural Transformation of the Public Sphere.* Trans. T. Burger and F Lawrence. Cambridge, MA: MIT Press.

Hall, Peter. 1993. Policy Paradigms, Social Learning, and the State: The Case of Economic Policymaking in Britain. *Comparative Politics* 25:275–96.

– and David Soskice. 2001. *Varieties of Capitalism.* Oxford: Oxford University Press.

Harmon-Jones, E., and J. Mills. 1999. *Cognitive Dissonance: Progress on a Pivotal Theory in Social Psychology.* Washington, DC: American Psychological Association.

Häusermann, Silja. 2008. What Explains the 'Unfreezing' of Continental European Welfare States? The Socio-Structural Basis of the New Politics of Pension Reforms. Paper read at the American Political Science Association Annual Meeting, Boston, 28–31 August.

Hay, Colin, and Nicola J. Smith. 2005. Horses for Courses? The Political Discourse of Globalisation and European Integration in the UK and Ireland. *West European Politics* 28(1):125–59.

Hirschman, Albert O. 1989. *National Power and the Structure of Foreign Trade.* Berkeley: University of California Press.

Hudson, David, and Mary Martin. 2010. Narratives of Neoliberalism: The Role of Everyday Media Practices and the Reproduction of Dominant

Ideas. In *The Role of Ideas in Political Analysis: A Portrait of Contemporary Debates* edited by A. Gofas and C. Hay. London: Routledge.

Jobert, B. 1989. The Normative Frameworks of Public Policy. *Political Studies* 37:376–86.

Kinderman, Daniel. 2005. Pressure from Without, Subversion from Within: The Two-Pronged German Employer Offensive. *Comparative European Politics* 3:432–63.

Kingdon, John. 1984. *Agendas, Alternatives and Public Policies*. New York: Longman.

Kuhn, Thomas. 1970. *The Structure of Scientific Revolutions*. 2nd ed. Chicago: University of Chicago Press.

Lehmbruch, G. 2001. Institutional Embedding of Market Economies: The German Model and its Impact on Japan. In *The Origins of Nonliberal Capitalism: Germany and Japan in Comparison*, edited by W. Streeck and K. Yamamur. Ithaca: Cornell University Press.

Levy, Jonah. 2000. France: Directing Adjustment? In Scharpf and Schmidt, *Welfare and Work In the Open Economy*. Vol. 2.

Locke, Richard, and Lucio Baccaro. 1999. The Resurgence of Italian Unions? In *The Brave New World of European Labor*, edited by A. Martin and G. Ross. New York: Berghahn.

Machlup, Fritz. 1969. If Matter Could Talk. In *Philosophy, Science and Method: Essays in Honor of Ernest Nagel*, edited by S. Morgenbessser, P. Suppes, and M.G. White. New York: St Martin's Press.

Majone, G. 1989. *Evidence, Argument, and Persuasion in the Policy Process*. New Haven: Yale University Press.

Mansbridge, Jane. 2009. Deliberative and Non-Deliberative Negotiations. Harvard Kennedy School Working Paper No. RWP09–010.

Marier, Patrik. 2008. Empowering Epistemic Communities: Specialist Politicians, Policy Experts and Policy Reform. *West European Politics* 321 (3):513–33.

McNamara, Kathleen. 1998. *The Currency of Ideas: Monetary Politics in the European Union*. Ithaca: Cornell University Press.

Merrien, François-Xavier. 1997. *L'État-providence, Que Sais-Je*. Paris: Les Presses Universitaires de France.

Muller, Pierre. 1995. Les politiques publiques comme construction d'un rapport au monde. In *La construction du sens dans les politiques publiques. Débats autour de la notion de référentiel*, edited by A. Faure, G. Pollet, and P. Warin. Paris: Harmattan.

Mutz, D.C., Paul M. Sniderman, and Richard A. Brody. 1996. *Political Persuasion and Attitude Change*. Ann Arbor: University of Michigan Press.

Palier, Bruno. 2005. Ambiguous Agreement, Cumulative Change: French Social Policy in the 1990s. In *Beyond Continuity: Institutional Change in Advanced Political Economies*, edited by W. Streeck and K. Thelen. Oxford: Oxford University Press.

– 2006. Long Good Bye to Bismarck? Changes in the French Welfare State. In *Changing France*, edited by P. Culpepper, P. Hall, and B. Palier. New York: Palgrave Macmillan.

Parsons, Craig. 2003. *A Certain Idea of Europe*. Ithaca: Cornell University Press.

Pierson, Paul. 2004. *Politics in Time: History, Institutions, and Social Analysis*. Princeton: Princeton University Press.

Prasad, Monica. 2006. *The Politics of Free Markets: The Rise of Neoliberal Economic Policies in Britain, France, Germany, and the United States*. Chicago: University of Chicago Press.

Radaelli, Claudio M. 2002. The Italian State and the Euro. In *The European State and the Euro*, edited by K. Dyson. Oxford: Oxford University Press.

Regini, Marino, and Ida Regalia. 1997. Employers, Unions and the State: The Resurgence of Concertation in Italy. *West European Politics* 20:210–30.

Rein, Martin, and D.A. Schön. 1994. *Frame Reflection: Toward the Resolution of Intractable Policy Controversies*. New York: Basic Books.

Risse-Kappen, Thomas. 1994. Ideas Do Not Float Freely: Transnational Coalitions, Domestic Structures, and the End of the Cold War. *International Organization* 48 (2):185–214.

Rothstein, Bo. 2005. *Social Traps and the Problem of Trust*. Cambridge: Cambridge University Press.

Sabatier, Paul, and Hank C. Jenkins-Smith, eds. 1993. *Policy Change and Learning: An Advocacy Coalition Approach*. Boulder, CO: Westview Press.

Scharpf, Fritz W. 2000. Economic Changes, Vulnerabilities, and Institutional Capabilities. In Scharpf and Schmidt, *Welfare and Work In the Open Economy*. Vol. 1: *From Vulnerability to Competitiveness*.

– and Schmidt, Vivien A. 2000. *Welfare and Work in the Open Economy*. 2 vols. Oxford: Oxford University Press.

Schmidt, Vivien A. 2000. Values and Discourse in the Politics of Adjustment. In *Welfare and Work in the Open Economy*. Vol. 1: *From Vulnerability to Competitiveness*.

– 2002. *The Futures of European Capitalism*. Oxford: Oxford University Press.

– 2003. How, Where, and When Does Discourse Matter in Small States' Welfare State Adjustment? *New Political Economy* 8 (1):127–46.

– 2006. *Democracy in Europe: The EU and National Polities*. Oxford: Oxford University Press.

– 2007. Trapped by Their Ideas: French Elites' Discourses of European Integration and Globalization. *Journal of European Public Policy* 14 (4):992–1009.

– 2008. Discursive Institutionalism: The Explanatory Power of Ideas and Discourse. *Annual Review of Political Science* 11: 303–26.

– 2009. Putting the Political Back into Political Economy by Bringing the State Back Yet Again. *World Politics* 61 (3):516–48.

– 2010. Taking Ideas and Discourse Seriously: Explaining Change through Discursive Institutionalism as the Fourth New Institutionalism. *European Political Science Review* 2 (1):1–25.

Seabrooke, Leonard. 2006. *The Social Sources of Financial Power.* Ithaca: Cornell University Press.

– 2007. The Everyday Social Sources of Economic Crises: From 'Great Frustrations' to 'Great Revelations' in Interwar Britain. *International Studies Quarterly* 51:795–810.

Searle, John. 1995. *The Construction of Social Reality.* New York: Free Press.

Stein, Janice, ed. 1989. *Getting to the Table: The Processes of International Prenegotiation.* Baltimore: Johns Hopkins University Press.

Stiller, Sabina. 2007. Innovative Agents versus Immovable Objects: The Role of Ideational Leadership in German Welfare State Reforms. Radboud University, Nijmegen.

Streeck, Wolfgang. 2009. *Re-Forming Capitalism: Institutional Change in the German Political Economy.* Oxford: Oxford University Press.

– and Kathleen Thelen. 2005. Introduction: Institutional Change in Advanced Political Economies. In *Beyond Continuity: Institutional Change in Advanced Political Economies,* edited by W. Streeck and K. Thelen. Oxford: Oxford University Press.

Taylor-Gooby, Peter. 1991. Attachment to the Welfare State. In *British Social Attitudes: The 8th Report,* edited by R. Jowell. Aldershot, UK: Dartmouth.

Teague, Paul. 2006. Social Partnership and Local Development in Ireland: The Limits to Deliberation. *British Journal of Industrial Relations* 44 (3):421–43.

Tiberghien, Yves. 2007. *Entrepreneurial States: Reforming Corporate Governance in France, Japan, and Korea.* Ithaca: Cornell University Press.

Toulmin, Stephen. 1958. *The Uses of Argument.* Cambridge: Cambridge University Press.

Verdun, Amy. 2000. *European Responses to Globalization and Financial Market Integration: Perceptions of EMU in Britain, France and Germany.* Basingstoke, UK: Macmillan. New York: St Martin's Press.

Winch, Peter. 1958. *The Idea of a Social Science and its Relation to Philosophy.* London: Routledge.

Zaller, J. 1992. *The Nature and Origins of Mass Opinion.* New York: Cambridge University Press.

3   Transnational Policy Paradigm Change and Conflict in the Harmonization of Vehicle Safety and Accounting Standards

TONY PORTER

What impact does transnationalism have on policy paradigm change? This chapter focuses on three aspects of policy paradigm change that have become more prominent as transnationalism has become more extensive. These are the increased impact of conflicts between *national* policy paradigms; the greater importance of *trans*national policy networks; and changes in the relationship between the ideational qualities of a policy paradigm and more material factors with which these ideas interact. As noted in the Introduction, the study of policy paradigms has evolved not just by applying a fixed conception of what a paradigm is to an increasing variety of cases and policy developments such as transnationalism, but also by continually re-examining and reworking the concept of a policy paradigm itself. The three aspects of transnational policy paradigm change that this chapter examines also suggest a need to further rework the concept of a policy paradigm.

The chapter assesses the significance of these practical and conceptual changes by examining two cases of transnational policy paradigms: vehicle safety standards and accounting standards. In both cases harmonization has involved policy paradigm clashes that relate to differences in US and EU regulatory traditions – but with very different outcomes. In the case of accounting, a US-oriented paradigm that incorporates important international elements is becoming dominant globally, while in the case of vehicle safety, the European-oriented paradigm with certain international elements is winning out.

Reconceptualizing Policy Paradigm Change in a Globalizing Environment

What is a policy paradigm and how does it relate to its external environment? We can define a paradigm as a set of ideas that have three features: they come in large packages; these packages have sufficient autonomy or self-referentiality that they are not simply reflections of empirical patterns; and these packages of ideas can have an influence on practice, including the practice of policy (Hall 1993), industry (Dosi 1982), or science (Kuhn 1970). While the merits of the notion of a paradigm can still be disputed, there is sufficiently wide acceptance that these general features of ideas are evident in some important policy cases, such as the shift from Keynesian policies to monetarism, that we can take this approach to ideas as a starting point and explore its potential and limits.

In recent decades the importance of transnational phenomena for national political systems has been elevated. In part this effect involves the increased importance of phenomena that have always exceeded the boundaries of nation states, such as diplomacy or trade, but it also involves the emergence of new phenomena. For much of the twentieth century states were able to insulate their national policy processes quite well from transnational phenomena. It is not surprising then that, when Hall (1993) developed his path-breaking analysis of policy paradigms, he focused primarily on the relevance of a policy paradigm to understand the interaction of actors and ideas that occurred at the level of a nation state. However, in the ensuing years the need to understand the effects of transnational phenomena has become pressing. Not only have traditional transnational phenomena become more important, but new aspects of transnationalism within and across borders have also become evident.

One useful way to analyse the increased effect of traditional transnational phenomena on national policy paradigms is to draw from the long and extensive history of the study of international relations. The dominant theme in this history is the state-centric realist idea that world politics is shaped by the conflict between states, and that the most powerful states always win. We may expect then that, as international interactions between states intensify, differing national paradigms will come into conflict and the paradigms associated with the most powerful states will supplant paradigms associated with weaker states, perhaps directly through state-to-state interactions, or perhaps by the powerful state manipulating international institutions. Alternatively, when power is more evenly distributed across the most powerful states, a negotiated compromise may lead to a new paradigm that includes elements of each powerful state's national policy paradigm, particularly if some degree of harmonization is in their mutual interest. These are types of paradigm change that might display the characteristics of change that are usually associated with paradigms, namely, long periods of incremental change interrupted by a relatively sudden wholesale change, but for very different reasons than have usually been identified in the literature inspired by Hall.

A secondary theme in this history that has challenged the state-centric realist emphasis on powerful states is the idea that international institutions and practices have sufficient autonomy to exert an influence on national policies that is more than the expression of the political power of other states. There is a long history of identifying such influences, and the older literature will alert us to the possibility that intergovernmental organizations such as the International Monetary Fund or the Organization for Economic Cooperation and Development may play a role in formulating or strengthening policy paradigms that is comparable to the role played by states at the national level.

However, there is also a great deal of theorizing that suggests that today transnationalism has become much more complex. In this chapter I focus especially on two contemporary features of transnational institutions that are highly relevant to policy paradigms. The first concerns the boundary between the realm of ideas, with which paradigms are usually associated, and material factors. The second concerns the degree to which the type of dramatic change that has usually been associated with paradigms involves a wholesale change in the *content* of the paradigm rather than a recombination of existing elements. I discuss each in turn. In each case the visibility of changes at the global level can be an inspiration for reworking the policy paradigm concept, but the effects of these changes are also present at the national level, and their relevance is just as great for national policy processes as for global ones.

Ideational/Material Entanglements and Policy Paradigm Change

A distinctive feature of our contemporary world is its knowledge intensity. Now, even at the international level, where hard military power has sometimes been seen as the only force that matters, it is widely recognized that ideas play an important role in shaping the actions of states. Yet the knowledge intensity of international affairs goes well beyond the reliance of states and other international actors on policy ideas. It is increasingly evident that the ideational is entangled with the material in ways that challenge the assumptions of many theories. This is most obvious in financial markets, where derivatives are a set of commitments based on complex risk models but also are products with enormous material values and effects, or where computer protocols allocate values and manage rules in ways that, in effect, are identical to decisions made by thinking human actors. More generally, best practices, which have become important transnational policy instruments, are simultaneously a set of ideas about how things should be done and an accumulation of actual physical behaviours.

Hall's influential analysis of policy paradigms highlighted certain distinctive features of paradigms that have tended to be associated with their autonomous ideational properties. Following Kuhn, Hall's model is one in which a relatively integrated and autonomous system of ideas lodges itself in a state, only to change when an accumulation of anomalies or a growing number of critics leads to the creation of a new paradigm, which then replaces the old one. What is the source of the paradigm's integration and autonomy? Hall suggests that it is the ideas and the language used to communicate them: 'Like a Gestalt, this framework is embedded in the very terminology through which policymakers communicate about their work, and it is influential precisely because so much of it is taken for granted and unamenable to scrutiny as a whole' (1993, 279). This paradigm, then, is reinforced by the social institutions associated with the state.

Moving away from this model to consider variations in the ideational/material entanglements of paradigms is important in exploring the impact of transnationalism on the longevity and the propensity to change of policy paradigms. The ideational elements of policy paradigms may be entangled with national or local histories whose persistence is enabled by their inscription in material artefacts, such as industrial technologies, regulatory manuals, or built environments.[1] Globalization has been characterized as a process of disembedding from local contexts of social relations facilitated by expert systems of knowledge and finance (Giddens 1990). However, this disembedding has a material aspect as well. Trans-border technologies such as airports or the hard wires that implement visions of borderless financial markets display ideational/material entanglements. Moreover, like other older technologies such as railways or the automobile, the technologies themselves can have a paradigm-like character because they come in very large-scale integrated systems that are characterized by incremental change punctuated by a wholesale shift to a new system after a crisis or a long accumulation of problems (Dosi 1982). If sets of integrated ideas, including policy paradigms, are entangled with such technologies, then their paradigm-like qualities can be reinforced. If these technologies extend across borders, then the policy paradigms entangled with them may be less associated with the state. When policy paradigms and the materiality of technology are entangled, the latter can be a source of paradigm change or it can inhibit change and contribute to the longevity of policy paradigms.

A widely recognized restructuring of the state further enhances the significance of such entanglements of ideational and material elements of policy paradigms. This restructuring has been given various labels in different research traditions, including 'regulatory capitalism' (Levi-Faur and Jordana 2005), 'governmentality' (Larner and Walters 2004), the 'disaggregated state' (Slaughter 2004; Hansen and Salskov-Iversen 2008), or the 'new public management.' All these terms suggest that there is a shift from more centralized command and control to governance mechanisms where general models, guidelines, or benchmarks are used to make a more decentralized set of actors implement policy by regulating their own conduct. Vertical chains of command decline in importance relative to networks and horizontal coordination. The policy landscape becomes a more hybrid mix of public and private actors and rules, some of which enjoy considerably greater autonomy than before. This includes the strengthening of private authority nationally and transnationally, where business actors create and manage rules that traditionally would have been seen as the prerogative of states (Cutler, Haufler, and Porter 1999). Hall's model and the case he chose to illustrate it are especially well suited to more traditional, centralized policy making, where a set of integrated ideas shapes the decisions of top policy makers, who then pull the appropriate levers to implement policy. However, for more disaggregated forms of governance the ideas need to extend much further along the chain of implementation. In many cases the complexity of particular semi-autonomous fields of activity in this chain will lead to quite distinctive sets of ideas that are entangled with the material aspects of those fields, and this materiality is likely to influence transnational processes of change. These semi-autonomous fields may have key characteristics of policy paradigms, but their centre of gravity may have shifted away from the state. I argue below that both accounting standards and vehicle safety regulation are examples.

Paradigm Change: Wholesale Replacement or Recombination of Existing Elements?

The structure of international affairs makes it less likely than is the case at the national level that paradigm change will involve the wholesale replacement of one system of thought by another. At the national level it is not uncommon for one party to be defeated and for another party with a quite different set of ideas to gain control of the government. Even if a single party retains control of the national government, the centralized character of that control means that, if that party is persuaded by a new set of ideas, it can implement them thoroughly. At the international level, in contrast, power is distributed across a great variety of states, and it is likely that the replacement of one set of ideas by another will involve processes of policy transfer and diffusion that are more uneven and gradual than is the case nationally.

As the study of global governance has evolved, there has been an increased recognition that structures of transnational authority are more likely to involve sustained horizontal and often informal coordination among states than the construction of formal bureaucratic international organizations that tell states what to do. Certainly, powerful states can work with international institutions to pressure weaker states to adopt particular policies, but the power of state sovereignty as an organizing principle puts limits on this influence. Even large, formal intergovernmental organizations such as the United Nations and the International Monetary Fund are intended to promote the interests of their member states and are constrained in trying to do more. Transnational policy networks can involve hybrid mixtures of public and private actors, adding further complexity. The disaggregation of the state that was discussed above contributes to this complexity but also means that lessons drawn from more horizontal forms of governance at the global level are more applicable to the national level than they were in the twentieth century, when the organizational differences between the two levels were much greater.

Despite the complexity of transnational governance, certain integrated sets of ideas can develop considerable coherence and persistence at the international level. These can be big general ideas such as environmental sustainability or the market-oriented policies that came to be labelled the Washington consensus, but they can also be more focused technical bodies of knowledge such as the motor vehicle safety standards and the accounting standards that this chapter examines below. They may be managed by public officials, private actors, or a mixture of both. How can such ideas display the patterns of discontinuous longevity and change that are usually seen as a defining feature of paradigms? The previous section emphasized the material entanglements of these ideas, but also important is the way in which paradigm change can result from a dramatic recombination of existing elements in a new paradigm rather than a wholesale replacement of the elements of one paradigm by the elements of another.

The concept of an *assemblage,* which originated in art as a reference to a collection of objects with prior uses and relationships that are brought together into a new meaningful relationship with one another (Seitz 1961), is an especially useful way to express this idea. Elements of one assemblage can 'plug into' others, and the roles they play can change over time. Sassen (2006; see also Ong and Collier 2005) has fruitfully used this concept to analyse the subtle ways in which a part of a state that at one point in time played a primarily domestic role has become part of a global structure of authority while retaining its domestic linkages. The *enrolment* of networks of humans and objects into such assemblages is an important feature of power.[2] The concept of enrolment suggests that power is obtained in complex environments not by commanding compliance but rather by linking these networks to a particular program of action. The chain of action that a network represents can reorient itself from a national to a transnational level and establish new transnational linkages in doing so. However, paradigm change can also occur more exclusively at the national or global levels if networks of action that have been oriented towards one organizing principle begin to reattach themselves to a different one.

The discontinuous character of these shifts can be explained from a more sociological perspective that emphasizes the importance of frames for guiding action (Djelic and Sahlin-Andersson 2006) or from a more rationalist perspective that emphasizes the sunk costs associated with existing practices and the cost effectiveness for most networks of awaiting an accumulation of signals from other networks that a new status quo will work before making the costly adjustments required to jump on board (Simmons and Elkins 2004). In both cases the discontinuity can be related to the power of a program to enrol decentralized networks of activity rather than to capture the thinking of those at the top of a chain of command. This model of paradigm change is different from Hall's, and it is likely to be especially relevant transnationally, where there is an absence of centralized authority.

Operationalizing This Approach

How might we operationalize these theoretical points in a way that makes them applicable to particular cases of policy paradigms and that allows their theoretical contributions to be assessed relative to alternative approaches? One task is to determine whether there is evidence of conflicts between states in which the more powerful states successfully promote their national policy paradigms against others, perhaps with the assistance of an intergovernmental organization. We also need to contrast two conceptions of the way in which policy paradigms function: one, consistent with Hall's approach, which traces the integration and cohesion of a set of ideas to the character of the ideas themselves, albeit with a link to the effectiveness of the policies they inspire; and a second, which stresses the ability of a paradigm in which the ideational and material are already entangled to draw together relatively autonomous and far-flung humans, objects, and networks to manage complex problems. In the first approach, change results when one paradigm weakens from anomalies and from the growth of external challengers and then is replaced all at once by another. In the second approach, rather than replacement, change instead can involve a recombination of existing elements in the construction of a new assemblage in which networks of action, mixing ideational and material elements, are linked to other networks in new ways. In empirically assessing the relative merits of these conceptions it will be important to pay close attention, in the process of change, to the character of the boundaries between the ideational and the material and between a paradigm and its environment.

Two Cases: Vehicle Safety and Accounting Standards

Attempts at the global harmonization of vehicle safety and accounting standards have been very actively pursued since the mid-1990s. Both are important issue areas. Vehicle safety standards are important in addressing the deaths of more than a million people in road crashes worldwide, along with as many as 50 million injured.[3] Accounting standards are essential for the assessment and comparison of corporate financial reports that in turn are essential for stock trading, investing, and financial markets more generally. Both cases differ from policies carried out in a more centralized 'command and control' fashion, such as macroeconomic policy, since they instead involve standard setting that is set apart from government and is reliant on direct private sector involvement in the creation or implementation of rules to a greater degree. As noted above, this type of regulation is becoming an increasingly important aspect of public policy, and meaningful comparison across the two cases is facilitated by their similarities in this respect.

We shall see that both cases involve clashes between a US-oriented policy paradigm and a European-oriented one. In both cases lack of harmonization was seen as a problem for international business actors, creating unwanted costs in moving from one jurisdiction to another. These business concerns about costs exhibit a degree of tension with other public policy goals that would require that standards not converge on a lowest common denominator (goals of reducing road carnage and enhancing the stability of financial markets). In both cases an international institution became the locus of efforts to develop global standards: 'global technical regulations' (GTRs) at the World Forum for Harmonization of Vehicle Regulations, ('World Forum'), at the UN Economic Commission for Europe (UNECE) and International Financial Reporting Standards (IFRS) at the International Accounting Standards Board (IASB).

Despite their similarities, the outcomes of these harmonization efforts have been quite different: in accounting, global standards that most closely resemble the US paradigm have enjoyed very rapid growth and acceptance, while in the vehicle case global standards have displayed relatively little progress and the European-oriented paradigm is becoming dominant. This different outcome of harmonization efforts across the two cases of vehicle safety and accounting standards provides a good opportunity to assess the merits of the theoretical approaches set out above in explaining these different outcomes of processes of paradigm change. This section discusses each case in turn before comparing them.

Vehicle Safety Standards

The global harmonization of vehicle safety standards has been complicated by the persistence of two very different policy paradigms.[4] In the highly integrated production system of the US and Canada vehicle safety regulation has been based on a manufacturer's 'self-certification' model. In this model a regulatory agency (in the US, the National Highway and Transport Safety Administration, the NHTSA) or department (Transport

Canada in Canada) sets out relatively general vehicle safety standards. Manufacturers are then given a great deal of discretion in how they design and produce vehicles to meet those standards. They conduct tests on their vehicles and present these data to the regulator, who then may conduct random spot tests. However, the major compliance mechanisms are the threat of private litigation and the recall of vehicles that are found to fall short of compliance once they are out on the road. This self-certification paradigm dates from the 1970s, when it was constructed in response to the types of auto safety problems dramatically revealed in Ralph Nader's *Unsafe at Any Speed* (1965).

In sharp contrast, the paradigm governing vehicle safety in Europe has been a 'type-approval' model. In this model government-approved laboratories establish more specific safety criteria for the design and construction of vehicles and parts, and manufacturers must establish that they meet these criteria before they are allowed to sell the vehicles. Compliance therefore occurs through an interaction between government and firms before the vehicle is marketed, while in the North American paradigm it occurs in the market, where there is a much higher degree of interaction between consumers and firms.

The first efforts at international harmonization of standards occurred at the UNECE's Working Party 29 (WP.29), created in 1952. It has focused on harmonizing regulations in the areas of active and passive safety (crash avoidance and crashworthiness) as well as two non-safety issues: environment and energy use. Until 1998 WP.29 reflected primarily European concerns. In its early years its focus was on solving regulatory problems that arose from vehicles being driven or sold across European borders. The first harmonized standard, for headlamps, was agreed in 1956, and a more extensive agreement concluded two years later, the '1958 Agreement,' has provided the framework for WP.29's subsequent work. Before 1998 there were no contracting parties to the 1958 agreement other than European countries and their immediate neighbours, but the transnational character of the industry and the eagerness of countries to exchange information about vehicle regulation led non-European nations to participate in WP.29. The US and Canada participated from the start, and Japan and Australia attended WP.29 meetings for two decades before they became contracting parties to WP.29's agreements (UNECE 2002).

In 1998 WP.29 was renamed the World Forum for Harmonization of Vehicle Regulations to mark efforts to transform it into a more global organization. In addition to the name change, a new 1998 agreement was signed, entering into force in 2000. This agreement does not supersede the 1958 agreement but rather works alongside it. As of 2007 the 1998 agreement had twenty-nine contracting parties.[5] In contrast to WP.29's prior practice the new agreement initiated the creation of 'global technical regulations' (GTRs)[6] – common global standards that it was hoped would be incorporated into national regulations around the world, including in North America. It also called for recognition of both type approval and manufacturers' self-certification. In contrast to its relatively detached stance in earlier phases of WP.29's development, the US was strongly supportive of this new global initiative. Despite the new globally oriented 1998 agreement, the particular importance for Europe of the 1958 agreement did not disappear. Indeed, the accession of the EU to WP.29's 1958 agreement in 1998 has facilitated increased linkages between EU regulations and the World Forum.

Considerable effort has been devoted to the development of GTRs, but progress has been very slow. While more than twenty-three additional initiatives to create new GTRs or amend existing ones had been recorded by late 2007, only five GTRs had been established, and only one of these (for door locks) was significant for auto manufacturers. By comparison the NHTSA administers over sixty Federal Motor Vehicle Safety Standards (FMVSS). Seven years after the 1998 agreement entered into force, the pace of GTR adoption has not unreasonably been characterized by a US representative at the World Forum as 'less than glacier speed.'[7]

More important than the GTR process have been regional initiatives. Not surprisingly, the Canadian government has been very actively seeking to harmonize Canadian vehicle safety standards with those of the US. Elsewhere, however, by far the prevailing trend has been harmonization with the World Forum's European-oriented 1958 agreement, based on the type-approval model. This is especially evident in the important Asian markets. The public/private Japan Automobile Standards Internationalization Center (JASIC), established in 1987, has played a leadership role in Asia in promoting convergence with World Forum regulations, especially with the 1958 agreement. JASIC established and implemented a contract with the APEC Secretariat, which formed the major part of APEC's Road Transport Harmonization Project. This project involved creating a detailed inventory of the state of the region's vehicle safety standards and the challenges involved in harmonizing them. JASIC has also provided a great deal of information and encouragement to regional regulators on participating in and following the World Forum regulations and on vehicle safety regulation more generally, including through its website and presentations at regional meetings.

The main emphasis in Asian discussions, heavily promoted by JASIC, has been to adopt the World Forum's 1958 agreement's type-approval system (including the delegation of testing to third parties). Adoption requires countries to mutually recognize certificates based on the regulations agreed under the 1958 agreement. There are some exceptions to this enthusiasm for type-approval regulation. South Korea has developed a self-certification system as an option and accordingly has greatly enhanced its recall system, while other countries (Australia, Brunei, Singapore) accept a manufacturer's self-certification for some parts of vehicles.[8] JASIC and other actors are enthusiastic about the goal of the 1998 agreement to bring together North American self-certification systems with the rest of the world's emphasis on type approval. Overall, however, the slow pace of the GTRs has guaranteed that the 1998 agreement will not be a significant counterweight to the rapid movement in Asia towards the 1958 agreement. Elsewhere in the world, regional agreements have not been as important; instead, certain individual countries have adopted type-approval systems that are more consistent with the 1958 agreement's standards than with the North American self-certification system.

Accounting Standards

In accounting, too, global harmonization of standards has been inhibited by differences between European and American policy paradigms.[9] In the United States accounting has long been oriented towards financial reporting in capital markets. The inevitable conflict of interest that can occur when firms hire accountants to create ostensibly independent verifications of their financial condition historically was handled by the creation of the private sector American Institute of Certified Public Accountants (AICPA), which provided reputational incentives to hold accountants accountable and also became involved in the setting of standards, the Generally Accepted Accounting Principles (GAAP). In 1973 responsibility for setting standards was shifted from the AICPA, and an independent private sector body, the Financial Accounting Standards Board (FASB), took over standard setting. Over time government oversight and support through the Securities and Exchange Commission (SEC) also increased, but the process nevertheless was dominated by the private sector. The FASB itself is a private sector body; the trustees who set its direction are representatives primarily of the private sector; and the standards setters, while not representing firms, generally have had extensive careers in accounting firms.[10] The very heavy dominance of the US market by the 'Big Four' accounting firms further enhances their ability to influence standard setting. Following the Enron scandal, in which Arthur Andersen, one of what were then the 'Big Five' accounting firms, failed to reveal financial wrongdoing and subsequently collapsed, responsibility for auditing of accounting was shifted from the AIPCA to a newly created Public Company Accounting Oversight Board (PCAOB), the members of which are appointed by the SEC.

The US GAAP have been distinctive not just because of their orientation towards capital markets and private sector governance, but also because of their highly legalistic approach. Largely in response to the threat of private legal action, accountants demanded ever finer detail in standards.[11] Excessive legalistic detail ('financial engineering') was seen as having contributed to the Enron scandal: many of the questionable treatments of Enron's financial data by accountants were within the letter of the complex detailed rules but violated what should have been the spirit of the standards – legal complexity was used to obscure the company's financial condition.

In contrast to the capital markets-oriented US paradigm, in continental Europe accounting was traditionally much more closely linked to taxation. Consequently, governments were much more heavily involved in standard setting. For instance, from 1947 accounting standards in France were written by a government agency, the Conseil national de la comptabilité (CNC), a group made up primarily of public servants, which included five trade unionists alongside a number of other non-accounting experts (Eaton and Porter 2008). Outside Britain and the Commonwealth, which was influenced by the more market-oriented approach of the British, the state-oriented approach was common. These divergent approaches mean that for twenty-five years the efforts to harmonize accounting standards at the International Accounting Standards Committee (IASC), which was established in 1973, were very slow and tended to involve an insistence on national representation (Eaton 2004). Until the late 1990s this slow pace, combined with the lure for foreigners of participation in the disproportionately large US capital markets, seemed to be leading to de facto global dominance of the US GAAP. For instance, an increasing number of European firms were beginning to report using the US GAAP, and the US SEC seemed to have an enormously powerful lever in its ability to require foreign firms and investors to use the US GAAP if they wished to participate in US capital markets.

In 2001 the IASC was transformed into the International Accounting Standards Board (IASB), which marked a significant change in direction for the harmonization process. The number of representatives on the board was reduced from seventeen part-time members to twelve full-time and two part-time members. It was made clear that they would be selected on the basis of expertise rather than geographical representation. A four-level structure was created with a separation between the trustees, who would manage the finances and appointments to the board; the board, which would focus solely on standard setting, free from direct external influence in its technical work; a Standards Advisory Council, which provided a consultative mechanism for actors not on the board; and a Standing Interpretations Committee, which would deal with ongoing interpretive questions.

The signal sent by the creation of the IASB was mixed. On the one hand, it represented a level of professionalization and institutional autonomy at the international level that seemed at odds with the idea that the US GAAP, run by the FASB and the US SEC, might become hegemonic. On the other hand, the loss of the principle of national representation, the similarities in the structures of the IASB and the FASB, the prominent role that big US-based accounting firms was likely to play in the new arrangement, and the appointment of Sir David Tweedie of the UK as the IASB's first chair led to a widespread perception that the IASB was a vehicle to promote the global dominance of Anglo-American accounting. At its creation the IASB became a prime example of transnational private authority, since it was a private sector rule-making body with a high degree of autonomy. The highly concentrated character of the accounting industry, which is also dominated internationally by the Big Four firms, reinforces the private aspects of transnational governance in accounting.

The history of the IASB since its creation indicates that, while the IASB's practices are closer to the US FASB's than to the state-oriented accounting process present earlier in continental Europe, it is not simply promoting US standards. On the contrary, a key difference and advantage of international accounting standards over the GAAP that was recognized by the SEC in the aftermath of the Enron scandal was the more principles-based and less legalistic character of the former. The IASB's standards are being adopted rapidly around the world, including most significantly in the European Union, thus greatly increasing their credibility relative to the US GAAP. While the EU has complained very vocally about the IASB's imposition on Europe of certain US-oriented practices, it seems clear that the influence of jurisdictions outside the US on standard setting at the IASB will be much greater than if the FASB's US GAAP had continued to become the de facto global standards. Indeed, following the global financial crisis of 2008, US concerns about European influence in the IASB were voiced, and the expectation that Asia would be given more influence was expressed by Tweedie and by Asian officials, making the importance for the IASB of balancing these competing pressures more evident.

Following the crisis, the SEC, the FASB, and the IASB reaffirmed their commitment to an intensive process of collaboration to promote convergence between the US GAAP and the IASB standards in anticipation that ultimately the latter will be accepted in the US. While the crisis made this convergence more difficult, especially with regard to differences in the degree to which financial assets should reflect their current market prices ('mark to market'), as opposed to amortized historical values, it also increased political support for convergence, most significantly from the G20 leaders. The mark to market approach was widely seen as having contributed to the crisis when certain markets froze and the market value of the instruments in them collapsed. The effects on the general public and markets in other countries raised questions about the adequacy of the IASB's own accountability, which in turn led to important constitutional changes in the IASB, most notably the creation of the new Monitoring Board of public authorities. While there is a possibility that the increased politicization and complexity of accounting standards following the crisis will lead to a breakdown of international harmonization, it is more likely that it will lead to an increase in the IASB's ability to manage and balance competing political pressures, reinforcing the transnational character of accounting standards, especially considering the costs of turning back when most national jurisdictions have already adopted the international standards. In this regard there are similarities between the impact of the crisis on the fate of the euro and the fate of the IASB.

Comparing Vehicle Safety and Accounting Standards

These two cases provide an interesting comparison. Despite their apparent similarities, the outcomes of the clash between the European-oriented and American-oriented paradigms were quite different. In the case of accounting, a new paradigm, the IASB's international standards, is replacing the other ones. In vehicle safety standards a comparable new global paradigm has been relatively unsuccessful; instead, the European-oriented type-approval paradigm has gained influence. This fact allows us to test models of paradigm change against the evidence to see which is better able to account for these outcomes. Since both cases are transnational, they also allow lessons to be drawn about the significance of the transnational dimension for models of paradigm change.

Hall's Approach

How might Hall's model be applied to these two cases? Can we treat the paradigms involved as integrated cohesive sets of ideas that explain the different outcomes with reference to an accumulation of anomalies and the recruitment into the debate by state actors or external actors who then together install a new paradigm? The most promising application of this approach to these cases is to highlight the anomalies in the excessively detailed US GAAP revealed by the Enron scandal and to compare them with the lack of such anomalies in the vehicle safety case. In the vehicle safety case the most comparable anomaly was the costs to transnational firms of complying with different regulatory paradigms in different markets, but this did not challenge the foundational assumptions of the paradigm in the way that the anomalies in accounting did. In both cases external actors in the form of multinational businesses and their associations were important, yet by themselves do not explain the differing outcomes; when combined with the differences in anomalies, however, they can provide a plausible explanation of the emergence of a new paradigm in accounting but not in vehicle safety.

There are, nevertheless, some important shortcomings to this explanation. The use of the notion of anomalies in this way tends to black-box the changes that occurred and to characterize them as problems that are restricted to their relationship to the internal operation of the paradigm. Such an emphasis on anomalies and state recruitment of external actors obscures both the role of variations in materiality in explaining these differences and the agency of external actors in initiating the anomalies and the responses to them, not just by making demands on the state, but by creating or failing to create new international practices – or to use the language introduced above, by enrolling humans, objects, and networks into a new assemblage. Moreover this emphasis on anomalies and external actors cannot explain the differences outside North

America and Europe in the two cases. Why would a European-oriented solution become dominant in Asia in vehicle safety, while a US-oriented solution became dominant in Asia in accounting? A focus on anomalies and recruitment of external actors does not provide an explanation.

The Role of Powerful States

Since the same set of state actors is involved in each case, there are some limitations to the degree that the conventional realist international relations emphasis on the relative power of states can help explain this case. One can always offer tautological explanations about how outcomes necessarily reflect the self-interested calculations of states, but these are not useful analytically. Nevertheless, one can certainly attribute part of the success of the European-oriented 1958 agreement and the global ascendancy of the IASB rather than the US GAAP to the growth in power of the EU relative to the US. As well, the greater role played by Japan in pushing an alternative to a US paradigm in vehicle safety but not in accounting undoubtedly reflects in part the greater relative power of Japan in automobiles compared with finance. Finally, one could argue that the US today is relatively more powerful in finance and accounting than in automobile manufacturing and this explains its success in bringing about a US-oriented global paradigm in the former but not the latter. However, European financial and monetary integration, including the growth of the euro and of European financial exchanges, the growth of massive monetary reserves accumulating in East Asia, and the ongoing size of the US market for vehicles should caution us against putting too much emphasis on these differences in relative power in the two issue areas.

Boundary Blurring: The Ideational and the Material

What can we say about the entanglement of the ideational and the material in these cases? At a more macro level the differences between the US GAAP and the accounting paradigm that was common historically in continental Europe are clearly related to differences in the structure of the economy, differences that have been highlighted by the varieties of capitalism literature. These macro-level connections to different forms of capitalism apply as well to the differences between the self-certification and type-approval paradigms in vehicle safety. The enthusiasm for markets, minimal government, and private litigation in the US are generalized features of the US political economy that are evident in this case, while the greater general reliance on governments in Europe in other issue areas is consistent with the heavier European reliance on government labs for vehicle testing. The economies, cultures, and legal systems to which these bodies of ideas are connected give them a material weight that is significant and can account to some degree for the persistence of the differences between the European-oriented and American-oriented paradigms. However, these macro-level factors are similar enough in the two cases that they cannot be used to explain the different outcomes that they display.

At a more micro level the entanglement of the ideational and material differs significantly in the two cases. Accounting standards themselves, like other soft-law instruments, involve both ideational and material qualities. The standards are a form of integrated knowledge, but they also have a material quality, including the inflexibility they possess for an accountant, who cannot deviate from them and the way in which they can establish the financial value of firms in the market, something usually seen as material. Accounting standards also achieve their enduring quality through their inscription in books of standards, annual reports, computing software, and training manuals. However, they differ significantly from vehicle safety standards. The knowledge contained in a vehicle safety standard is entangled with the physical properties of the vehicle part and that part's environment, which could include the road, the vehicle as a whole, lighting conditions, and the bodies of passengers. Permissible safety tolerances require complex estimates of the physical effects of these elements colliding in crashes. Even the test instruments, such as crash test dummies representing different body sizes, have a complex materiality.

In the two cases the interaction of the standards with the firms to which they apply also differs. Accounting can have a significant material effect on a firm in affecting its cost of capital and even its organization. Financial data produced by accountants can be used as performance and control measures for individuals and divisions within a firm. Intense political controversies over accounting standards for stock options, which revolved around whether they would damage the US lead in innovative high-tech start-ups, where they are used to motivate executives, are a good example. Nevertheless, the material resistance and cost of altering accounting standards associated with such effects are likely to be considerably less on average than in the case of vehicle safety standards, where the tooling of the production line and test labs, as well as the coherence of any particular part with the car as a whole, have a much greater materiality.

Such differences in the entanglement of the ideational and material affect not just the difficulty of measuring and narrowing differences between American and European standards, but also the way in which the material weight of differences in varieties of capitalism interacts with the standard-setting process. In other words, although the jurisdictional differences by themselves cannot account for the different outcomes, one can see that the impact of the interaction of jurisdictional differences with the greater materiality of standard setting in the vehicle safety case makes harmonization much more difficult. Overall, then, differences in the entanglement of ideational and material factors in the two cases are important in explaining the fact that the clash of regional and national paradigms has resulted in a successful new global paradigm in accounting but not vehicle safety.

Variation in the situation in the rest of the world outside Europe and America is also related to the entanglement of ideational and material factors. In the accounting case the rest of the world is moving quickly towards the IASB's global but US-oriented standards, while in the vehicle safety case it is moving quickly towards the European-focused type-approval model of the World Forum's 1958 agreement. Why? The greater compatibility with Europe of models of capitalism elsewhere, including a greater role for government, cannot by itself explain this difference in outcomes, since it should affect the two cases similarly. However, the greater micro-level materiality of vehicle standards and testing is important. The interaction of the vehicle with its driving environment varies more across the regions than do the interactions of accounting standards with capital markets. The massive costs of design and crash testing of vehicle parts relative to accounting make it much more difficult to adopt a US-type private-sector-oriented solution in the developing world. The World Forum's 1958 agreement comes with ready-made, well-defined procedures for compliance and testing that governments can implement, while the successful adoption of a self-certification model requires a government to manage a set of more complex mechanisms involving firms, courts, and consumer groups.

Wholesale Paradigm Replacement or a New Assemblage of Recombined Elements?

Points made above about the interaction of jurisdictional factors with standard setting are relevant here as well. For instance, the courts and consumer groups that are essential to the effective operation of the self-certification model of vehicle safety are relatively autonomous and devote only a small proportion of their time to vehicle safety issues. This situation is captured more effectively by the assemblage conception of paradigms.

In accounting, a highly integrated body of complex standards is linked to far-flung chains of interaction with humans, objects, and networks that run through standards-setting boards to accountants and their spreadsheets; to the inventory and sales flows of the firm's products; to professional accountancy organizations; to stock markets and other financial exchanges; to the legal support offered by governments; to the financial press; to senior managers in firms issuing annual reports; and in large institutional investors deciding where to place their funds. The private character of the IASB and the dominance of the Big Four accounting firms contribute as well to offsetting the impact of national differences. In some cases it is hard to say with precision the direction of enrolment in these interactions. Is the FASB enrolling the SEC or the other way around? While the directionality of these types of enrolment cannot be established with confidence in each case, it is clear that overall, and despite important failures such as Enron or the accounting failures revealed by the 2008 global financial crisis, accounting is remarkably unified, effective, and functional at mobilizing all its connections with these humans, networks, and objects to address the problem of establishing the value around which it is organized. There are very few sets of transnational rules that play such a central, detailed, daily role in activities of such enormous economic value. The strength of an accounting paradigm such as the IASB's standards is reliant in part on the integration and complexity of its ideas. The integration is evident at the level of the standards themselves, which ultimately need to be used to provide an overall financial picture of the firm in which the value of the parts is aggregated into overall values, but also in the rules for using the standards. For instance, the IASB provides a 'Framework for the Preparation and Presentation of Financial Statements.' However, the strength of accounting is also dependent on the interaction of these standards with the other relatively autonomous parts of the assemblage that it constitutes.

In vehicle safety the standards are no less technical, but they are much less integrated. To some degree, like accounting, the performance of one standard depends on the performance of another. For instance, standards governing 'roof crush' (the performance of roofs in crashes) and door locks interact with seat belt standards, since the movement of an occupant in a crash that is permitted by belts will have consequences for injuries from roof crush or doors flying open. Moreover, general engineering, bio-medical, and physics knowledge is drawn upon to assess vehicle safety risks and performance across all standards. However, each vehicle safety standard is also connected to distinct and relatively autonomous chains of humans, networks, and objects. For instance, windshields are connected to glass makers, models of light refraction under differing conditions, wipers, glazing chemicals, sunlight, rain, dust, and eyesight. Brakes and brake hoses are connected to the materials used to construct them, the likely road conditions the car will be experiencing, the weight and speed of the car, the reaction times of the driver, and the quality of road construction, among other factors. The two parts involve very different test instruments and processes. Automobile manufacturing, like accounting, is an oligopolistic industry, but the assemblage of human and objects that it involves is less easily integrated. From the standard setter's point of view, the differences in implementing two accounting standards – for instance, one on inventories and one on leases – are less.[12] While the ultimate referents of accounting standards are diverse (e.g., a piece of intellectual property, a financial derivative, and a bolt) they are presented to accountants in an already aggregated and refined state that makes comparison and integration easier.

The pathways that connect standard setters with the use of the products also vary. Both road networks and financial networks, the media through which these two products primarily travel, are relatively autonomous. These networks as a whole and particular parts of them (such as a freeway interchange or a financial exchange) have their own logics and parameters that also influence in predictable ways the flow of the products through them. Both have a materiality. However, the financial networks are more connected internationally and more commensurable. An example of the difference this makes is evident in the differing reactions of consumers to internationalization efforts in the two cases. In accounting there was little concern expressed by investors, who are already globally active, that the IASB is physically located in London. In contrast, the consumer groups that monitor vehicle safety standards in the US were very concerned about the distance to Geneva and asked US regulators to press for some World Forum meetings to be held in Washington, DC.

Overall, then, both vehicle safety and accounting paradigms involve integrated and relatively autonomous bodies of knowledge that are remarkable in their ability to mobilize far-flung humans, networks, and objects, but the integration in the vehicle case is less and the relative autonomy of the humans, networks, and objects that it enrols into its assemblage is greater. Thus, it is not surprising that the reconfiguration of the various humans, networks, and objects in a new assemblage and paradigm was accomplished in the accounting case but not in the vehicle safety case.

Conclusion

This chapter has suggested that it is useful to make the concept of policy paradigm change more suited to a transnationalizing world by considering distinctive characteristics of the international environment, especially differences in the power of competitive states and the role of international institutions, and by altering the degree to which paradigms that might be lodged in particular states are seen as deriving their integration and cohesion from the system of ideas itself. In place of more purely ideational paradigms, this chapter has proposed a concept of policy paradigms in which the ideational and material are entangled, and in which paradigms are an assemblage of related but autonomous elements in which integration and boundaries are constructed and reversible.

The changes in the paradigms involved in the two cases, vehicle safety and accounting standards, clearly cannot be understood without reference to transnational actors and institutions. Cross-border harmonization is a key aspect of both stories. The key problem to explain is why the outcomes in these two cases were very different despite their many similarities, with a US-oriented but global paradigm succeeding in the accounting case and a European-oriented paradigm succeeding in the vehicle standards case. The model of an accumulation of anomalies and critics leading to the overturning of a paradigm performs poorly in explaining these differences. While it can help explain the abandonment of the older European approach to accounting, it cannot explain the different outcomes or other aspects of the cases such as why actors outside existing paradigms in Europe and North America choose one or another paradigm.

Consistent with realist international relations theory, differences in the distribution of power across state actors provided a partial explanation of the different outcomes by highlighting Japan's greater relative power in vehicle production compared with accounting and the impact that its active campaigning for European standards in Asia had on the vehicle safety standards case. However, the US remains very powerful in vehicle production and the multinational firms involved in the auto industry are oligopolistic and powerful enough that one might have expected global harmonization to have been more successful.

The comparison of the entanglement of ideational and material factors in the two cases and of the degree to which particular paradigms facilitated the mobilization and integration of diverse and relatively autonomous elements revealed significant variation across the two cases and explains well the differing outcomes. Vehicle safety standards involve interactions with a collection of diverse auto parts, which in turn interact with elements in their physical environment, including the human body, the road, rain, light, and the physics of crashes and testing. By contrast, accounting standard setters interact with financial data that have been processed so that its diverse and often physical referents are already represented by relatively commensurable numbers. The degree of integration and autonomy involved in accounting standards is far greater than in vehicle safety standards. Thus, it is not surprising that a global paradigm is emerging in accounting but not in vehicle safety. These differences can also explain why the world outside Europe and North America is turning towards European standards in the vehicle safety case but US-oriented global standards in the accounting case. The greater difficulty of managing the physical properties of the former and of tailoring them to local conditions makes the government-oriented European standards more attractive than global standards that rely on multinational firms for their implementation, a problem that is less pronounced in the accounting case.

How generalizable are these findings, and what are their implications for the future of research on policy paradigm change? Both cautionary and encouraging points can be noted. On the cautionary side, it is important to carefully consider the character of a policy field before applying this type of analysis. Similarities in these two cases meant that certain variables were held relatively constant, including the power of multinational firms, the range of states involved, the lack of civil society involvement, and the degree of transnationalism. Other cases may be more exclusively national, firms and markets may play a smaller role, or particular powerful states may be more influential. In these cases this chapter's emphasis on the entanglement of the ideational and the material and on disaggregation may need to be tempered by devoting more attention to other variables, including state power and the role of non-governmental organizations.

On the encouraging side, it is likely that entanglement of the ideational and material and disaggregation will be increasingly common across policy fields and will continue to make clashing policy paradigms more common, varied, complex, and important. This is likely to be so even where other variables such as differences in state power are more significant than in these cases. The careful attention to detail that is needed to apply these ideas to particular policy fields and networks may reduce the ease with which generalizations can be applied, but the pay-off should be much better understanding of the impetus and obstacles to policy paradigm change in a transnationalizing world.

NOTES

1 This approach is inspired in part by actor network theory (Latour, 2005).
2 Enrolment is a concept drawn from actor network theory. For an interesting application of the concept that is similar to the approach taken here see Braithwaite and Drahos (2000). For a development of a more general social theory of assemblages see DeLanda (2006).
3 See World Bank/WHO (2004), which estimates that deaths and injuries are likely to increase by about 65 per cent over the next twenty years.
4 This section draws on the author's ongoing research on the harmonization of vehicle regulation. For an analysis of North American policy paradigms in vehicle emissions see Perl and Dunn (2007).
5 Agreement concerning the Establishing of Global Technical Regulations for Wheeled Vehicles, Equipment and Parts which can be fitted and/or be used on Wheeled Vehicles, of 25 June 1998. As of November 2007 the contracting parties consisted of Canada, US, Japan, France, UK, European Community, Germany, Russia, P.R. China, Republic of Korea, Italy, South Africa, Finland, Hungary, Turkey, Slovakia, New Zealand, Netherlands, Azerbaijan, Spain, Romania, Sweden, Norway, Cyprus, Luxembourg, Malaysia, India, Lithuania, and Moldova (listed in order of effective date). Status of the Agreement, of the Global Registry and of the Compendium of Candidates, World Forum report ECE/TRANS/WP.29/2007/92, 5 November 2007.
6 In most documents associated with WP.29 the acronym for global technical regulations is in lower case (gtr). In this paper the more standard convention of capitalizing acronyms is followed.

7 Ken Feith, Transcript of NHTSA Public Meeting on Global Agreement, 3 February 1999 (Docket 1988–4956–0013).
8 Draft Final Report, APEC Road Transport Harmonization Project 1998.
9 This section draws upon Eaton and Porter (2008) and Porter (2005). On accounting see also Mattli and Büthe (2005).
10 Part of the complexity of the US GAAP is a result of the multiple levels at which standards or interpretations can be made. In addition to the FASB's official standards, less authoritative but still significant standards can be issued by the AICPA's Accounting Standards Executive Committee (AcSEC), the Emerging Issues Task Force (EITF) and the FASB staff (SEC 2003, 2.A.iii).
11 For instance, Benston (2003, 1334) notes that 45 pages worth of FAS 133, 137, and 138 standards specifying fair value accounting for derivatives are supplemented by 158 pages of an implementation guide and 576 pages of a PricewaterhouseCoopers guide to their use.
12 The IASB labels the standards it has created 'International Financial Reporting Standards' (IFRS). The standards it has inherited from the International Accounting Standards Committee it labels 'International Accounting Standards' (IAS). Inventories are covered by IAS 2 and leases by IAS 17.

REFERENCES

Benston, George J. 2003. The Regulation of Accountants and Public Accounting Before and After Enron. *Emory Law Journal* 52:1325–51.
Braithwaite, John, and Peter Drahos. 2000. *Global Business Regulation.* Cambridge: Cambridge University Press.
Cutler, Claire A., Virginia Haufler, and Tony Porter, eds. 1999. *Private Authority in International Affairs.* Albany: SUNY Press.
DeLanda, Manuel. 2006. *A New Philosophy of Society: Assemblage Theory and Social Complexity.* London: Continuum.
Djelic, Marie-Laure, and Kerstin Sahlin-Andersson. 2006. *Transnational Governance: Institutional Dynamics of Regulation.* New York: Cambridge University Press.
Dosi, Giovanni. 1982. Technological Paradigms and Technological Trajectories. *Research Policy* 11 (3):147–62.
Eaton, Sarah. 2004. Is there a Doctor in the House? The Role of Crisis and Authority in the Development of the International Accounting Standards Board. Department of Political Science, McMaster University.

– and Tony Porter. 2008. Globalization, Autonomy and Global Institutions: Accounting for Accounting. In *Global Ordering: Institutions and Autonomy in a Changing World*, edited by L.W. Pauly and W.D. Coleman. Vancouver: UBC Press.

Giddens, Anthony. 1990. *Consequences of Modernity*. Stanford: Stanford University Press.

Hall, Peter A. 1993. Policy Paradigms, Social Learning, and the State: The Case of Economic Policymaking in Britain. *Comparative Politics* 25 (3):275–96.

Hansen, Hans Krause, and Dorte Salskov-Iversen, eds. 2008. *Critical Perspectives on Private Authority in Global Politics*. Basingstoke, UK: Palgrave.

Kuhn, Thomas. 1970. *The Structure of Scientific Revolutions*. 2nd ed. Chicago: University of Chicago Press.

Larner, Wendy, and William Walters. 2004. *Global Governmentality: Governing International Spaces*. London: Routledge.

Latour, Bruno. 2005. *Reassembling the Social: An Introduction to Actor-Network Theory*. Oxford: Oxford University Press.

Levi-Faur, David, and Jacint Jordana. 2005. The Rise of Regulatory Capitalism: The Global Diffusion of a New Order. *Annals of the American Academy of Political and Social Science* 598.

Mattli, Walter, and Tim Büthe. 2005. Accountability in Accounting? The Politics of Private Rule-Making in the Public Interest. *Governance* 18 (3):399–429.

Nader, Ralph. 1965. *Unsafe at Any Speed: The Designed-in Dangers of the American Automobile*. New York: Grossman.

Ong, Aihwa, and Stephen J. Collier. 2005. *Global Assemblages: Technology, Politics and Ethics as Anthropological Problems*. Malden: Blackwell.

Perl, Anthony, and James A. Dunn Jr. 2007. Reframing Automobile Fuel Economy Policy in North America: The Politics of Punctuating a Policy Equilibrium. *Transport Reviews* 27 (1):1–35.

Porter, Tony. 2005. Private Authority, Technical Authority, and the Globalization of Accounting Standards. *Business and Politics* 7 (3): Article 2.

Sassen, Saskia. 2006. *Territory, Authority, Rights: From Medieval to Global Assemblages*. Princeton: Princeton University Press.

Securities and Exchange Commission (SEC). 2003. *Study Pursuant to Section 108(d) of the Sarbanes-Oxley Act of 2002 on the Adoption by the United States Financial Reporting System of a Principles-Based Accounting System*. Accessed 2003. Available from www.sec.gov/news/studies/principlesbasedstand.htm.

Seitz, William C. 1961. *The Art of Assemblage*. New York: Doubleday.

Simmons, Beth A., and Zachary Elkins. 2004. The Globalization of Liberalization: Policy Diffusion in the International Political Economy. *American Political Science Review* 98 (1):171–89.

Slaughter, Anne-Marie. 2004. *A New World Order.* Princeton: Princeton University Press.
United Nations Economic Commission for Europe (UNECE). 2002. *World Forum for Harmonization of Vehicle Regulations (WP.29): How it Works; How to Join It.* New York and Geneva: United Nations.
World Bank/World Health Organization. 2008. *World Report on Road Traffic Injury Prevention.* 2004. Accessed 4 April 2008. Available from http://www.who.int/violence_injury_prevention/publications/road_traffic/world_report/en/index.html.

4 Constructing a Transnational Policy Paradigm in the European Union: The Case of GMO Risk Regulation

GRACE SKOGSTAD

Two distinct paradigms have developed in the European Union (EU) and the United States (US) with respect to the regulation of genetically modified organisms (GMOs), products of modern biotechnology.[1] These paradigmatic differences were fully apparent in the complaint the US brought to the World Trade Organization (WTO) in 2004 against EU policies affecting the approval and marketing of genetically modified (GM) crops. Defending its besieged biotechnology policies, the EU made a number of arguments. First, the technologies that produce GMOs are new and GMOs therefore cannot be treated as 'like' or 'equivalent to' their non-GMO counterparts; second, determining GMOs' advantages and risks is 'scientifically complex' and their long-term consequences – to human, animal and plant life and health, as well as the environment – are 'relatively unknown'; and third, the 'inherent characteristics' and potential risks of GMOs 'require them to be subject to rigorous scrutiny' to ensure they do not cause harm (European Communities 2004, 5, 1, 3). By contrast, the US government's submission to the WTO articulated an alternative epistemic understanding of GMOs. It stated that the current products of biotechnology are simply 'the latest technique' – and the most 'precise' technique – of many centuries of genetically engineering plants in order to improve their productivity and functionality, stressed the benefits of GMOs with no mention of any potential harms, and argued that GMOs had a 'proven safety record' (US 2004, 4, 9). Its own domestic regulations do not view GM foods as novel; indeed, their 'substantial equivalence' to non-GM foods exempts GM foods from pre-market regulatory approval in the United States.

Besides the divergence of its epistemic framework from that of the US, another feature of the EU GMO paradigm is noteworthy. It, and the regulations based upon it, are controversial not only across the Atlantic but within the European Union itself. Indeed, the contestation that surrounds the regulations based on the EU GMO paradigm and the unwillingness of some member states to implement and comply with these rules denote the failure of the EU GMO epistemic framework to acquire the 'taken for granted' quality that marks a Kuhnian/Hall paradigm.

Its divergence from the US model and its controversy provoke a question about the EU GMO paradigm that is at the centre of this book. To what degree are both features of the EU GMO paradigm attributable to its transnational scope, that is, its applicability across all European Community/EU member countries? How does the institutional context within which transnational paradigms are constructed in the EU bear on their constituent elements and the likelihood of consensus around paradigmatic elements? How have transnational actors, both within and outside the EU, through their strategic interactions and discourses within this institutional context, shaped the development of the EU's GMO risk regulation paradigm?

To answer these questions and to address the role and impact of transnational actors and transnational institutions in paradigm development, the chapter begins theoretically in part 1, where it conceptualizes policy paradigm development as a conflict-prone exercise in knowledge-making. It posits that the apparent settlement of epistemic controversies at a given juncture need not end controversy about their legitimacy. The act of inscribing knowledge claims in public policies and institutional procedures is thus usefully distinguished from the subsequent process of acceptance of these same knowledge claims as legitimate, including by competing epistemic factions. Part 1 also demarcates the factors important in accounting for why some knowledge claims prevail over their competitors at a given point in time: 'the positional advantages,' resources, and legitimacy of competing discourse factions; the fit between competing factions' epistemic ideas, and the broader normative context; and systemic-wide events that intersect with knowledge-making activities in sectoral policy arenas. Arguing that transnational paradigms are prone to a hybrid character, it posits that this characteristic, as well as the positional advantages and discursive strategies of competing epistemic coalitions, make it difficult to settle epistemic controversies in transnational paradigm development, contribute to their ongoing controversy, and handicap societal acceptance and legitimation of paradigmatic knowledge claims.

Parts 2 and 3 of the chapter discuss the development of the current EU GMO paradigm. Part 2 focuses on the initial period of EU GMO paradigm construction from the late 1980s through to the mid-1990s, when an episteme that emphasized the novelty and risks of GMOs succeeded in displacing its rival episteme that presented GMOs as neither novel nor riskier than traditional plants in order to become the basis for regulating GMOs in the EU. This outcome is attributed to both the positional advantage of the GMOs-as-novel-and-risky coalition, as well as the fit of its ideas with polity-wide goals and norms. Part 3 examines the subsequent evolution of the EU GMO paradigm after it lost legitimacy in the late 1990s. This account stresses the impact on GMO paradigm development of two systemic changes. The first was a crisis of legitimacy in transnational governance within the EU; its effect was to weaken the authority of unelected state actors, in particular at the EU level, and to strengthen that of non-state actors speaking on behalf of consumer interests. More specifically, this systemic crisis strengthened the authority of a transnational advocacy coalition opposed to GMOs that successfully linked knowledge claims of GMOs novelty and risks to the need to strengthen norms of transparency, accountability, and public participation in policy making. The second systemic development was global/WTO rules; they lent legitimacy to the claims of a pro-biotechnology coalition that GMO risks were scientifically knowable. In the EU context of systemic policy goals of competitiveness and market integration, these two competing discourses had to be reconciled, and the result was a GMO paradigm that was a synthesis of the two competing discourses.

The incorporation of the premises of an episteme into public policies does not necessarily end controversy around the constitutive ideas of the paradigm, and part 4 documents and addresses why the EU GMO risk regulation paradigm continues to be contested. Part 5 concludes by drawing lessons for conceptualization of policy paradigms and theories about their development from the continuing controversy around EU GMO knowledge making. Throughout, the analyses draw on primary documents, interviews with European policy makers, and secondary literature.

Transnational Policy Paradigm Development

Theorizing about transnational paradigm development begins with the observation that paradigm construction is an exercise in knowledge making: that is, it entails 'constitut[ing] social order by molding the underlying epistemic frameworks that guide the definition of social problems, the classification of social kinds [ontological frameworks], and the evaluation of social behaviors' (Miller 2007, 331). Not surprisingly, then, paradigm development is often seen to be the work of epistemic communities of technical experts; decision makers turn to them to classify social phenomena, particularly when there is uncertainty around their meaning, and to prescribe appropriate courses of action with respect to them (Haas 1992). Indeed, communities of experts have been credited with considerable influence in the construction of epistemic consensus around transnational paradigms, for example, with respect to capital accounts liberalization (Chwieroth 2007) and central bank independence (McNamara 1998).

However, knowledge-making activities are neither an exercise solely for professionally trained experts nor one devoid of conflict. Others besides professionally or scientifically trained experts also claim possession of knowledge. This possibility is enhanced in policy domains where expert knowledge is continuing to be built. Moreover, efforts to meld political authority and expert authority (Miller 2007, 332) often falter as disagreements emerge across experts and between them and non-experts on the 'truth status of knowledge claims' (ibid., 330). Such disputes over credible knowledge claims appear in the domestic arena, but they are especially likely to bedevil transnational policy paradigm construction. Understandings about what constitutes credible knowledge – and the respective roles of experts, state actors, and even citizens in its constitution – are entangled with values, historic contingencies, and the bias of institutional settings, all factors that are likely to differ more across countries than within them and thereby to yield different national discourses about knowledge (Gottweis 1998; Jasanoff 2005). One should therefore not be surprised to discover cases (e.g., GMO risk regulation) where attempts to privilege one set of knowledge claims over another, or even to synthesize them – the stuff of transnational paradigm development – have proven contentious.

What shapes the outcome of a contestation of epistemic frameworks at a given point in time? To answer this question, the analyses here turn to the persuasion and powering dynamics of the coalitions that line up behind competing epistemes, looking at both the discursive fit of their epistemic ideas with the broader normative context and their positional advantage within the transnational institutional framework. Normative and epistemic frameworks in the wider (regional or global) polity give the discursive advantage to social and political actors who deploy their resources (of information and public and media support, for example) strategically and frame their epistemic discourses in ways that resonate with other ideas and norms in good standing in the polity (Cortell and Davis 2000; Checkel 1997). The transnational institutional setting – with its decision-making norms and rules for pooling and delegating political authority – determines whose epistemic claims get a hearing and have influence and, as well, the possibility for consensus-building around competing knowledge claims. At the same time, there is still likely to be an element of contingency in the outcome of contestation over epistemes/paradigms, as developments exogenous to the policy domain intersect with knowledge-making activities in unanticipated ways (Hall 1993; Schmidt 2001; Garzon 2006).

As in a domestic policy paradigm, the knowledge claims that triumph initially as the scripts for transnational policy making are likely to be particularly consequential. Analysts have documented the dynamics of 'positive feedback' that lend resilience to the ideas that initially constitute public policies and give them an advantage over their competitors (Pierson 2000 2004). Even in the face of controversy over their appropriateness, any deviation from embedded ideas will be resisted not only by their promoters but also by earlier opponents who have subsequently configured their behaviour to be consistent with the inscribed episteme (ibid.). Paradigm change thus normally hinges upon changes in institutional decision rules that either shift resources to proponents of alternative epistemic frameworks, or create the conditions for incumbent political actors to alter their epistemic assumptions (Hall 1993; Howlett and Ramesh 2002). In the case of transnational paradigms, whose scope of application, as embedded in public policies, extends across a number of countries, changes to their epistemic scripts will also ordinarily require the support of multiple political actors. Thus, changes usually will be difficult.

While the high threshold of consensus needed to change transnational policy paradigms can lend them further resilience, it does not necessarily end controversy around them. The institutional framework within which they are developed is likely to make transnational paradigms hybrids of competing knowledge claims, and this hybrid character can ensure continuing controversy insofar as no epistemic community is fully satisfied with the outcome. Even when inscribed in public policies, policy paradigms thus may fail to be internalized as consensual knowledge. The broader normative and epistemic context, particularly when it is in transition, can continue to be discursively deployed by strategic actors to undermine the legitimacy of the inscribed paradigm.

In explaining the constitution of the EU GMO risk regulation paradigm over time, and the controversy that surrounds it, the discussion below draws attention to changes in the structural and normative context of decision making in the EU. Institutional and normative changes have enhanced the role of non-state transnational actors and shaped their resources and strategies for advancing their competing claims of good governance for risk regulation. We will look first at structural changes: formal institutional changes have led to a larger role for the European Parliament, alongside the Council of Ministers and the European Commission, in EU policy making. Informal changes, intended to bolster the legitimacy and effectiveness of decision making by unelected officials in transnational structures, have given non-governmental actors a greater role in transnational policy development in the EU. This development is EU-wide (Risse-Kappen 1995; Kohler-Koch and Eising 1999; Pollack 2005; Eberlein and Grande 2005), but a crisis of legitimacy in risk regulation for food product safety in the late 1990s has made it particularly prominent in EU GMO risk regulation. At the same time, structural changes in the global political economy have granted the World Trade Organization regulatory authority, including over matters of food safety and trade. These global institutional changes heighten the role of the WTO, as well as extra-EU (especially North American-based) private and public actors, in the EU GMO policy process.

Along with this change in the institutional context towards even greater transnational political activity, transnational GMO paradigm development in the EU has also been shaped by a shifting normative context. In the EU, 'input legitimacy' norms have gathered strength; they stress democratic procedures, public participation, and attentiveness to public concerns in policy formulation (Scharpf 1999, 7). These norms sit uneasily alongside 'output legitimacy' norms that stress effective policy outcomes and grant authority to experts, including scientists, to define the common good in a way that is consistent with external standards of appropriate behaviour (ibid.). Output legitimacy norms dominate in the WTO, where scientific experts are viewed as authoritative on matters of GMO risk regulation. In the context of governing by transnational policy networks, the result of efforts to reconcile this tension between input and output legitimacy norms is a hybrid GMO risk regulation paradigm that does not fully satisfy either of the knowledge-making communities that have formed around GMO risk regulation.

The discussion now turns to the early stage of constructing the EU GMO paradigm, when two truth claims about GMOs tangled.

Phase 1 of Constructing the EU GMO Paradigm

GMOs are created by recombinant DNA (rDNA) techniques that involve transferring a particular gene from one organism to another in order to create a new organism with a desirable trait. GM corn varieties, for example, are inserted with genes from a microbe (bacillus thuringiensis, or Bt) that is toxic to predatory insects; other GM plants are inserted with genes to make them resistant to pests. If scientists can agree on what the techniques of rDNA entail, they, society, and governments have not always agreed on whether GMOs are novel, what their risks are, the balance of their risks to benefits, and, consequently, whether and how to regulate GMOs risks.

In the 1970s and 1980s, as GM plants were developed first in the laboratory and subsequently tested in field trials in Europe and the United States, two knowledge-making claims or discourses emerged about GMOs. The first, described as a scientific rationality paradigm (Isaac 2002), rested on the knowledge claim that any risks that GMOs present can be controlled. To the question – what is the difference between a product created by genetic engineering technologies and one produced by other means? – the answer was 'nothing – or at least nothing to merit specific legislation to regulate them.' This epistemic view presented genetic engineering as a key technology of future industrial competitiveness and prosperity and urged a regulatory framework that did not discriminate against it and allowed the benefits of biotechnology to be fully exploited (Cantley 1995). Advanced by the biotechnology industry and many scientists, this epistemic discourse around GMOs prevailed in the United States, where it became the basis for a regulatory framework that relied on existing laws to control any risks posed by GM products (US 1985, 1991; Jasanoff 2005, chap. 2).

The second epistemic discourse stressed that the process of genetic modification was a novel one and that GMOs posed unique risks to the environment, human health, and society (Gottweis 1998, 249–54; Toke 2004; Jasanoff 2005).[2] Vigorously advanced by national Green parties and environmental groups in the EU, it was particularly influential in Germany, where it was supported by the Green and Social Democratic parties (Jasanoff 2005, 58–61; Gottweis 1998), but it also gained credence in the United Kingdom and in the European Union.

In the EU, the first epistemic view, that rDNA posed no significant novel hazards and hence there was no need for special legislation to regulate products of biotechnology, took hold initially in the early 1980s. It did so under the influence of scientists, the biotechnology industry, a number of member states, and those within the European Commission then responsible for biotechnology policy (Gottweis 1999, 73; Cantley 1995, 530). Nonetheless, the second discourse – of GMOs as novel and risky – largely won out by the early 1990s. The evidence was Directive 90/220, the Deliberate Release Directive, which specified procedures to authorize GMOs for licensing and sale in the EU. Directive 90/220 singled out GMOs for regulatory oversight on the rationale that the release of GMOs into the environment could have 'irreversible' effects, and so 'action by the Community relating to the environment should be based on the principle that preventive action should be taken' (CEC 1990). The directive required member states to undertake a case-by-case assessment of the potential risks to the environment of a new GMO prior to its authorization for cultivation and commercial marketing in their country. Because GMOs might also have risks to human health, a risk assessment of each GMO's impacts on human health was also required.

Why did the epistemic understanding of GMOs as novel and risky, and therefore in need of rigorous regulation, prevail in this initial stage of developing the EU GMO paradigm? The answer is found in first placing the GMO debate in the wider context. EU polity-wide goals of a single internal market, to which member states had committed themselves in the 1987 Single European Act, threatened to be derailed when member states such as Denmark and Germany launched national initiatives to regulate biotechnology. Their legislation raised the real possibility of divergent GMO regulatory standards across member states and, as Directive 90/220 stated explicitly, made an EU-wide regulatory framework necessary in order to avoid 'unequal conditions for competition or barriers to trade [in GMO products] ... thus affecting the functioning of the common market' (CEC 1990; see also Cantley 1995).

Once the need for an EU regulatory framework became evident, factors of positional advantage, resources of political support, and the ability to capitalize on the broader normative context of public scepticism about GMOs influenced which knowledge claims around GMOs won out. After 1985 those in the European Commission who appeared to have earlier prevailed in eschewing the need for GMO-specific legislation lost their positional advantage as a cross-national network of Green parties and environmental groups found allies for their knowledge claims (of GMOs as risky) in the three institutions whose support was needed to pass EU-wide legislation: the European Parliament, the European Commission, and the European Council of Ministers (Gottweis 1998, 245). The European Parliament, whose rejection of Commission legislation could be overruled only by unanimity within the Council of Ministers, argued in a 1987 report that there were 'special risks associated with genetic engineering methods' and there were, to date, no 'reliable scientific methods for assessing the medium and long-term effects of the irreversible release of GM organisms into the environment' (as quoted in Cantley 1995, 543, 542). A proposal in the Parliament for a five-year ban on the sale of certain products of genetic engineering was defeated by a single vote (ibid.). In the European Commission, the Environment Directorate, which had acquired legislative responsibility for environmental legislation around GMOs, laid the epistemic groundwork for what eventually became Directive 90/220. It linked the precautionary regulation of hazards of genetic engineering to market harmonization and argued that public mistrust of genetic engineering warranted a common regulatory framework to allow the European biotechnology industry to succeed (Gottweis 1999, 79). These views resonated with countries like Germany, Netherlands and Denmark in the Council of Ministers and, as noted earlier, with the European Parliament (Cantley 1995; Gottweis 1999; Patterson 2000; Gaskell and Bauer 2001; Gaskell et al. 2001). The biotechnology industry, which opposed singling out GMOs for regulation, was too weak and poorly organized to counter this argument effectively (Greenwood and Ronit 1992; Cantley 1995, 559).

The political struggle over truth claims around GMOs and whether/ how they were to be regulated in the EU was an exercise in mutually constituting political and expert authority. Those who argued GMOs were novel entities with unpredictable risks, as well as those who argued the opposite view, sought to mobilize scientific arguments to support their position. As Gottweis (1999, 77) observes, 'Political reasoning was ... always supported by reference to scientific arguments, while scientific reasoning inevitably relied on arguments from the political discourse.' Scientific arguments could not settle the controversy around GMOs' risks, but reference to broader norms of environmentalism appeared to assist the discursive coalition that emphasized the risks and novelty of GMOs. The 'environment,' Gottweis (1999, 69) argues, had become 'a core value in the political arena,' and this normative context lent legitimacy to environmental groups and Green parties and their GMO sceptical arguments.[3]

As a compromise among competing truth claims, Directive 90/220 failed to settle the controversy over GMOs. It was not fully satisfactory to those who thought genetic engineering was a largely unpredictable and difficult-to-control technology and who believed assessment of GMO risks should also include their social, economic, and ethical risks (Gottweis 1998, chap. 6). Nor did its requirement to assess every GMO's risks appease those who argued that there were no scientific grounds to treat GMOs differently from their non-GMO counterparts. The latter – the biotechnology industry and branches within the European Commission responsible for industry and research – worried that the onerous regulatory framework would stifle the competitiveness of the European biotechnology industry.[4]

Industrial competitiveness goals and lobbying by a now better organized biotechnology industry led to initiatives in the European Commission over 1993–4 to streamline the EU GMO approval process and to harmonize it with international practice (CEC 1994; Cantley 1995, 647–51). After 1995 global rules under the rubric of the World Trade Organization clarified what international practice entailed. The WTO Sanitary and Phytosanitary (SPS) Agreement, implemented in 1995, requires that health and safety measures, such as those for GM products, be based on scientific assessments of risks. It also requires food and safety measures to be based on international standards where they exist and mandates the Codex Alimentarius Commission (Codex) to establish such international standards. Countries that adopt Codex standards are deemed to be in compliance with the SPS Agreement and WTO law. The WTO has very strong powers to enforce the SPS Agreement. Countries that are found to be in violation of the SPS Agreement – for example, by erecting barriers to entry of a food product from another country – are required to bring their measures into conformity with the Agreement or face WTO-imposed sanctions from the exporting country.

Efforts commenced to harmonize the EU GMO regulatory framework on international epistemic principles. The major legislative initiative in this regard was the 1997 Novel Food and Novel Food Ingredients Regulation. It allowed the manufacturer of a novel (GM) food that was judged to be substantially equivalent to an existing food to produce only a scientific justification for the claim, not a risk assessment of the GM food (CEC 1997). This regulation, consistent with guidelines issued by the OECD in 1993 and endorsed by the United States, stated that GM foods that were 'substantially equivalent' to an existing food or food component could be treated in a similar manner with respect to their safety. The Novel Food Regulation appeared to mark a shift away from the epistemic premise that genetic engineering was an inherently risky process. However, another of its provisions, requiring novel foods to be labelled, also suggested the resilience of the idea of GMOs as risky. Before further steps could be taken towards US paradigmatic principles, a crisis in the legitimacy of the EU with respect to food product safety regulation altered the institutional and normative context of EU GMO paradigm development.

Phase 2: Paradigm Development in the Wake of a Systemic Legitimacy Crisis

From 1997 onward, a handful of EU member states began to ban the import and cultivation of GM products within their country, despite these products' having been approved for EU-wide marketing by EU level institutions.[5] No new applications for GMO release in the European Union were approved after October 1998, and in June 1999 member states in the Council of (Environmental) Ministers formally announced that they would not approve any new GMOs until Directive 90/220 was reformed. The suspension of GMO authorizations signalled a loss of legitimacy of the transnational GMO regulatory framework and, indeed, of the EU as a transnational decision maker in this policy domain.

The short-term cause of the loss of the regulatory framework's legitimacy was the European Commission's approval of, first, a GM soya in April 1996 and then a GM maize (corn) in early 1997, against the wishes of member states. The Commission had acted – legally – on the advice of an EU committee of scientific experts, which concluded that the products posed no risks. Not all experts agreed with the claim, however, and this division of knowledge claims, publicized by the media, allowed environmental, consumer, and other organizations that were critical of GMOs to mobilize public opposition against GM products (Murphy and Levidow 2006, 3). Public opposition to GMOs led some member states (Austria, Italy, Luxembourg, and France) to ban the EU-approved products in their country and other member states to support their fellow EU-members' actions by subsequently refusing to abide by the existing EU GMO regulatory framework.

What had caused an already sceptical European public to become even more leery of GM products? The answer is found in the successful discursive strategies of transnational consumer and environmental groups as well as of members of the European Parliament. They were able to interpret simultaneous developments in other policy arenas in a manner that reinforced their own truth claims about GMOs and undermined the knowledge-making authority of national and EU scientific experts and regulators (Bernauer and Meins 2003; Ansell, Maxwell, and Sicurelli 2006). Three developments in the broader context were particularly important in creating opportunities for strategic actors to reinforce the public's already negative opinion of GM foods and their worries about GMOs' environmental risks (on public opinion, see Eurobarometer 2001,26; on the importance of these developments, see Jasanoff 2005; Ansell 2006; Pollack and Shaffer 2009).

The first development was the BSE or 'mad cow' debacle.[6] National and EU regulatory authorities had earlier relied on the opinion of scientists that the disease found in animals, first, was unrelated to animal feed produced from rendered animal parts and, second, could not be transmitted to humans eating beef. In March 1996, a month before the Commission approved the sale of the GM soy over member state objections, the British government announced that it had earlier erred in saying there was no threat to consumer health. Consumer and environmental groups successfully framed the regulatory lapse as evidence of government failure, of scientists (on whom national and Commission regulators had relied for faulty advice about the safety of eating meat from BSE-infected cattle) turning a blind eye to consumer safety, and of the risks of industrial farming methods and its technologies (Chambers 1999; Gaskell and Bauer 2001; Jasanoff 2005). Consumer groups adroitly used the EU's mismanagement of the BSE crisis to enhance their legitimacy as champions of consumer interests.[7] The European Parliament used the crisis to force a major reorganization of responsibility inside the European Commission for food safety issues – including for GM foods – that left it in the hands of a Consumer Directorate (Skogstad 2001).

Further, the BSE debacle, in conjunction with other food safety crises, helped to change the normative context of risk regulation in the EU by lending vigour to the precautionary principle. As incorporated in the 1997 Treaty of Amsterdam, the precautionary principle obliges governments to act to avoid harm in the event of scientific uncertainty and not to wait for a risk to be confirmed by scientific evidence (CEC 2000).

The principle signals that 'doubt and uncertainty concerning the safety of a product can justify recourse to protective measures' (Noiville 2006, 309) and shifts the burden to GMO advocates to demonstrate that they pose an acceptable or no risk.

The second development in the institutional and normative context was economic globalization within the WTO regulatory framework.[8] In December 1996, just before the EU approved for licensing a GM maize developed by the American biotechnology company Monsanto, the United States, supported by Canada, challenged the ban on hormone-fed beef that the EU had implemented in 1985 with wide popular support. By 1998 the United States and Canada had successfully argued before the WTO that the SPS Agreement (discussed earlier) prohibited the import of American hormone-fed beef. The beef hormone dispute was followed by a second trade action by the United States against the EU. In the wake of its de facto moratorium on GM product approvals, the United States, supported by the two other major exporters of GM products, Canada and Argentina, first threatened to instigate, and then in 2003 launched a formal challenge to the EU's de facto moratorium.[9] The complainants argued – eventually successfully – that the SPS Agreement required that imports of foods and plants (like GM products) be restricted only when a scientific risk assessment demonstrated that they were unsafe.

These American-led globalization developments were differently framed by GMO opponents and GMO proponents. For anti-GMO activists, the events represented an effort by the US to use WTO rules to enforce its 'industrial model' of agriculture on the EU. Environmental groups, such as Greenpeace and Friends of the Earth, and, subsequentially, organizations representing small farmers, argued that the United States, as the world's major producer and exporter of GM seeds, animal feed, and foods, was seeking once again to undermine EU public policies.[10] Anti-GMO activists were able to make resistance to biotechnology 'a surrogate for resisting America's imperial power' (Jasanoff 2005, 8; see also Ansell 2006). For Commission officials, particularly trade officials, and the organization representing the biotechnology industry, Europabio, these trade disputes and economic globalization required closer harmonization of the epistemic principles of the EU GMO regulatory framework with those in the global trading regime. Closer alignment was needed both to avoid trade frictions and to ensure the competitiveness of the EU biotechnology industry.[11]

The third contextual development that intersected with the GMO debate was ongoing European political and economic integration. By the late 1990s criticisms of the democratic deficit of the EU had made norms of transparency, accountability, and public participation crucial to the legitimacy of EU-level governance (Eriksen and Fossum 2000; Horeth 1999; Majone 1999, 2000). The significance of these input legitimacy norms (Scharpf 1999, 7) – and the need for the EU to adhere to them – was explicitly recognized by the European Commission in its July 2001 White Paper on Governance. Referring directly to the biotechnology and food safety crises, the White Paper acknowledged that 'a better informed public increasingly questions the content and independence of the expert advice that is given.' It also stated that a wider range of inputs 'beyond the purely scientific' was needed, as was overcoming the opaqueness of expert committees (CEC 2001a, 35). This perception, that 'the confidence of the European consumer in science and politics is totally gone'[12] and had to be restored, shaped both the process and content of EU GMO regulatory paradigm development in the late 1990s and early 2000s.

Recognition on the part of EU decision makers of the EU's only 'partial' legitimacy (Ansell 2006, 343) resulted in a prominent role for civil society groups in the transnational policy networks that attempted to build a consensus on EU GMO regulatory governance (Skogstad 2003; Abels 2005; Borrás 2006; Kurzer and Cooper 2007). By virtue of their legal authority over decision making, the European Commission and the European Parliament were central nodes in these transnational networks. Besides bilateral meetings of civil society groups with individual members of the European Parliament (MEPs), monthly meetings organized by an MEP brought together commission officials, MEPs, representatives of the biotechnology industry, environmental groups, and other civil society actors. Commission officials in responsible directorates (health, environment) engaged in extended deliberations with civil society groups, too, in an attempt to forge a compromise between two competing knowledge claims: those of the biotechnology industry (and most scientists), who stressed the ability to scientifically determine and manage whatever risks GMOs posed, and those of environmentalists and consumers, who were much more sceptical of the benefits of GMOs and more risk averse. The two responsible commissioners linked the need to provide the European public with 'a high level of protection for human health and the environment based on science' to goals of ending the de facto moratorium on licensing GMOs so as to allow society 'to profit from the benefit of these new technologies.'[13]

Interviews with state and non-state actors who were insiders to the policy deliberations provide insight into shifts in discursive strategies that took place as a result of the social learning that Hall (1993) describes as characterizing paradigm development.[14] For its part, the biotechnology industry learned that, with public opinion running overwhelmingly against GMOs, it could not simply dismiss the concerns of consumers and environmentalists about the risks of GMOs. For their part, anti-GMO activists, such as Greenpeace, recognized that their preference for a ban on GMOs (on grounds of their risks) could not be sustained and that they could still largely accomplish that goal by making GMO licensing conditional on labelling of these products. For both competing epistemic factions, mandatory labelling of GM products to give consumers 'the right to know' and also thereby the means to reject GM products, was the social learning that enabled compromise on a regulatory framework whose objective was to recommence GMO licensing in the EU.

In short, much as during the first phase of GMO risk regulation paradigm development, the outcome of efforts to restore legitimacy to the EU transnational GMO regulatory framework was shaped by the institutional and normative context of transnational policy formulation. This context enabled strategically positioned actors to advance their competing knowledge-making claims, but it also gave them incentives to moderate their claims sufficiently to enable agreement on the rules under which GMOs would be licensed for sale in the EU.

As reflected in the regulatory reforms implemented over the period 2002–4, the compromise was a hybrid of competing knowledge-making claims about GMO risks and their knowability. On the one hand, the original epistemic claim of genetic engineering as a novel and risky technology persists and is extended. Every GM seed/plant must undergo a scientific risk assessment in order to confirm that it poses no environmental or human health risks (CEC 2001b). Similar provisions apply to GM foods (ibid. 2003a). In addition, new precautionary measures were implemented to require long-term monitoring of the cumulative long-term effects of GMOs, and traceability provisions require GM products to be tracked from 'farm to fork' in order to enable their removal from the marketplace in the event of a safety issue (ibid. 2003b).

On the other hand, there are, simultaneously, clear efforts to strengthen the authority of the epistemic claim that GMOs' risks are knowable and can be ascertained scientifically. Although decision makers in EU institutions have the final say on whether to authorize GMOs for licensing, the task of assessing GMO risks no longer resides with commission-appointed scientific committees. Instead, it is delegated to an independent

scientific body, the European Food Safety Authority (EFSA). The alloca-
tion of responsibility for risk assessment to EFSA's scientific committees
was, argues Chalmers (2005, 654), an effort to allow independent scientists to 'frame the debates' around GMO risks.

The hybrid GMO paradigm, despite its effort to synthesize competing knowledge claims around GMOs, did not ensure its legitimacy.

Phase 3: GMO Paradigm Internalization and the Legitimation Gap

Controversy continues around GMOs in the EU, constituting evidence
that the epistemic principles within the existing GMO regulatory
framework – that scientific experts can ascertain the risks of GMOs and
that GMOs are not inherently risky – have yet to acquire legitimacy
and a 'taken for granted' status. Public opinion surveys show that the
majority of the European public continues to view plant biotechnology with scepticism and to see GM foods as neither useful nor mor-
ally acceptable (Gaskell et al. 2006; European Commission 2008, 66).[15]
The antipathy to GMOs varies across member states, stronger in some
countries than in others.[16] A handful of EU member states continues to
be reluctant to approve the licensing of GMOs, despite the advice of EU
advisory scientific committees that they pose no risks to the environment or human health. Further, despite the WTO's ruling their behaviour illegal (as discussed further below), some member states continue
to ban GMOs in their countries (Skogstad 2008).

GMO risk regulation in the EU illustrates that disputed knowledge-
making claims can plague policy paradigms and weaken their legitimacy. This conundrum appears to be especially problematic for
transnational policy paradigms that are the outcome of transnational
politics and governing structures. Although national decision-making
bodies can face difficulties in legitimizing policy paradigms when there
has been considerable societal discord around them, the legitimacy of
democratically elected national governments itself usually is not disputed. National governments by and large can rely on this reservoir
of diffuse public support, even when they enact policy decisions with
controversial epistemic and normative claims. The same situation does
not necessarily hold for transnational governing institutions like the
EU that necessarily rely on delegated authority and in so doing clash
with popular democratic norms of control and accountability (Skogstad
2008). The endemic competition between national governments and

transnational structures of authority in the EU weakens the incentives of national governments to support unpopular EU-level decisions (Tiberghien 2009).

The possibility that political and expert authority with respect to GMO risk regulation will be melded in the European Food Safety Agency (EFSA) has been undermined by contestation around its advice and very role. The GMOs that have been licensed for import into the EU have been approved by the European Commission, acting on the advice of scientific committees in EFSA, but without the consent of a qualified majority of member states. Not surprisingly, then, both member states and environmental groups (Friends of the Earth Europe 2004) have questioned the integrity of EFSA`s scientific opinions, including what they view as its failure to recognize the uncertain state of scientific knowledge of GMO environmental risks (Levidow 2006). The European Commission has taken steps to enhance the authority of EFSA's knowledge-making role, for example, by requiring it to work more closely with member states' scientific experts, to explain in detail when its opinion differs from that of member states' experts, and to take a longer term precautionary approach of the environmental and health effects of GMOs (AgraFocus 2006, 36). Only time will tell whether such initiatives will shore up the authority and legitimacy of EFSA and the scientific premise on which it relies, that is, that GMO risks are knowable.

Time will also reveal the impact on EU GMO paradigm development of the WTO ruling in European Communities – Biotech Products, the dispute between the European Union and the world's major exporters of GM products (WTO 2006). The United States, Canada, and Argentina challenged both the EU's 1999 suspension of authorization of new GMOs and some member countries' bans on GMOs that had received EU-level approval. They asserted that these actions were illegal in the absence of scientific risk assessments to support such bans. The EU defended its actions on the grounds of the scientific uncertainty of GMO risks and argued that it needed time to assess those risks: 'The science necessary to assess the risks . . . and in particular any long term, indirect, or delayed effects, has had and is having a hard time to catch up with the rapid development of new GM products. The science traditionally used in risk assessment is deterministic (some say reductionist) by nature, and that means that it had a difficult time to apprehend all the properties of highly complex organisms, the interaction between organisms, and the full picture of the ecosystems and agroecosystems that might be affected' (CEC 2004, 4).

The WTO panel did not agree. It issued a ruling consistent with the scientific rationality paradigm, that is, that the risks of GMOs are knowable and can be ascertained scientifically. The fact that scientific information and data on GMO risks were still limited did not justify the long-term suspension of approval of product-specific measures. The precautionary measures in the SPS Agreement can justify only short-term measures. Nor could member state bans on specific GM products be justified; since EU-level risk assessments had been conducted on the same GMOs, relevant scientific evidence was not insufficient. The WTO ruling appears to lead to the conclusion that, after a certain point, a country has to decide whether a product is safe or not, regardless of the degree of uncertainty surrounding it (Poli 2007; Franken and Burchardi 2007).

Conclusion: Drawing Lessons for Transnational Policy Paradigms

The case of EU GMO risk regulation provides a number of insights into the questions at the fore of this text. First is how best to conceptualize policy paradigms. The analyses here have highlighted the epistemic principles of paradigms, recognizing that cognitive and normative ideas are usually entangled. Ontological ideas about what GMOs are – how novel, how risky – are closely linked to normative ideas about their desirability (GMO Compass 2010). Sectoral paradigmatic ideas do not 'float freely' from either their agents (Risse-Kappen 1994) or their context. They need to have a cultural match with acceptable norms and epistemic understandings in the broader society.

Analyses elsewhere suggest that the EU's distinct (from American) food culture helps to explain its attitudes towards techniques of modern agriculture, including plant biotechnology (Echols 1998). Consistent with Tony Porter's argument in chapter 3, the EU GMO case also suggests the entanglement of ideational and material factors. GMO regulatory paradigms cannot be isolated from their environmental context, including the systems of agricultural and food production in which GMO crops are raised and consumed. The EU's structure of small-scale agriculture, balancing traditional and increasingly organic farming, it is argued, has had a bearing on epistemic and normative beliefs about GMOs (Toke 2004). For example, Kurzer and Cooper (2007) find anti-GMO sentiment in Europe to be strongest where an alliance of organic farmer associations and environmental and consumer associations has coalesced around the potential harms of agricultural biotechnology to the environment, farming, culinary traditions, and health and food safety. In short, rather than epistemic communities of scientific experts having authority across national contexts (Drori et al. 2003), the process of mutually constituting expert and political authority is heavily conditioned by features of the local material and normative context.

Second is the matter of how paradigms change and to whom persuasive discourses must be made. In terms of processes of change, EU GMO risk regulation lends support to Hall's (1993, 280) characterization of paradigm change as 'more sociological than scientific' and to Vivien Schmidt's reminder in chapter 2 of this book that the 'bottom-up communications of the public' are important to paradigm development. Transnational environmental groups, such as Greenpeace and Friends of the Earth (Europe), as well as other transnational organizations representing farmers, were particularly successful in their bottom-up communicative discursive interactions with the European public. Along with transnational groups representing European consumers, this anti-GMO coalition also had some success in their coordinative discursive interactions with the policy actors (state and non-state) who adhered to an alternative paradigm of the novelty/risks and desirability of GMOs. Although the latter were not persuaded to adopt the anti-GMO paradigmatic principles, they were persuaded of the need to adjust their strategies (on labelling GM products, for example) in order to make GMOs more acceptable to the public and hence to move their position closer to the pro-GMO understanding of GMOs as not inherently risky and as beneficial to society.

Third, further to how paradigms change, the GMO case suggests the stickiness of initial knowledge-making claims. Early cognitive ideas (of GMOs as novel with unique risks) have persisted. Top-down initiatives at the EU level that portended an evolution away from these ideas in the mid-1990s were thwarted by a systemic-wide crisis in EU regulatory governing. As noted in the Introduction to this book, crises are often understood to be moments that engender transformative change by facilitating discourses of paradigm failure. The failure of the EU GMO regulatory framework took place against a broader crisis in the authority and legitimacy of transnational state officials. It entailed a failure of the cognitive assumption that regulators – including transnational regulators – could be trusted. This lesson, and the consequent alteration of ideas about acceptable risk regulation procedures, lent vigour to the discourse of those who had initially succeeded in inscribing their epistemic claims about GMOs' novelty and risks in EU legislation.

Fourth, and further to the above, EU GMO risk regulation indicates how developments in other policy sectors, and their timing, can spill over to affect sectoral policy paradigms. Widespread acknowledgment of regulatory failure in food safety policies (the BSE crisis) at the very time the first imports of GMOs were arriving in the EU stopped in their tracks paradigmatic-changing initiatives towards deregulating GMO licensing. Theories of policy paradigm development thus need to be attentive to developments in neighbouring policy sectors, as well as those in the broader normative and institutional context, that can either undermine or bolster the legitimacy of alternative ideational frameworks.

Fifth, the diffuse legitimacy of political authorities appears to affect the legitimacy of policy paradigms, particularly those whose development has been riddled with controversy over epistemic and normative claims. The weak legitimacy of the EU's supranational governing institutions has undoubtedly handicapped their capacity to shore up support for the GMO risk regulation paradigm. More generally, compared with domestic policy paradigms, transnational policy paradigms are likely to face larger obstacles to their inscription as legitimate templates because they cannot draw on the reservoir of diffuse support that national democratic governments usually enjoy.

Finally, the EU GMO case sheds some light on another question addressed in this collection: does the EU represent a special case of transnational paradigm development, with limited lessons for understanding the possibilities and dynamics of transnational paradigms elsewhere? It may well do so. Incentives to develop transnational paradigms are arguably stronger in the EU than they are across countries that are less economically and politically integrated. Strong incentives – to maintain the common market – explain the persistence of efforts to build a consensus on the constitutive principles of the GMO regulatory paradigm, even while efforts to bridge the EU and US GMO regulatory paradigms have languished. At the same time, its political architecture – with multiple veto players, norms of horizontal accountability of member states to one another, popular democratic norms, and supranational institutions with weak legitimacy – make consensus building on paradigms difficult in the EU, and arguably more so than across countries with fewer veto players and weaker democratic norms. Still, Porter's attention to an EU paradigm in both accounting and vehicle safety standards in the preceding chapter suggests that there is no one politics or model of policy paradigm development in the EU. In policy domains that do not witness a high degree of mobilization of transnational advocacy groups, where knowledge claims are settled, and/or where private actors comprise the crucial transnational actors, transnational paradigm development in the EU may well look similar to that across other jurisdictions.

NOTES

1 Both European Community (EC) and European Union (EU) are used; EC refers to the pre-1992 period and EU to the union following the 1992 Maastricht Treaty. The terms GMOs, plant biotechnology, genetic engineering, and genetic modification are used interchangeably.

2 These risks have been more fully elaborated over time and include environmental risks to non-target insects that feed on the GM crop and find it toxic and to the wild relatives of GM plants that may be overwhelmed by more resilient GM plants; the health risks to humans who consume GM plants and foods and have an allergic or toxic reaction; and the social and economic risks from dislocation and loss of jobs from the technology.

3 Cantley (1995, 666) reports data that show that environmental organizations were the most trusted group on biotechnology in polls conducted in 1991 and 1993, 52.6 per cent and 60.8 per cent naming them in answer to the question 'Who do you trust most to tell you the truth about biotechnology?' The data are Eurobarometer data. Public authorities were trusted by 20.4 per cent and 16.8 per cent in 1991 and 1993, respectively, and industry by 6.0 per cent and 5.6 per cent, respectively.

4 In 1999, 69 per cent of GM crops were grown in the U.S. and only 0.03 per cent in Europe (Directorate-General for Agriculture 2000, table 1.2).

5 Italy, France, Luxembourg, Greece, and Denmark were the five countries that effectively started the de facto moratorium on GMO approvals.

6 BSE was linked to feeding livestock cow meal that was composed of rendered remnants of other (including diseased) animals.

7 Eurobarometer data show that in 1999 Europeans trusted consumer (55 per cent), medical (53 per cent) and environmental (45 per cent) organizations more than they did national public authorities (15 per cent); as reported in Jasanoff (2005, 87).

8 Another structural contextual change is the emergence of a global environmental regime based in the United Nations Environmental Program. The Cartagena Protocol on Biosafety, negotiated by the signatories to the 1992 Convention on Biological Diversity, adopted in December 2000 and in effect since September 2003, applies to trade in living, modified organisms (LMOs;

referred to here as GMOs). The Biosafety Protocol allows countries to restrict imports of LMOs on precautionary grounds. The WTO Panel in the *Biotech Products* dispute refused to consider whether EU regulations were consistent with the Biosafety Protocol because, although the EU was a party to the Biosafety Protocol, the United States was not (WTO 2006).

9 American soybean and corn exports to the EU are estimated to have dropped by $1 billion in sales as a result of the EU suspension of GMO approvals (Zarelli 2000, 6–7).

10 In France, the farm union leader José Bové was particularly effective in framing GM products and WTO trade rules as an exercise in seizing control from European farmers and consumers over decisions about what they could grow and eat.

11 For the Commission view, see CEC (2002).

12 This comment was made by the EU counsellor to the United States at a conference, 'The Future of Food Biotechnology' held in Washington, DC, in 2001. See AgraEurope (2001).

13 Joint Statement of the Environment Commissioner, Margot Wallstrom, and Commissioner for Health and Consumer Protection, David Byrne. Press release, February 2001, Brussels. Trade officials in the Commission publicly warned that the standstill on GMO authorizations made the EU vulnerable to legal action within the WTO. See AgraEurope (2001).

14 The claims made in this paragraph are based on information obtained in interviews conducted in Brussels in February and December 2001 and October 2003 with officials in the Commission, the European Parliament, and environmental and consumer organizations.

15 GMO Compass (2010) reports Eurobarometer data showing that public opinion on GMOs is improving, but in no EU member state does a majority have a positive view of the technology. It concludes, 'Even the EU's recently overhauled regulatory framework for GMO authorisation and labelling has yet to make Europeans more accepting of food made from genetically engineered plants.' Further, 'the public is clearly concerned about potential risks to human health and the environment.'

16 Opposition to GM foods is stronger in Austria, Germany, Greece, and France than in Italy and Spain.

REFERENCES

Abels, G. 2005. The Long and Winding Road from Asilomar to Brussels: Science, Politics and the Public in Biotechnology Regulation. *Science as Culture* 14 (4):339–53.

AgraEurope. 2001. US/EU Clash over GM Labeling and Tracing Inevitable. EP/6.

AgraFocus. 2006. EU Promises Greater Transparency on GMOs. Brussels.

Ansell, Christopher. 2006. The Asymmetries of Governance. In *What's the Beef? The Contested Governance of European Food Safety*, edited by C. Ansell and D. Vogel. Cambridge, MA: MIT Press.

– Rahsaan Maxwell, and Daniela Sicurelli. 2006. Protesting Food: NGOs and Political Mobilization in Europe. In *What's the Beef? The Contested Governance of European Food Safety*, edited by C. Ansell and D. Vogel. Cambridge, MA: MIT Press.

Bernauer, Thomas, and Erika Meins. 2003. Technological Revolution Meets Policy and the Market: Explaining Cross-national Differences in Agricultural Biotechnology Regulation. *European Journal of Political Research*, 42:643–83.

Borrás, S. 2006. Legitimate Governance of Risk at the EU Level? The Case of Genetically Modified Organisms. *Technological Forecasting and Social Change* 73 (1):61–75.

Cantley, Mark F. 1995. The Regulation of Modern Biotechnology: A Historical and European Perspective. In *Biotechnology: Legal, Economic and Ethical Dimensions*, edited by D. Brauer. Weinheim: VCH.

Chalmers, Damien. 2005. Risk, Anxiety and the European Mediation of the Politics of Life. *European Law Review* 30:649–74.

Chambers, Graham. 1999. The BSE Crisis and the European Parliament. In *EU Committees: Social Regulation, Law and Politics*, edited by C. Joerges and E. Vos. Oxford: Hart.

Checkel, Jeffrey. 1997. *Ideas and International Political Change: Soviet/Russian Behavior and the End of the Cold War*. New Haven: Yale University Press.

Chwieroth, Jeffrey M. 2007. Neoliberal Economists and Capital Account Liberalization in Emerging Markets. *International Organization* 61 (2):443–63.

Commission of the European Communities (CEC). 1990. Council Directive of 23 April 1990 on the deliberate release into the environment of genetically modified organisms 90/220/EEC. *Official Journal of the European Communities* L (117/15):8.5.90.

– 1994. BCC Communication: Biotechnology and the White Paper on Growth, Competitiveness and Employment – Preparing the Next Stage. Brussels.

– 1997. Regulation (EC) No. 258/97 of the European Parliament and of the Council of 27 January 1997 concerning novel foods and novel food ingredients. *Official Journal of the European Communities* L (43/1):14.2.97.

– 2000. Communication from the Commission on the Precautionary Principle. COM(2000). Brussels.

- 2001a. European Governance: A White Paper. *COM (2001) 428.* 2001a. Accessed 27 July. Available from http://eur-lex.europa.eu/LexUniServ/site/ en/Com/2001/Com2001_0428en01.pdf.
- 2001b. Directive 2001/18/EEC of the European Parliament and of the Council of Ministers of 12 March 2001 on the deliberate release into the environment of genetically modified organisms and repealing Council Directive 90/220/EEC. *Official Journal of the European Communities* L (106):1–39.
- 2002. Communication from the Commission to the Council, the European Parliament, the Economic and Social Committee and the Committee of Regions: Life Science and Biotechnology – A Strategy for Europe. COM(2002) 27. Brussels.
- 2003a. Regulation (EC) No. 1829/2003 of the European Parliament and of the Council of 22 September 2003 on genetically modified food and feed. *Official Journal of the European Union* L (268):1–22.
- 2003b. Regulation (EC) No. 1830/2003 of the European Parliament and of the Council of 22 September 2003 concerning the traceability and labeling of genetically modified organisms and traceability of food and feed products from genetically modified organisms and amending Directive 2001/18/EC (16). *Official Journal of the European Union* L (268):24–8.
- 2004. Oral Statement of the European Communities at the first meeting of the Panel with the Parties, European Communities – measures affecting the approval and marketing of biotech products (DS291, DS292, DS293). Geneva.
Cortell, Andrew, and James Davis. 2000. Understanding the Domestic Impact of International Norms: A Research Agenda. *International Studies Review* 2 (1):65–87.
Directorate General for Agriculture. 2000. Economic Impacts of Genetically Modified Crops on the Agri-Food Sector. Brussels: Commission of the European Communities.
Drori, S. Gili, John W. Meyer, Francisco O. Ramirez, and Evan Schofer. 2003. *Science in the Modern World Polity: Institutionalization and Globalization.* Stanford: Stanford University Press.
Eberlein, Bukhard, and Edgar Grande. 2005. Beyond Delegation: Transnational Regulatory Regimes and the EU Regulatory State. *Journal of European Public Policy* 12 (1):89–112.
Echols, M.A. 1998. Food Safety Regulation in the European Union and the United States: Different Cultures, Different Laws. *Columbia Journal of European Law* 3:525–43.
Eriksen, Erik Oddvar, and John Erik Fossum. 2000. *Democracy in the European Union: Integration Through Deliberation?* New York: Routledge.

Eurobarometer. 2001. Europeans, Science and Technology. Brussels: Directorate General for Research 55 (2).

European Commission. *Attitudes of European Citizens towards the Environment: Report. Special Eurobarometer. 295, Wave 68.2.* Accessed 2008. Available from http://ec.europa.eu/environment/barometer/pdf/report2008_environment_en.pdf.

European Communities. 2004. European Communities – Measures Affecting the Approval and Marketing of Biotech Products. First Written Submission by the European Communities. DS291, DS292, DS293. Geneva.

Franken, Lorenz, and Jan-Erik Burchardi. 2007. Beyond Biosafety – An Analysis of the EC-Biotech Panel Report. *Aussenwirtschaft* 62:77–106.

Friends of the Earth Europe. 2004. *Throwing Caution to the Wind: A Review of the European Food Safety Authority and Its Work on Genetically Modified Foods and Crops.* Available from http://www.foeeurope.org/GMOs/publications/EFSAreport.pdf.

Garzon, Isabelle. 2006. *Reforming the Common Agricultural Policy: History of a Paradigm Change.* New York: Palgrave Macmillan.

Gaskell, George, and Martin W. Bauer. 2001. *Biotechnology, 1996–2000.* London: Science Museum.

Gaskell, George, Paul Thompson, and Nick Allum. 2001. Worlds Apart? Public Opinion in Europe and the USA. In Gaskell and Bauer, *Biotechnology, 1996–2000.*

Gaskell, George, et al. 2001. Troubled Waters: The Atlantic Divide on Biotechnology Policy. In Gaskell and Bauer, *Biotechnology, 1996–2000.*

– 2006. Europeans and Biotechnology in 2005: Patterns and Trends. Eurobarometer 64.3. A Report to the European Commission's Directorate General for Research.

GMO Compass. *An Overview of European Consumer Polls on Attitudes to GMOs.* 2010. Accessed 12 January 2010. Available from http://www.gmos-cmpass.org/eng/news/stories/415.an_overview_european-consumer_polls_attitudes_gmos.html.

Gottweis, Herbert. 1998. *Governing Molecules: The Discursive Politics of Genetic Engineering in Europe and the United States.* Cambridge, MA: MIT Press.

– 1999. Regulating Genetic Engineering in the European Union. In B. Kohler-Koch and R. Eising, *Transformation of Governance in the European Union.*

Greenwood, Justin, and Karsten Ronit. 1992. Established and Emergent Sectors: Organized Interests at the European Level in the Pharmaceutical and the New Biotechnologies. In *Organized Interests and the European Community,* edited by J. Greenwood, J.R. Grote, and K. Ronit. London: Sage.

Haas, Peter M. 1992. Introduction: Epistemic Communities and International Policy Coordination *International Organization* 46:1–35.

Hall, Peter A. 1993. Policy Paradigms, Social Learning, and the State: The Case of Economic Policymaking in Britain. *Comparative Politics* 25:175–96.

Horeth, M. 1999. No Way Out for the Beast? The Unsolved Legitimacy Problem of European Governance. *Journal of European Public Policy* 6 (2):249–68.

Howlett, Michael, and M. Ramesh. 2002. The Policy Effects of Internationalization: A Subsystem Adjustment Analysis of Policy Change. *Journal of Comparative Policy Analysis: Research and Practice* 4:31–50.

Isaac, Grant. 2002. *Agricultural Biotechnology and Transatlantic Trade.* Oxford: CABI.

Jasanoff, Sheila. 2005. *Designs on Nature: Science and Democracy in Europe and the United States.* Princeton: Princeton University Press.

Kohler-Koch, Beate, and Rainer Eising. 1999. *The Transformation of Governance in the European Union.* London: Routledge.

Kurzer, Paulette, and Alice Cooper. 2007. What's for Dinner? European Farming and Food Traditions Confront American Biotechnology. *Comparative Political Studies* 40 (9):1035–58.

Levidow, Les. 2006. EU Agbiotech Regulation. *Soziale Technik* 3:10–12.

Majone, Giandomenico. 1999. The Regulatory State and Its Legitimacy Problems. *West European Politics* 22 (1):1–13.

– 2000. The Credibility Crisis of Community Regulation. *Journal of Common Market Studies* 38 (2):273–302.

McNamara, Kathleen. 1998. *The Currency of Ideas: Monetary Politics in the European Union.* Ithaca: Cornell University Press.

Miller, Clark A. 2007. Democratization, International Knowledge Institutions, and Global Governance. *Governance* 20 (2):325–57.

Murphy, Joseph, and Les Levidow. 2006. *Governing the Transatlantic Conflict over Agricultural Biotechnology.* Abingdon, UK: Routledge.

Noiville, Christine. 2006. Compatibility or Clash? EU Food Safety and the WTO. In *What's the Beef? The Contested Governance of European Food Safety,* edited by C. Ansell and D. Vogel. Cambridge, MA: MIT Press.

OECD. 1993. *Safety Evaluation of Foods Derived by Modern Biotechnology: Concepts and Principles.* Paris: OECD.

Patterson, Lee Ann. 2000. Biotechnology Policy: Regulating Risks and Risking Regulation. In *Policy-Making in the European Union,* edited by H. Wallace and W. Wallace. Oxford: Oxford University Press.

Pierson, Paul. 2000. Not Just What but When: Timing and Sequence in Political Processes. *Studies in American Political Development* 14:72–92.

– 2004. *Politics in Time: History, Institutions, and Social Analysis.* Princeton: Princeton University Press.

Poli, Sara. 2007. The EC's Implementation of the WTO Ruling in the Biotech Dispute. *European Law Review* 32:705–26.

Pollack, Mark A. 2005. Theorizing EU Policy-Making. In *Policy-Making in the European Union*. 5th ed., edited by H. Wallace, W. Wallace, and M.A. Pollack. Oxford: Oxford University Press.

– and Gregory C. Shaffer. 2009. *When Cooperation Fails: The International Law and Politics of Genetically Modified Foods*. New York: Oxford University Press.

Risse-Kappen, Thomas. 1994. Ideas Do Not Float Freely: Transnational Coalitions, Domestic Structures and the End of the Cold War. *International Organization* 48 (2):185–214.

– 1995. Bringing Transnational Relations Back In: Introduction. In *Bringing Transnational Relations Back In: Non-State Actors, Domestic Structures and International Institutions*, edited by T. Risse-Kappen. Cambridge: Cambridge University Press.

Scharpf, Fritz. 1999. *Governing in Europe: Effective and Democratic?* New York: Oxford University Press.

Schmidt, Vivien A. 2001. The Politics of Economic Adjustment in France and Britain: When Does Discourse Matter? *European Journal of Public Policy* 8:247–64.

Skogstad, Grace. 2001. The WTO and Food Safety Regulatory Policy Innovation in the European Union. *Journal of Common Market Studies* 39 (3):485–505.

– 2003 Legitimacy and/or Policy Effectiveness? GMO Regulation in the European Union. *Journal of European Public Policy* 10 (3):321–38.

– 2008. Supranational Regulation and Contested Accountability: The Case of GMO Risk Regulation in the European Union. EUI Working Paper SPS No. 2008/7.

Tiberghien, Yves. 2009. Competitive Governance and the Quest for Legitimacy in the EU: The Battle over the Regulation of GMOs Since the Mid-1990s. *Journal of European Integration* 31 (3):389–407.

Toke, D. 2004. *The Politics of GM Food: A Comparative Study of the UK, USA and EU*. London: Routledge.

United States (US). 1985. *Biotechnology: The U. S. Department of Agriculture's Biotechnology Research Efforts*. Briefing Report. To the Chairman, Committee on Science and Technology. House of Representatives. Gaithersburg, MD: U.S. General Accounting Office

– 2004. European Communities – Measures Affecting the Approval and Marketing of Biotech Products. First Submission of the United States. WT/DS291, 292, and 293.

– 1991. Congress. House Committee on Agriculture. Subcommittee on Department Operations, Research, and Foreign Agriculture. Review of

Current and Proposed Agricultural Biotechnology Regulatory Authority and the Omnibus Biotechnology Act. Washington, DC.

World Trade Organization (WTO). 1998. *EC Measures Concerning Meat and Meat Products (Hormones): Report of the Appellate Body.* Geneva: WTO.

– 2006. European Communities – Measures Affecting the Approval and Marketing of Biotech Products. Reports of the Panel. WT/DS291/R, WT/DS292/R, WT/DS293/R.

Zarelli, S. 2000. International Trade in Genetically Modified Organisms and Multilateral Negotiations: A New Dilemma for Developing Countries. UNCTAD/DITC/TNCD/1. Geneva: UNCTAD.

5 Same-Sex Unions Legislation and Policy Paradigms: Something Borrowed, Yet Something New

KELLY KOLLMAN

The regulation of family relationships has been revolutionized in many western democracies over the past two decades. In 1990 only one state in the world, Denmark, legally recognized the relationships of same-sex couples who wished to enter state-sanctioned unions. Today only four democracies in Western Europe and North America withhold such recognition at the national level: Greece, Italy, Mexico, and the United States (see table 5.1). I have argued elsewhere (Kollman 2007, 2009) that the broader European polity, which in addition to the European Union (EU) includes the Council of Europe and informal transnational networks of policy makers and advocacy groups, has acted as an important catalyst for adoption of same-sex union (SSU) legislation in Western Europe. Through the implementation of various policies, non-binding recommendations, and court decisions, the European Union (EU), European Court of Human Rights (ECtHR), and several pioneering states have helped to define the rights of lesbian, gay, bisexual, and transgender (LGBT) people as human rights. Advocacy groups working at both the national and the transnational levels been able to cobble together these disparate decisions and policies to forge and disseminate a non-binding, soft-law norm for the legal recognition of same-sex relationships.

The influence of the European SSU norm on domestic policy outcomes fits well with theories of international socialization offered by constructivist scholars in international relations (Finnemore 1996; Risse and Sikkink 1999; Checkel 2001). In these accounts domestic policy change results, in part, from the creation and promulgation of new norms by international actors – either foreign states, intergovernmental organizations and/or transnational advocacy networks – and efforts by

Table 5.1
Same-sex unions policy in western democracies by policy type

Marriage	Registered partnership	Unregistered partnership	No recognition
Netherlands (2001)	Denmark (1989)	Portugal (2001)	Greece
Belgium (2003)	Norway (1993–2009)	Austria (2003)	Italy
Spain (2005)	Sweden (1995–2009)		US
Canada (2005)	Iceland (1996–2010)		
Norway (2009)	France (1999)		
Sweden (2009)	Germany (2001)		
Portugal (2010)	Finland (2001)		
Iceland (2010)	UK (2004)		
	Switzerland (2005)		
	Austria (2010)		
	Ireland (2010)		

these actors to encourage recalcitrant states to comply with the norm through sanctions, persuasion, and, in truly successful cases, the internalization of the norm. Although helpful, constructivist accounts often leave underspecified the process by which international norms lead to domestic policy change. Constructivists still have not done an adequate job of mapping out how domestic political actors, structures, and culture filter, subvert, or incorporate international normative pressure for change. It is here that the 'ideas' literature in comparative politics developed by scholars such as Peter Hall (1993), Sheri Berman (2001), and Mark Blyth (1997) can be of help. Two aspects of this work in particular appear useful for fleshing out the manner by and circumstances under which the dissemination of international norms will lead national political elites to adopt new policies. The first, the subject of this volume, is Hall's much used notion of policy paradigm shifts. Hall reminds us that far-reaching policy change often results from the replacement of old ideas by a new paradigm that redefines core policy goals as well as the instruments and resources used to reach those goals. Policy change is usually preceded by a contest between two competing sets of ideas. The second useful insight is these scholars' broader analysis of how domestic institutions, culture, history, and discourse either privilege or disadvantage new ideas.

Both insights are necessary to fully explain how a soft-law norm for relationship recognition has had such a profound effect on policy outcomes in Western European countries over the past decade. The norm, of course, did not act alone. By the time it was created and disseminated in the late 1990s and early 2000s, cultural change in western countries had already undermined these societies' commitment to traditional definitions of family and exclusive state support of this particular family model. This shift in values in and of itself was not enough, however, to induce change in long-standing family policy in most societies. Traditionally, the goal of family policy has been the protection and promotion of a narrowly defined cultural institution, namely, the nuclear family made up of a married heterosexual couple and their biological children. The European SSU norm, with its emphasis on rights and equality, gave national LGBT movements, policy makers, and publics a specific alternative framework for (re)defining the goals of family policy by conceptualizing civil relationship recognition as a bundle of rights (and duties) that the state bestows on citizens to help them create loving, intimate relationships. This change in the fundamental goals underpinning family policy represents the policy paradigm shift under scrutiny in this chapter.

To make these arguments and to illustrate the processes by which the European SSU norm has catalysed domestic policy paradigm shifts, I examine the evolution of the same-sex union debate in Germany over the past thirty years. I argue that Europe has been particularly important in the German case because of a number of domestic barriers to SSU adoption that existed in that country well into the 1990s. These barriers included a relatively radical LGBT movement, the presence of strong Christian democratic parties, comparatively moderate levels of secularization, and a 'special protection of marriage' clause in the German constitution.[1] Marriage and rights discourses have been seen as anathema to many of those in the German LGBT movement, who have critiqued both as relics of the corrupt bourgeois, patriarchal state. The fall of the Berlin Wall did much to enhance the legitimacy of rights-based rhetoric within the German Left, but the existence of a successful European LGBT rights movement helped mainstream German LGBT organizations legitimately to redefine themselves as human rights organizations. Similarly, the task of the Red-Green government in 2000 to redefine the core goal of family policy from the protection of a specific cultural institution to the creation of a right and support for family life for all couples regardless of their sexuality was made easier by the existence of the European SSU norm. The SSU norm thus first helped induce a shift in the fundamental goals of the mainstream German LGBT movement before it was used to catalyse a shift in family policy goals. Given the institutional barriers supporters of relationship recognition had to overcome, it is simply not plausible to think that this shift in movement or policy goals would have been possible without Europe's influence, at least not in the near term.

The rest of the chapter proceeds as follows. The next section briefly outlines both constructivist theories of international norm influence and Hall's theory of policy paradigm shifts. It argues that we can gain a better understanding of when and how international norms cause domestic policy change by integrating key insights from these two literatures and outlines how this argument unfolds in the German SSU case. The third section traces the development of a soft-law norm for relationship recognition within European institutions and policy networks. The fourth section examines the effect this European norm had on family policy in the newly reunified Germany. In the first half of this section I argue that the norm caused many mainstream German LGBT groups to redefine themselves more explicitly as human rights organizations. In the second half I posit that the existence of the norm and its endorsement by European institutions and countries also played a crucial role in convincing German policy makers and the public that the goal of family policy should be to bestow rights, not to promote the traditional nuclear family to the exclusion of all other family forms. The final section offers conclusions and discusses the implications of these findings.

International Norms and Domestic Policy Paradigm Change

As the introductory chapter of the volume outlines, there are several ways in which transnational actors and processes of transnationalism can affect domestic policy paradigms. In the SSU case the main mechanism of international influence has been the normative pressure a transnational network of SSU supporters has been able to exert on domestic policy elites and publics to legally recognize same-sex couples. The ability of non-binding, soft-law norms to induce domestic policy change, although not necessarily policy paradigms, is by now a well-established proposition in international relations theory. In the human rights field, Thomas Risse and Kathryn Sikkink's spiral model of socialization offers a succinct but theoretically powerful way of conceptualizing how state elites and national publics can come to internalize a human rights norm created in the international sphere. Synthesizing instrumental, persuasion, and habituation theories of norm compliance, Risse and Sikkink posit that initially state adherence to a human rights norm often results from pragmatic cost-benefit calculations, but through international engagement states may come to internalize and perhaps even institutionalize the norm over time (1999, 16–35). To generalized accounts of international socialization such as Risse and Sikkink's spiral model, constructivist scholars have added more mid-range theory about how norms have effects in domestic settings and why the influence of an international norm varies across societies (Checkel 1999, 2001; Cortell and Davis 1996; Keck and Sikkink 1998; Price 1998). Although these authors have developed broadly useful frameworks for analysing national norm reception, their treatment of domestic structures and values often remains superficial, concentrating on simple macro-level structures such as open vs. closed states or somewhat amorphous concepts such as 'cultural match' or the domestic 'salience' of international norms.

Strangely, international relations (IR) constructivists have largely ignored work done in comparative politics on the role that ideas play in policy change, which could add a great deal of flesh to their accounts of domestic norm reception. Hall's (1993) theory of policy paradigm change can be of great help here. His key insight is that policy learning is a broad category that contains several different phenomena within it. He distinguishes between three different levels of policy change and learning. In the first level of change policy makers adjust the settings of policy instruments in order to better fulfil the policy's overarching goals. The instruments and goals themselves are left largely intact. Second-order change occurs when new policy instruments are adopted but overarching goals remain in place. Third-order change refers to the overhaul of policy settings, instruments, and, perhaps most important, the hierarchy of goals that structure the entire policy area. The latter type of change is likely to occur only when the ideational or cognitive framework that supports the priority of these policy goals and corresponding instruments is discredited and replaced with a new interpretive framework. This framework is what Hall refers to as a policy paradigm (277–81).

Different orders of policy change correspond to different types of politics. First- and second-order changes largely follow the model of bureaucratic politics or technocratic incrementalism. The more dramatic third-order change of a policy paradigm shift is a very different beast. Here the technocrats lose out to the policy evangelists as elected politicians, social movement groups, think tanks, and the media enter into the fray and take sides, either defending the old paradigm or espousing the tenets of the new one. A shift to the new framework is more likely to occur, of course, if the ideas contained in the old framework have lost legitimacy and/or are no longer able to explain implementation outcomes. Hall points out that third-order change is likely to be more sociological than scientific in nature, as the belief systems that underpin a policy paradigm cannot be fully confirmed or disconfirmed by empirical evidence alone. To understand this process we must examine how political and societal structures, cultural systems of meaning and policy discourse, come to promote certain ideas and discredit others; we also have to examine how actors espousing the ideas in the new paradigm gain or fail to gain authority to institutionalize their policy goals and instruments (1993, 279–81; on the importance of discourse for policy change see also Schmidt 2002). It seems quite clear that IR constructivists are generally interested in this type of third-order policy change where interaction with international society leads states and domestic publics to redefine their core goals, interests, and perhaps even to refashion their identities. The IR accounts of domestic socialization described above, however, are indeterminate precisely because they have no theory of paradigm replacement or a fully developed theory of how domestic political structures, values, or discourse shape which paradigms will fail or succeed.

Insights from both IR constructivist literature and work done by comparativists on the ideational sources of policy change are necessary to understand the adoption of a same-sex unions law in Germany and, I suspect, in many other Western European states. The European SSU norm and its endorsement by prominent European institutions and states helped supportive German policy activists both to get the issue of relationship recognition onto the political agenda and to frame it as a rights issue. The task of initiating a discourse about the right to legal relationship recognition for same-sex couples was no mean feat in Germany. Not only was the traditional family policy goal of protecting heterosexual marriage firmly entrenched in German law and strongly supported by the two Christian democratic parties, but many segments of the LGBT movement itself were hostile to the idea of same-sex marriage and defining themselves as human rights organizations. As constructivist theories of international socialization would posit, the SSU norm catalysed policy change by inducing policy activists, political elites, and eventually the public to internalize new values and ideational frameworks. It did so first by helping domestic LGBT activists to redefine the core goals of the mainstream movement and later by persuading German policy makers and the public to rethink the normative basis of family policy.

The concept of policy paradigm change helps explain how the norm came to have an effect. As Hall would predict, the European SSU norm was given a hearing in Germany because the normative basis of the traditional family policy paradigm had begun to erode. Higher rates of divorce, increasing numbers of single-parent households, and greater tolerance towards homosexuality all had undermined the primacy of the nuclear family in German society. The campaign to legally recognize same-sex couples, however, challenged the core goals of family policy more overtly than previous family reform movements, which had been promoted largely by feminist activists. The old goals of protecting the traditional family model simply could not support an SSU law; the purpose of family policy had to be redefined. The European 'relationship recognition as a human right' norm provided the necessary new framework. The very public debate over the registered partnership (RP) law that occurred in Germany in 1999–2002 had all the earmarks of Hall's paradigm shift, as the public, policy activists, the media, and political parties took centre stage, espousing two largely incommensurate visions of the role the state should play in defining and recognizing families. Although the newly elected Red-Green coalition government was able to adopt a registered partnership law in 2000, before this debate had been settled, the incoherence of the original law and the court challenges launched against it by the Christian democratic parties make clear that the paradigm shift was far from complete at this point. It took time, argumentation by SSU supporters, as well as a series of decisions by German courts, which with the help of European jurisprudence eventually fully endorsed a rights-based approach to family policy, to firmly reconstitute the underlying policy goals. By the beginning of 2010, as is evidenced by an expansion of the original law and an endorsement of the anti-discrimination goals embedded in the registered partnership law by Germany's two Christian democratic parties, the paradigm shift in German family policy was largely complete.

The German case also highlights two aspects of policy paradigm shifts that are not well explained in either the IR constructivist or comparative policy literatures. First, the European norm has caused policy change through a dual paradigm shift in Germany. Not only has it led policy elites to re-conceptualize the goals of family policy, but it first

helped convince many domestic LGBT organizations to redefine themselves explicitly as human rights organizations. In the 1970s and 1980s
many LGBT groups utilized the rhetoric of sexual liberation and sought
to critique the heterosexual model of marriage rather than to redefine
state relationship recognition as a rights issue. Constructivist scholars
have long noted that international norms influence both the arguments
domestic NGOs are able to make and how policy elites view an issue,
but they generally have not examined how international norms cause
movements to redefine their core goals or identities. Similarly, comparative politics scholars have generally examined only shifts in policy
paradigms and have failed to note the importance of major shifts in
movement goals that often precede them.

Finally, although I argue that the SSU norm has caused a policy paradigm shift in Germany by helping to redefine the core goals of family
policy, Hall's third-order change, the key instruments utilized in SSU
legislation, namely, civil relationship recognition and bestowing certain rights and duties on monogamous couples, have largely been borrowed from the marriage model. This makes the policy paradigm shift
appear less radical than is often the case in paradigmatic change. To
call SSU laws anything less than a paradigm shift, however, ignores
just how profound a change in goals the new laws represent and how
interwoven into the fabric of society traditional definitions of family
were in most western countries until very recently. SSU laws are not a
case of normal policy making.

The Creation and Dissemination of a European Norm
for Same-Sex Relationship Recognition

European gay and lesbian organizations have formed cross-border associations since the late nineteenth century. In the 1980s, however, these
networks began to take on a more stable character as the advocacy organizations that comprise them became more professional and focused
on political lobbying. Today the European LGBT advocacy network is
held together by the International Lesbian and Gay Association-Europe
(ILGA-Europe). The broader ILGA organization is a global umbrella
association made up of over 400 organizations from over 70 countries. In
the mid-1990s the association was reorganized into six regional groups.
ILGA-Europe was the first regional group to form and remains the
most active of these new organizations. At about the same time,
ILGA-Europe became an unapologetic human rights NGO. Before

the 1990s the rights rhetoric of the European LGBT movement was often muted by more sweeping calls for sexual and later queer liberation (Beger 2004).

In shifting to a human rights framing of the movement, ILGA-Europe borrowed from a well-established social movement paradigm that has been used by numerous groups such as racial minorities, feminists, and indigenous peoples. The paradigm defines lesbians, gay men, bisexuals, and transgender persons as a minority group that is seeking to gain the same rights as heterosexuals. The rights turn of the movement allowed the organization to take part in and graft their demands onto discussions about the European human rights regime that were high on the EU's and Council of Europe's agendas in the early 1990s in the wake of the fall of the Berlin Wall. Although many of ILGA-Europe's demands, such as relationship recognition, seemed quite radical to decision makers in these institutions, the demands were more conservative than many European LGBT groups had been espousing a decade and a half before. Not surprisingly, given this shift in movement rhetoric, by the late 1990s human rights organizations such as Amnesty International and Human Rights Watch had also become an important part of the European LGBT advocacy network. This network has promoted the rights of LGBT people both by acting as a conduit of knowledge and best practice for national LGBT groups and by lobbying European institutions to adopt decisions and policies that enhance the legal standing of gays, lesbians, and transgender persons in European law and policy (Kollman 2007).

The campaign to include sexual orientation in the European human rights regime began in earnest in the mid-1980s. In 1984 a committee in the EU's European Parliament (EP) published *Sexual Discrimination at the Workplace*, which included sexual orientation in its call for more comprehensive anti-discrimination protections. It was followed ten years later by another EP report entitled *Equal Rights for Homosexuals and Lesbians in the EC*. Known as the Roth Report after the German MEP who drafted it, the report condemned discrimination against Europe's gays and lesbians in a wide range of areas and for the first time criticized European governments for excluding same-sex couples from national marriage laws. The EP has included a section on sexual orientation in all of its annual reports on the state of human rights in Europe since the publication of this report (Beger 2004, 33–7). ILGA-Europe lobbied heavily for and participated informally in the drafting of this publication (interview, EC official, 23 Aug. 2003).

Although non-binding, these reports did a great deal to define discrimination against lesbians, gay men, and bisexuals as a human rights issue both at the European level and within member states. Throughout the 1990s the European LGBT network increased its influence, becoming a founding member of the EU's Social Platform of NGOs in 1995 and gaining official consultative status at the Council of Europe in 1998. In 1997 the European LGBT rights network scored its biggest victory when EU member states agreed to include sexual orientation as a category of non-discrimination in the new EU Amsterdam Treaty, which came into force in 1999. The Amsterdam Treaty was the first binding international treaty to include sexual orientation in its anti-discrimination clauses. In 2000 the EU quickly made use of this new legal competence and adopted an Employment Equality Directive that prohibits discrimination in the workplace based on sexual orientation (Council of the European Union 2000).

The European LGBT rights network has also had successes at the Council of Europe's European Court of Human Rights, which is independent of the EU. ILGA-Europe and other LGBT rights organizations have helped gay men and lesbians bring suits in the court against European governments that they claim have violated their rights. These court decisions, for example, have forced the UK government to include gay men and lesbians in their military and across Europe have forbidden the use of sexual orientation as grounds for curtailing parental rights and forbidden the criminalization of homosexual behaviour (Beger 2004, 27–33). More recently the ECtHR has begun to address the issue of relationship rights. In the 2003 Karner v. Austria ruling, the ECtHR held that homosexual partners must be granted all the rights and benefits that non-married, heterosexual couples receive (ECtHR 2003). Although this ruling does not require signatory countries to adopt SSU laws, the implication of the decision is that governments should grant same-sex couples all the benefits enjoyed by non-married, different-sex cohabitants. By the beginning of the 2000s the European LGBT advocacy network had been able to cobble together these various decisions, reports, and policies to create and disseminate a clear, if still controversial, soft-law norm against sexual orientation discrimination and for the legal recognition of gay and lesbian relationships.

This norm and the transnational network of LGBT advocacy organizations and policy makers that support it have influenced domestic policy debates about same-sex unions in important ways. First, policy developments within prominent European institutions and pioneering

Nordic countries have made it easier for national LGBT organizations to put same-sex unions on national policy agendas and to legitimately frame relationship recognition as a human rights issue. Second, many national policy elites, particularly those from the left-leaning parties, appear to be internalizing the European norm for relationship recognition. Policy documents from Germany, the UK, and the Nordic countries reveal that elites cite reports and decisions from European institutions as well as the laws of other European countries to justify their own support of new same-sex union policies. Interviews with policy elites in Germany and Austria confirm that European norms and examples have helped to convince national elites that passing a same-sex union law is both timely and the right thing to do (Kollman 2007, 2009). Taken together, these processes have had a profound effect on national SSU policy outcomes (see table 5.1).

However, this account presents a picture of a rather seamless process of international norm creation and dissemination that obscures many of the domestic political processes that have made SSU policy adoption possible. In fact, policy change did not result simply from the creation of a new international norm for SSU recognition by transnational LGBT activists. Just as important to this story is how the new norm and its framing of family policy as a human rights issue has helped to induce paradigm shifts – both in LGBT movement and policy goals – in domestic political settings. Cultural and demographic changes in Europe since World War II have undermined the normative framework upon which western states' exclusive promotion of heterosexual marriage was based. Although many western states have created alternative legal institutions such as domestic partnerships or cohabitants laws, it was not until these governments were faced with calls for same-sex relationship recognition that the old family policy goal of protecting a traditional cultural institution came under direct threat. To ask for this recognition, LGBT groups had to convince policy makers and publics that civil relationship recognition is a bundle of rights, benefits, and duties to which all citizens, regardless of their sexual orientation, should have access. The wider European polity's endorsement of this idea, coupled with the decline of the nuclear family and increased tolerance of homosexuality in many western societies, has made this fundamental shift in family policy goals possible in a very short period of time. As will be argued below, the influence of the European SSU norm has been particularly important in Germany, where several domestic barriers to SSU adoption existed.

The *Lebenspartnerschaftsgesetz*: The Changing Face of German Family Policy[2]

Although Germany has experienced many of the same demographic changes, such as higher divorce and lower marriage rates, as have undermined the universality of the nuclear family model in other European countries, family policy has been slow to change in the Federal Republic (for statistics on changing German family structure see Dorbritz, Lengerer, and Ruckdeschel 2005). Unmarried, different-sex, cohabitating couples do enjoy some rights in German law, but their legal status is quite limited compared with that of other European countries (Ostner 2001). Until the registered partnership law was passed in 2001, almost none of these privileges extended to same-sex couples, despite relatively high levels of tolerance towards homosexuality in Germany (see table 5.2). Indeed in the late 1990s several cultural and institutional barriers to reforming family policy existed in the newly reunited Federal Republic. Although Germany was more secular than it had been in the 1960s and 1970s, in 1998 Germans still attended church in higher numbers than citizens of any of the other seven countries that had previously adopted a same-sex union law. High levels of religiosity and the presence of conservative religious values have been among the greatest barriers to SSU adoption in western democracies, as is evidenced by the fact that the two remaining non-adopter countries in Western Europe – Italy and Greece – have comparatively very high levels of religiosity (Kollman 2007; see table 5.3).

In Germany these religious values are well represented in the political system via the two Christian democratic parties, the Christian Democratic Union (CDU) and its Bavarian sister party, the Christian Social Union (CSU), which sit together in the national parliament. The early dominance of CDU/CSU governments during the founding years of the Federal Republic helps explain the conservative nature of family policy in Germany, in particular the insertion of the much analysed Article 6 into the German Basic Law (Herzog 2005). This article guarantees the 'special protection of marriage and the family.' Although gender neutral, this clause has been interpreted by the German courts to mean heterosexual, monogamous marriage. The institutionalization of this definition of family in the Basic Law has made German lawmakers extremely cautious about creating alternative legal partnership forms for either different or same-sex couples.

The final barrier to SSU adoption in Germany was the nature of the LGBT movement. Having failed to recreate many of the homophile

Table 5.2
Tolerance of homosexual behaviour in western democracies

Country	International Social Survey, 1998/99*	Pew Global Attitudes Survey, 2002**
Denmark	60	n/a
France	51	77%
Germany	51 (ex-East) / 56 (ex-West)	83%
Italy	32	72%
Netherlands	77	n/a
United Kingdom	46	74%
United States	31	51%

 * The ISS measures responses to a feeling thermometer about homosexual behaviour, which range from 0–100; 0 being homosexual behaviour is always wrong and 100 being homosexual behaviour is never wrong. The national number represents the modal response for that country.
** The Pew Survey is simply the percentage of respondents from that country that answered yes to the question 'do you think homosexuality should be accepted?' Sources: The Pew Global Attitudes Project. 2007. *Spring 2007 Survey.* http://pewglobal.org/reports/pdf/258topline.pdf. International Social Survey Program. 1999.

Table 5.3
Same-sex union legislation and religiosity (percentage monthly church attendance)

	Marriage	Registered partnership	Unregistered partnership	No Recognition/ defence of marriage
Low religiosity		France (17) Denmark (19) Norway (13) Sweden (12) Finland (12)		
Medium religiosity	Netherlands (35) Belgium (36)	Germany (31) UK (24) Switzerland (34)	Austria (35)	
High religiosity	Canada (42) Spain (44)	Ireland (88)	Portugal (42)	Greece (55%) Italy (47)

Source: M. Minkenberg (2002). Religiosity is measured by median levels of church attendance from 1980 to 1998 as reported in three different World Values Surveys. The numbers in parentheses represent the percentage of the population that reported attending church at least once a month, averaged over the three surveys. The values for church attendance in Greece, not included in World Values Surveys, are from the 2002 European Social Survey.

organizations that existed in Germany during the Weimar era, the West German gay and lesbian movement lay relatively dormant until the wave of student protests in the late 1960s (Adam 1995). The gay and lesbian organizations that formed during this period reflected the intellectual foundations of the student movement and were highly critical of the West German bourgeois state and society. As a result the movement largely eschewed a rights-based framing of their demands and instead sought to foment cultural and sexual liberation. Although more conservative elements of the gay men's movement did periodically agitate for more narrow legal reforms, including same-sex relationship recognition, no permanent, national LGBT rights organization formed in Germany until the 1990s. Unlike their counterparts in the Nordic countries, relationship recognition was simply not a priority – indeed quite the opposite – for the German movement throughout most of its post-war history.

Yet despite these barriers to change, the Lebenspartnerschaftsgesetz (LPartG) adopted in 2000 was one of the first major reforms the Red-Green coalition government was able to enact. The law created a registered partnership scheme that allows gay and lesbian couples to take part in a public ceremony, use a common last name, and receive certain rights, duties, and benefits from the state. Perhaps not surprisingly, given the barriers discussed above, the original LPartG law had a difficult birth and, unlike the RPs in the Nordic countries, it withheld many of the rights and benefits associated with civil marriage, including tax benefits and adoption rights. In 2004, after a crucial decision supporting the original law had been handed down by the Federal Constitutional Court, the Red-Green government expanded the registered partnership law to include certain tax benefits for same-sex registered partners and the right of so-called stepchild adoption, which allows a registered partner to adopt their spouse's biological child. Since 2004 these benefits have been expanded further through a series of court decisions, one of them handed down by the EU's European Court of Justice.

How can we explain this change in light of the barriers that existed to family policy reform in Germany? I argue that the importation of the European norms against sexual orientation discrimination and for same-sex relationship recognition by certain political actors helped induce a dual paradigm shift in the Federal Republic. The first shift occurred within the LGBT movement after a national rights-based organization, the Lesben- und Schwulenverband in Deutschland (LSVD; Lesbian and Gay Federation in Germany), formed in the early 1990s. This organization utilized its European connections first to legitimize a rights-based identity of the movement and then to lobby both the German public and government for legal change. The European norm helped the fledging LSVD to reconstitute the core goals of the German LGBT movement. This change was not a mere repackaging of old goals in new rhetoric but represented a genuine shift in the mainstream movement's goals and identity.

The second shift more clearly resembles Hall's policy paradigm change. After coming to power in 1998, the Green Party was able to use the European SSU norm to convince its Social Democratic Party (SPD) allies, other policy elites, and parts of the German public that relationship recognition was a rights issue. Family policy, this argument went, should be defined as the recognition and promotion of stable, loving relationships, not as the exclusive protection of the heterosexual nuclear family. Further, state recognition of relationships entails bestowing certain rights and benefits on these couples, not promoting heterosexual marriage to the exclusion of all other partnership forms. To do otherwise results in unfair discrimination against the growing number of individuals who either choose not to marry or are barred from marriage because of their sexuality. As will be illustrated below, without the existence of the European norm and supporting network, it is doubtful that the German LGBT movement or the Green Party would have been able to induce these paradigm shifts, and these shifts almost certainly would not have occurred as quickly or as early as they did (Kollman 2009).

From Liberation to Rights: Reconstituting the Goals of the Mainstream German LGBT Movement

Interwar Weimar Germany is often credited with being the birthplace of the first modern gay and lesbian movement. Tragically, this movement was crushed by the Nazi dictatorship that grabbed power in 1932. The re-founding of West German democracy after the war under the tutelage of successive CDU/CSU governments was not an auspicious environment in which to recreate the German lesbian and gay movement, and indeed nothing like the milieu that existed during Weimar reappeared. Sex between men was not decriminalized in West Germany until an SPD-led government was elected in 1969 (Herzog 2005). It took the advent of the student protest movements in the 1960s to reinvigorate German lesbian and gay culture. Many of the organizations that formed in the early 1970s considered themselves to be part of a larger New Left movement that sought to overthrow the bourgeois, patriarchal state (Adam 1995, 81–96). The use of this New Left liberation rhetoric led to a movement in which political lobbying for legal reform based on rights claims was often viewed as suspect.

Perhaps less obviously, the liberation framing of the movement also created a deep divide between gay men and lesbians. Many of the lesbian organizations associated themselves with the autonomous feminist movement and did not seek to form coalitions with gay men. Throughout the 1980s there were several attempts to create a national, rights-based LGBT organization; most of them ended in failure. The most prominent of these organizations, the Bundesverband Homosexualitaet (BVH; Federal Association of Homosexuality), which was formed in 1986, disbanded after a bitter dispute over whether same-sex marriage should constitute a core goal of the movement (Bruns 2006). Lesbian feminist groups also grappled with the issue of same-sex marriage and relationship rights during the late 1980s. The well-known group Lesbenring officially rejected the idea of making marriage a desirable goal for the movement in 1989 after years of intensive debate (Heinicke 2007). The gay and lesbian movement in Germany thus entered the 1990s without a national organization in place, divided about overarching goals, and largely unwilling to use rights rhetoric to lobby for relationship recognition or other legal reforms. Had the Berlin Wall not come down in 1989, precipitating German reunification a year later, it is unlikely that this situation would have changed significantly for years.

Among the diverse set of rights-based, civil society groups that came together in late 1989 to protest against the repressive East German communist dictatorship was a relatively small association of gay men.[3] In the aftermath of the fall of the Berlin Wall in 1990 this organization, which now called itself the Schwulenverband in Deutschland (SVD; Gay Federation in Germany), very quickly registered as an official association. The group made a strategic decision to become a German-wide organization and to lobby the newly reunified German government for legal reform. Unsurprisingly, given its origins in the East German democratization movement, the SVD was and remains an unapologetic human rights organization (LSVD 2006). The founding of the SVD coincided with the creation of ILGA-Europe and the latter's own shift from a focus on sexual liberation to the common humanity of LGBT people and their rights. (L)SVD has been one of the more active organizations in ILGA-Europe and has both helped shape that organization's strategy as well as used European legislative victories to its advantage in the German political setting (interviews, ILGA-Europe 28 Oct. 2005,

LSVD 21 Nov. 2005). These connections helped reinforce the human rights orientation of the SVD by illustrating how successful rights rhetoric has been in other countries and in lobbying European institutions. SVD became the primary conduit by which European human rights norms were imported and incorporated into the German LGBT movement. Although certain factions within the movement have remained sceptical of this new identity and related movement goals, German politicians and the public have reacted favourably to the SVD's rights and equality-based campaigns. For the first time, the LGBT movement was consistently using a discourse and a movement paradigm that the German public and policy makers could understand.

The most successful of the SVD's early human rights-based campaigns was the Aktion Standesamt, which was carried out in 1992. The action involved over 200 gay and lesbian couples who attempted to get married at city halls in various cities. The campaign, which used the example of the newly adopted registered partnership law in Denmark to support its claims of marriage rights for same-sex couples, resulted in several unsuccessful court cases (Berliner Senatsverwaltung fuer Bildung, Jugend und Sport 1994). More important, however, it gained widespread media coverage and brought the issue of relationship rights as human rights to the attention of the general German public and mainstream politicians (LSVD 2002). Two years later, in 1994, the SVD again made use of its European connections to lobby the German MEP, Claudia Roth, to incorporate several of their demands – including the opening of marriage to same-sex couples – into her influential European Parliament report (LSVD 2006). This EP report, coupled with the positive public response to the *Aktion Standesamt,* did a great deal to put LGBT rights, including relationship rights, onto the German political agenda. By 1996 the leadership of the SVD had persuaded several prominent lesbian activists to join the organization, which was then renamed the Lesben- und Schwulenverbands in Deutschland (LSVD; Lesbian and Gay Federation in Germany). In the short span of just six years the LSVD managed to do what no West German organization in the post-war era had been able to accomplish, namely, create a national organization that uses human rights claims to improve the legal standing of gay men and lesbians in German society. Perhaps more important, it permanently shifted both how mainstream LGBT organizations defined themselves and the overarching goals they sought to pursue. While the rhetoric of liberation and lesbian feminism certainly still exists within the movement today, this rhetoric clearly has been sidelined by the LSVD and its pursuit of rights reform. It is hard to imagine that such a dramatic shift of the movement paradigm would have been possible in reunified Germany without the endorsement that the rights rhetoric found within the wider European polity.

Getting the movement to embrace the goal of relationship recognition, however, was just the beginning. The passage of an SSU law required the movement to convince German policy makers and the public that state recognition of relationships was a rights issue, something neither the law nor German society at the time explicitly accepted. To accomplish this policy paradigm shift, LSVD and its supporters required allies inside the German political system, the example of Europe, and a little luck.

From Protecting a Cultural Institution to Bestowing Rights: Reconstituting the Goals of German Family Policy

Article 6 of the German Basic Law defined the overarching goal of family policy in the Federal Republic as the 'special protection' of heterosexual, monogamous marriage. The decline of the nuclear family as a lived form over the past four decades has not induced a moral panic in German society, but until the LPartG was adopted in 2000 neither had it led to thoroughgoing reform of the regulation of partnerships that occur apart from heterosexual marriage (Ostner 2001). If LSVD helped put same-sex unions on the political agenda, it was the Green Party that kept the issue front and centre by making it a key issue in its political program throughout the 1990s. Like the LSVD, the German Green Party has strong ties to its European counterparts and uses the European political sphere to help promote its political agenda at home. In the case of same-sex unions the European Parliament provided a particularly useful forum in which to advance its cause. The EP Roth Report, discussed above, which endorsed opening marriage to same-sex couples, was written and promoted by a prominent member of the German Green Party, Claudia Roth. The German Green Party thus both helped to create and deeply internalized the European SSU norm in the 1990s. Using key decisions within the EU and the example of SSU laws in Nordic countries to bolster their claims, prominent Green Party politicians such as Volker Beck and Claudia Roth very publicly began to question many of the core principles upon which family policy in Germany was based.

It was not until the Greens became part of the governing coalition in 1998, however, that passage of the LPartG had a chance of becoming a reality. International norms and new policy paradigms can gain a foothold in national political settings only when their key supporters either are in positions of authority or are in positions to influence authority. By becoming the junior member of the government coalition after the 1998 election, the Green Party gained both. The SPD and the Greens had included a promise to adopt a registered partnership law in their respective election programs in 1998, but the former had done so largely in an attempt to court the latter. The SPD did have passionate supporters of the LPartG in its parliamentary grouping, but these supporters were not well represented in the government that took power in late 1998. Many elected members of the SPD were leery of promoting a registered partnership law precisely because they feared the repercussions of redefining family policy in terms of rights. Not only were many lawmakers convinced that the German courts would overturn such a law as a violation of Article 6 of the Basic Law, but some members of the SPD leadership feared that many of their voters would also reject the rights arguments upon which the law was to be based.

The Greens and other supporters of the law used the European norm to convince the SPD leadership and the public of the legitimacy of defining state relationship recognition as a rights issue (interview, Green Party member, 18 Nov. 2005). Evidence of this European influence can be found in the coalition agreement that the SPD and Green Party signed in 1998. In announcing its intention to adopt a registered partnership law, the coalition agreement justifies its position by saying it is implementing long-standing recommendations of the European Parliament (SPD/ Buendnis 90-Die Gruenen 1998). The coalition appears to be invoking outside support for what many in the SPD considered a controversial law. Although somewhat hesitant and divided about supporting the reform, the SPD in the end did accept the new framing of family policy as a rights issue. In 2000 the Red-Green government submitted a bill entitled 'Draft of a Law to End the Discrimination of Same-sex Partnerships: The Life Partnership Bill,' which was based on the idea of ending state discrimination of same-sex couples (Deutscher Bundestag 2000a). Despite the initial reluctance of some members of the SPD, the change in government in 1998 was crucial to the success of the SSU law in Germany. As Hall suggests, paradigm change often occurs as a result of realigning elections that bring to power novel coalitions with new ideological commitments. There can be little doubt that the adoption of the RP law in Germany would not have been possible without the election of the country's first Red-Green government – not in 2000 anyway.

The LSVD and the Greens might have been successful in persuading the SPD that family policy was a rights issue, but the main opposition parties, the CDU/CSU and the liberal Free Democratic Party (FDP), had yet to be convinced. All three parties opposed the draft law. The very public debate that ensued over the registered partnership bill in 1999 and 2000 very clearly reflected two different and largely incompatible views of family policy. The CDU/CSU parliamentary grouping was particularly vociferous in its opposition. Their defence of the traditional family policy paradigm is visible in the following excerpt taken from a parliamentary resolution submitted by the CDU/CSU party grouping before the final reading of the LPartG bill in the Bundestag: 'we reject the government coalition's draft law out of constitutional and social political reasons. This draft law makes same-sex, unmarried partnerships almost the same as marriage in terms of its legal effects ... This is neither compatible with our model of marriage and family nor with the Constitution' (Deutscher Bundestag 2000b; translation by author).

The LPartG law that resulted from this parliamentary debate was much less comprehensive than the government had originally proposed. Because all bills that affect the federal states in Germany must also gain assent from the Bundesrat, the German Parliament's upper house, and because the Red-Green government knew the bill would not pass this chamber, it split it into two parts. The first part created the new institution and granted same-sex couples rights such as entitlement to adopt a common last name, the right to remain for non-German partners, and obligation for maintenance. This bill required approval only from the Bundestag, the lower house, where the government had majority support, and became the LPartG law. The second part, which contained many of the financial and tax benefits granted to married couples and did require approval from the Bundesrat, did not pass the upper chamber.

The splitting of the law may have allowed the Red-Green coalition to pass the draft bill, in somewhat meagre form, into law but it did not resolve the overarching tensions that now existed in German family policy. The shift to a new rights-based family policy paradigm was far from complete. Almost immediately after the Bundestag had adopted the LPartG law, three CDU- and CSU-governed Laender (federal states) launched a constitutional complaint against the law in the Federal Constitutional Court. These Laender governments asserted that the law violated the special protection of marriage clause, Article 6, of the German Basic Law. The Constitutional Court's decision, which it handed down on 17 July 2002, served largely to reinforce the new rights-based goals of German family policy. The court clearly accepted the Red-Green government's framing of the law as an anti-discrimination measure. It not only found that LPartG in no way threatened hetero-sexual marriage, but also let lawmakers know that they could bestow more of the rights and privileges associated with marriage on the new institution without violating the constitution (Federal Constitutional Court 2002; Miller and Roeben 2002). This decision did a great deal to solidify the law and the rights-based family policy paradigm in German political circles and in the eyes of the public (interviews, German jour-nalist, 18 Oct. 2005; CDU parliamentary staff member, 18 Nov. 2005). Edmund Stoiber, the CSU premier of Bavaria, who was running against Gerhardt Schroeder in a national parliamentary election and who at one point had threatened to make the repeal of LPartG a campaign issue, quietly dropped the subject. Indeed, there is little evidence that the law had much electoral salience. The FDP also dropped its opposi-tion to the law shortly thereafter and now supports LPartG's expan-sion. The most important consequence of the court's decision, however, was the confidence it gave the Red-Green government to expand the RP law to include greater financial benefits and, more controversially, stepchild adoption rights. The new law, Gesetz zur Ücberarbeitung des Lebenspartnerschaftsrechts, was adopted in 2004.

The court's decision clearly solidified the legitimacy of the LPartG law in Germany. But the reasoning behind this decision contained somewhat mixed messages about the equality principle embedded in the legislation. The court emphatically rejected the challenger's conten-tion that the RP law undermined marriage or that Article 6 forbade the German state from creating institutions that legally recognize other family forms. So far this logic is very much in keeping with the new rights-based paradigm. The court came to this conclusion, however, by holding that same-sex partners are fundamentally different from different-sex partners in that they cannot marry. In this way the RP law helps to address the legal discrimination that lesbian and gay couples face without undermining the institution of heterosexual marriage (Moeschel 2009). This reasoning allowed the Red-Green government to expand the law without violating Article 6 of the Basic Law, but it made it difficult for LGBT groups to campaign for the right to marriage, something the LSVD said it wanted eventually. It also made it easier for the courts subsequently to hold that same-sex registered partners do not have a constitutional right to the same privileges as married couples. The legislature could grant registered partners more of the rights and benefits associated with marriage if it so chose, as it had in the 2004 law, but the state was not constitutionally obliged to do so. Indeed, between 2004 and 2008 several German courts, including the Constitutional Court, denied same-sex registered partners additional rights and benefits using exactly this type of argumentation (ibid.).

This reasoning did not change significantly until a German court referred the Maruko v. Versorgungsanstalt der deutschen Buehnen case to the EU's European Court of Justice (ECJ) in 2007. The decision, which the ECJ handed down in April 2008, held that the EU Employment Equality Directive necessitated that pension schemes must give the same survivor's benefits to registered partners in Germany that married spouses enjoy (EC J 2008). The decision was clear. Equality meant that if member states chose to recognize same-sex couples in law – something the court did not and cannot force them to do – they should treat these couples as they do married spouses. To do otherwise is to engage in unlawful discrimination. Although the ECJ's decision applies only to how same-sex registered partners are treated in the workplace, the German Constitutional Court has clearly accepted and broadly applied the anti-discrimination argumentation of the ECJ decision. Through a series of decisions in 2009 and 2010, the Constitutional Court has found that withholding the rights and benefits that accrue to married couples from same-sex registered partners violates the German Basic Law (*Sueddeutsche Zeitung,* 9 Aug. 2009, 17 Aug. 2010). Once again Europe has played a crucial role in entrenching the new family policy paradigm in the German political and legal system.

It thus has taken almost decade since the passage of the original RP law for the shift from a traditional to a rights-based family policy paradigm to be completed. But shift it has. The evidence for this change in the goals of German family policy can be found in the relatively consistent, if slow, expansion of the original RP law by German policy makers and courts since its implementation in 2001. In addition, the new goals of German family policy also appear to enjoy widespread acceptance of by the general public. Opinion polls taken in Germany since the passage of the LPartG law consistently have shown that a majority of the public would support opening marriage to same-sex couples (Eurobarometer 2006). Perhaps most remarkably, the two Christian democratic parties now mention same-sex unions in their political programs; the CDU specifically states that the party accepts and endorses the LPartG law (CDU 2007; CSU 2007). This decision by the opposition parties to accept the legitimacy of LPartG was catalysed, in part, by the coming into force of the EU's Employment Equality Directive in 2006 as well as by the subsequent Maruko decision described above. The directive prohibits only workplace-based discrimination, but the fact that it includes sexual orientation in its anti-discrimination measures helped convince sceptical CDU/CSU policy makers that European law now considers the rights of gays and lesbians to be human rights (interview, LSVD 19 March 2008). From the beginning, normative pressure from Europe has played an important role in this paradigm shift in Germany. In the end, its influence has been profound. Although heterosexual marriage is still symbolically privileged in German law and important rights such as the ability to jointly adopt non-biological children are still withheld from same-sex registered partners, it is no longer considered permissible to withhold either state recognition or most of the rights and duties associated with marriage from same-sex couples. On the latter points there is no longer debate.

Conclusions and Implications

The case of German SSU adoption illustrates the usefulness of integrating insights from the ideas literature in comparative politics and IR constructivist scholarship. The creation and dissemination of a European norm for same-sex relationship recognition clearly influenced both the direction and the speed of SSU policy change in Germany, as constructivist theories of socialization would predict. But the mechanism by which international norms affect national policy outcomes is not fully explained by these theories. The SSU case demonstrates that transnational advocacy networks and the norms they promote can induce domestic policy paradigm shifts. The concept of policy paradigm change helps illustrate that the type of social learning in which constructivists are most interested – that is, learning that results in a redefinition of actors' core goals and/or identities – involves not just the internalization of new norms and policy ideas but also the replacement of their institutionally entrenched predecessors. As Hall has pointed out, these types of shift in underlying paradigms are highly political processes, which in democracies often involve tussles between the media, think tanks, political parties, and key social groups. The ability of new paradigms to induce thoroughgoing policy change is largely determined by the legitimacy of the old paradigm, the cultural resonance of the new paradigm, and how political institutions and processes structure this debate.

In the German SSU case, a European norm was able to catalyse change in the face of a firmly entrenched traditional family policy paradigm because of the declining cultural primacy of the nuclear family model, the changing nature of the LGBT movement in the newly reunified Germany, and the influence that the Green Party had on government in the late 1990s and early 2000s. The rights framing of family policy goals embedded in the European norm and its endorsement by key European institutions helped the relatively weak LSVD and Green Party to push through major policy change in the form of the registered partnership law in 2000. The incoherence and controversy surrounding the adoption of this law, however, illustrate the very real battle that was being fought over the fundamental goals of German family policy. In the end, it took almost ten years of argumentation by domestic supporters of same-sex relationship recognition and the influence of the EU's increasingly stringent anti-discrimination measures to convince sceptical German policy makers and members of the public to accept the premise of the rights-based family policy paradigm.

However, certain findings from the case do not fit neatly with the conventional wisdom of the two 'ideas' literatures. Policy paradigms are often portrayed as being induced by radically new ideas that change policy makers' and the public's perceptions and world views. Although the rights-based SSU norm has caused western states to change the fundamental goals on which family policy is based, the instruments states use to recognize same-sex couples look very similar to those used in the traditional marriage model – often, however, without the name itself. Far-reaching policy change may occur even in the absence of new instruments if core policy goals are reconstituted. The human rights paradigm that has come to dominate the LGBT movement is both less original and more conservative than sexual liberation or queer politics frames. Indeed, the less threatening nature of the SSU norm lies at the heart of its political success. As this case illustrates, movements and policy paradigms do not have to be radical to act as catalysts of what Hall describes as third-order policy change. Same-sex unions are thus both something borrowed and something new.

Finally, the role that societal actors played in inducing the family policy paradigm shift in Germany is more complicated than is often portrayed in policy learning accounts. Although Hall emphasizes the importance of interest groups in promoting a new policy paradigm, in the cases he examines interest group preferences are relatively stable; new paradigms simply allow them to better justify the promotion of these interests. In the German SSU case, policy change became possible only after the mainstream LGBT movement itself changed its core goals. Policy paradigm change followed in the wake of movement paradigm change; a dual paradigm shift was necessary. The European norm gave the movement the language, goals, and framework necessary to find political allies in the German political establishment and to work with these allies to define a common political project. The role that ideas and norms play in shaping movements is just as important as the role that they play in shaping policy outcomes. Dramatic policy change may well start with shifts in how movements or other societal groups define themselves and their overarching goals.

NOTES

1 In Germany there are two Christian democratic parties: the Christian Social Union (CSU) and the Christian Democratic Union (CDU). The former exists only in the Bundesland (federal state) of Bavaria; the latter exists in all the other Bundeslaender. As they are regionally separate, the two parties never compete against one another in elections and they sit as a single-party grouping in the national parliament. The CSU generally promotes policies that are more socially conservative than the CDU, reflecting the Catholic heritage of the Bavarian constituency that it represents.
2 This section of the chapter draws on an argument I have developed in Kollman (2007, 2009).
3 The LGBT movement in East Germany was not particularly well developed before the fall of the Berlin Wall. Because of the ideological nature of the communist East German regime, however, the government there did decriminalize sex between men slightly before its counterpart in West Germany. However, gay men and lesbians were routinely discriminated against in the former East Germany. See Herzog (2005) for an overview.

REFERENCES

Adam, B. 1995. *The Rise of a Gay and Lesbian Movement.* London: Twayne.
Beger, N. 2004. *Tensions in the Struggle for Sexual Minority Rights in Europe.* Manchester: University of Manchester Press.

Berliner Senatsverwaltung fuer Bildung, Jugend und Sport. 1994. *Lesben. Schwule. Partnerschaften.* Berlin: Berliner Senatsverwaltung fuer Bildung, Jugend und Sport.

Berman, S. 2001. Review: Ideas, Norms and Culture in Political Analysis. *Comparative Politics* 33 (2):231–50

Blyth, M. 1997. Review: Any More Bright Ideas? The Ideational Turn of Comparative Political Economy. *Comparative Politics* 29 (2):229–50.

Bruns, M. 2008. *Schwulenpolitik in der alten Bundesrepublik.* 2006. Accessed 12 March 2008. Available from http://old.lsvd.de/bund/schwulenpolitik.html

Checkel, J. 1999. Norms, Institutions and National Identity in Contemporary Europe. *International Studies Quarterly* 43 (1):83–114.

– 2001. Why Comply? Social Learning and European Identity Change. *International Organization* 55 (3):553–88.

Christlich Demokratische Union Deutschlands (CDU). 2007. *Freiheit und Sicherheit: Grundsatzprogramm der CDU.* Accessed 25 March 2008. Available from http://www.cdu.de/doc/pdfc/070701-leitantrag-cdu-grundsatzprogramm-navigierbar.pdf.

Christlich-Soziale Union (CSU). 2007. *Chancen fuer Alle – Grundsatzprogramm der CSU.* Accessed 25 March 2008. Available from http://www.csu.de/partei/partei/grundsatzprogramm/index.htm.

Cortell, A., and J. Davis. 1996. How Do International Institutions Matter? The Domestic Impact of International Rules and Norms. *International Studies Quarterly* 40 (4):451–78.

Council of the European Union. 2000. Council Directive 2000/78/EC establishing a general framework for equal treatment in employment and occupation.

Deutscher Bundestag. 2000a. Entschliessungsantrag der Fraktion der CDU/CSU zu der dritten Beratung des Entwurf eines Gesetzes zur Beendigung der Diskriminierung gleichgeschlechtlicher Gemeinschaften: Lebenspartnerschaftgesetz. Drucksache 14/4551.

– 2000b. Entwurf eines Gesetzes zur Beendigung der Diskriminierung gleichgeschlechtlicher Gemeinschaften: Lebenspartnerschaften (Lebenspartnerschaftsgesetz – LPartG). Drucksache 14/3751.

Dorbritz, J., A. Lengerer, and K. Ruckdeschel. 2005. Einstellungen zu demographischen Trendsund zu bevölkerungsrelevanten Politiken. Bundesinstitut für Bevölkerungsforschung beim Statistischen Bundesamt, Wiesbaden.

Eurobarometer. 2006. Standard Eurobarometer. *TNS Opinion and Social* 66 (Fall).

European Court of Human Rights (EctHR). 2003. Karner v. Austria, judgment of 24 July 2003, no. 40016/98, §36.

European Court of Justice (ECJ). 2008. Tadao Maruko v. Versorgungsanstalt der deutschen Bühnen, judgment of 1 April 2008; Case number Case C 267/06.

Federal Constitutional Court (Bundesverfassungsgericht). 2002. Entscheidungen. BverfG, 1BvF 1/01 vom 17.7.2002. Absatz-Nr (1–147).

Finnemore, M. 1996. *National Interests in International Society.* Ithaca: Cornell University Press.

Hall, Peter A. 1993. Policy Paradigms, Social Learning, and the State: The Case of Economic Policymaking in Britain. *Comparative Politics* 25:175–96.

Heinicke, E. 2007. *Festrede zu 25. Jahrestag des Lesbenring.* Accessed 11 Jan. 2008. Available from http://www.lesbenring.de/seiten/pm/festrede_25.htm.

Herzog, D. 2005. *Sex after Fascism.* Princeton: Princeton University Press.

Keck, M.E., and K. Sikkink. 1998. *Activists Beyond Borders: Advocacy Networks in International Politics.* Ithaca: Cornell University Press.

Kollman, K. 2007. Same-Sex Unions: The Globalization of an Idea. *International Studies Quarterly* 51 (2):329–57.

– 2009. European Institutions, Transnational Networks and National Same-Sex Union Policy: When Soft Law Hits Harder. *Contemporary Politics* 15 (1):37–53.

Lesben- und Schwulenverband in Deutschland (LSVD). 2000. *Pressemitteilung des LSVD: LSVD fordert CDU zum Ja-Wort auf. 30.06.2000.* Accessed 25 March 2008. Available from http://berlin.gay-web.de/homoehe/.

– 2002. Ratgeber zum LpartG. Guide to the Life Partnership Law.

– 2006. *Programm des Lesben- und Schwulenverbandes in Deutschland.* Accessed 28 March 2008. Available from http://www.lsvd.de/index.php?id=88&print=1&no_cahce=1.

– 2007. *Chronik.* Accessed 5 March 2007. Available from http://typo3.lsvd.de/25.0.html.

Miller, R., and V. Roeben. 2002. Constitutional Court Upholds Lifetime Partnership Act. *German Law Journal* 3 (8).

Minkenberg, M. 2002. Religion and Public Policy: Institutional, Cultural and Political Impact on the Shaping of Abortion Policies in Western Democracies. *Comparative Political Studies* 35 (2):221–47.

Moeschel, M. 2009. Germany's Life Partnerships: Separate and Unequal? *Columbia Journal of European Law* 16 (1):37–66.

Ostner, I. 2001. Co-habitation in Germany: Rules, Reality and Public Discourses *International Journal of Law and the Family* 15:88–101.

Price, R. 1998. Reversing the Gun Sights: Transnational Civil Society Targets Landmines. *International Organization* 52 (3):613–44.

Risse, T., and K. Sikkink. 1999. The Socialization of International Human Rights into Domestic Practices: Introduction. In *The Power of Human Rights,* edited by T. Risse, S. Ropp, and K. Sikkink. Cambridge: Cambridge University Press.

Schmidt, V. 2002. Does Discourse Matter in the Politics of Welfare State Adjustment? *Comparative Political Studies* 35 (2):168–93.

Slaughter, Anne-Marie. 2004. *A New World Order.* Princeton: Princeton University Press.

SPD / Buendnis 90-Die Gruenen. 1998. Aufbruch und Erneuerung-Deutschlands Weg in 21.

Jahrhundert. pdf document; downloaded 15 Sept. 2005.

Wintemute, R. 2005. From 'Sex Rights' to 'Love Rights': Partnership Rights as Human Rights. In *Sex Rights,* edited by N. Bamforth. Oxford: Oxford University Press.

6 Normative Contexts, Domestic Institutions, and the Transformation of Immigration Policy Paradigms in Canada and the United States

TRIADAFILOS TRIADAFILOPOULOS

For much of the nineteenth and twentieth centuries, liberal-democratic countries relied on racially discriminatory criteria for judging the suitability of would-be immigrants (Triadafilopoulos 2010).[1] Discriminatory approaches to the regulation of immigration drew inspiration from scientific theories of race and were buttressed by patterns of colonial domination premised on Europeans' 'civilizing mission.' The US National Origins Quota Act transposed the hierarchical logic of scientific racism into public policy by closely regulating the admission of European 'races' according to their putative assimilability. Other laws, such as the Chinese Exclusion Act, barred the door to 'unassimilable' non-Europeans altogether (Ngai 1999; Zolberg 2006). In the same spirit, Canada developed an immigration policy paradigm oriented toward maintaining Canada's identity as a 'white man's country' (Huttenback 1976; Roy 1989; Ryder 1991).

Although immigration remains a contentious issue, there has been a fundamental shift in what counts as legitimate criteria of exclusion among liberal-democratic countries in the post-World War II era (Joppke 2005a; Triadafilopoulos and Schönwälder 2006). Restrictions based on racial and ethnic categories are no longer acceptable and exclusions aimed at preserving national homogeneity are subject to scrutiny and contestation (Joppke 2005b). Consequently, states such as Canada and the United States that had used immigration policies to fashion national identities based on a white, Northern European 'core' population have experienced a profound demographic reorientation through the admissions of previously excluded groups (Bélanger and Malenfant 2005; Shrestha 2006).

This chapter examines the post-war transformation of immigration policy making in Canada and the United States. I argue that paradigm change in both countries was driven by shifting norms pertaining to race and human rights that cast discriminatory paradigms in a new, sharply critical light. Opponents of racial discrimination in immigration policy took advantage of this new normative context to highlight the lack of fit between the commitment to liberal norms and human rights of Canada and of the United States, on the one hand, and their respective extant policy paradigms, on the other. This pressure set in motion comparable processes of paradigm change, which I capture through the concepts of paradigm 'stretching,' 'unravelling' and 'shifting.'

Paradigm change in the two countries was subject to quite different political dynamics. Canada's institutional configuration granted the executive branch and the bureaucracy considerable autonomy, allowing policy makers to experiment with new ideas. A new paradigm that eschewed racial discrimination while maintaining a degree of selectivity based on immigrants' potential contributions to the Canadian economy emerged out of a process of trial and error led, in the main, by bureaucrats (Dirks 1995; Hawkins 1988; Kelley and Trebilcock 1998). Conversely, the greater openness of the American political system resulted in a more politicized process (Tichenor 2002; Zolberg 2006). As a result, the executive branch's effort to recast immigration policy in terms similar to Canada's was compromised. The end result was a patchwork solution, aimed at mollifying distinct and conflicting interests by granting preference to family members of American citizens and legally permanent residents rather than immigrants with work-related skills (as presidents Kennedy and Johnson had proposed).

I begin by outlining my argument regarding the interplay of shifting normative contexts and domestic politics and go on to apply the resulting analytical framework to better understand post-war immigration policy making in Canada and then in the United States. I conclude with a brief summary of the implications of the chapter's findings for understandings of internationalization and policy paradigm change.

Global Norms, Domestic Politics, and Paradigm Change

The division of the world into sovereign nation states makes international migration an anomalous process, as border crossing inevitably raises questions of membership. This is true of all international migrants, including temporary foreign workers, refugees, undocumented 'aliens,' and immigrants carefully selected according to their potential contributions to receiving states' economies (Carens 1987; Walzer 1981; Zolberg

1981, 1987). In traditional settler countries built on immigration, admissions policies serve as the initial gate of entry into both the territory of the state and its polity. Immigration policies thus define the boundaries of membership in nation states. Who 'we' are depends in part on who we admit into our 'national' space (Shuck 1985).

Decisions as to who should be admitted into the national space and on what terms are shaped by a host of factors, including traditions of nationhood, economic requirements, and perceived demographic need (Castles 1995; Hollifield 1992; Messina 2007). However, limiting our attention to these domestic variables obscures encompassing ideational structures that influence policy makers' positions on immigration policy across states. In particular, we must be sensitive to the influence of what the Stanford School sociologists refer to as 'global culture' – the broadly encompassing normative contexts that inform understandings of what constitutes appropriate conduct among states (Elliot 2007; Koenig 2008; Meyer et al. 1997; Finnemore 1996; Katzenstein 1996). In the sense employed in this chapter, normative contexts ground a particular era's moral foundations. Who we admit and on what grounds will have much to do with how we think about the morality of exclusion.

Two very different normative contexts shaped thinking on immigration policy in the twentieth century. The period from the turn of the century to the end of World War II featured a normative context shaped by scientific racism, imperialism, and intense nationalism (Fredrickson 2002; Füredi 1998; Lake and Reynolds 2008; Lauren 1996; Mazower 2008). These broad and deeply ingrained philosophic ideas influenced thinking on immigration across states. Immigrant selection was predicated on notions of racial 'suitability' understood in a biological sense, whereby certain inferior peoples were deemed incapable of contributing to the development of 'civilized' nations. Racial discrimination in immigration policy was defensible from the standpoint of both science and nation building; healthy nations depended on the admission of racially suitable immigrants and the strict control or exclusion of unsuitable races. Immigration policy complemented eugenics policies, such as sterilization (Hansen and King 2001). Both sought to protect the nation from threatening (because inferior) groups: domestic in the case of eugenics, external/foreign in the case of immigration policy.

The coherence and validity of this normative context and the policy paradigms it sustained was challenged at the midpoint of the twentieth century by a series of transformative events and processes, including the discrediting of scientific racism as a result of the war against fascism and revelations of Nazi atrocities, the related emergence of a global human rights regime, and decolonization. The post-war normative context established a new logic of appropriateness for states claiming a liberal-democratic identity, as the group-centred racism of the pre-war period gave way to an individualist ethic holding that all persons were endowed with fundamental rights regardless of their race, ethnicity, and nationality (Cairns 1999; Lauren 1996; Kymlicka 2007; Skrentny 2002). As a result, established policy paradigms came under pressure, as individual rights-based claims for equal treatment clashed with the rights-denying policies and practices they informed. As self-identifying liberal democracies, Canada and the United States were especially vulnerable to charges of hypocrisy made by domestic and international critics; pre-war policies that relied on discrimination no longer 'fit' with the prevailing normative context.

Yet, policy makers in Canada and the United States did not respond to this emergent dissonance by quickly reforming their immigration policies. On the contrary, as theories of path dependence would lead us to expect (Pierson 1993, 2000; Thelen 1999), they continued to engage in what Peter Hall (1993, 279) has usefully termed 'normal' policy making, 'adjust[ing] policy without challenging the overall terms of [their established] policy paradigm[s].' The changes that were introduced were limited to 'first and second order change': adjustments to the settings of policy instruments and, on occasion, more substantive changes to the instruments themselves (281–3). Nevertheless, pre-war policy paradigms continued to inform policy makers' understandings of immigration policy.

Yet, *pace* Hall, normal policy making did not reinforce existing paradigms; it undermined them. Normal policy making under changed normative contexts may usefully be thought of as paradigm 'stretching': small-scale first- and second-order changes undertaken by policy makers to co-opt critics represent efforts to bring established paradigms into line with new normative realities – to square paradigms based on a prior logic of appropriateness with that generated by a new order. Yet stretching fails to address the fundamental lack of fit between established paradigms and new normative contexts. Indeed, stretching may hasten the demise of the established order, as cautious gestures made to mollify critics concede the fundamental validity of their claims. This recognition of the incompatibility of the old order and the new emboldens critics, leading to more frequent and far-reaching demands for reform. As per Thomas Risse's 'spiral model' of norm diffusion (1999, 2000; Risse and Sikkink 1999), a process of discursive 'self-entrapment' drives the reform process forward, engendering what Seyla Benhabib (2009, 698–9) has usefully termed 'democratic iterations[:] complex processes of public argument, deliberations, and exchanges through which universalist claims are contested and contextualized, invoked and revoked, posited and positioned.' Subsequent adjustments of the existing paradigm undertaken during the course of democratic iterations further diminish its coherence, gradually undermining its utility as a guide for policy making. The consequent unravelling of policy paradigms that results from this recurrent stretching opens space for the introduction of new ideas in line with the ascendant normative context, grounding universalist principles in a new paradigm.

Hence, paradigm change is an incremental, evolutionary process (Thelen 2006; Peng and Wong 2008), albeit one instigated by profound changes in context during critical historical junctures (Capoccia and Keleman 2007; Hay 2002, 162–3). Using Hall's terms, normatively driven first- and second-order changes are necessary precursors to third-order change. While the kinds of change involved are indeed distinctive, they bear a common source: the lack of fit created when a paradigm developed under the terms of a historically specific normative context drifts into a new one. It is this 'friction' of clashing orders that drives paradigm change (Lieberman 2002; Orren and Skowronek 2004, 78–119).

How paradigm change proceeds will depend on the political context shaping policy makers' responses to lack of fit. In cases where executives and bureaucrats are insulated from the partisan arena, paradigm change may be very much in the spirit of 'puzzling' and 'social learning' – processes of trial and error shaped by the pursuit of relatively well-defined goals (Heclo 1974). Conversely, paradigm change is more likely to be driven by 'powering' where institutions give rise to a more politicized policy-making context. With regard to the cases at hand, divided government and the unique role of congressional committees in the American system led to a politicized process, in which defenders of the discriminatory paradigm could exploit veto points and joint decision traps to wage last-ditch efforts to preserve some vestiges of the old system (Tichenor 2002, 211–16). The lack of any comparable source of institutional leverage made such opposition in Canada futile. In the absence of any credible opposition, Canadian policy makers enjoyed wide latitude in crafting an internally coherent immigration policy paradigm through a process of trial and error.

These differences in institutional configuration had important consequences. Most notably, American restrictionists' success in pushing through a strong preference for family reunification in the 1965 Immigration Act thwarted the efforts of the administrations of first Kennedy and then Johnson to base immigration admissions on the country's economic needs. Critics of American immigration policy have since argued that the 1965 act's privileging of family reunification has led to a 'precipitous decline ... in the average skills of the immigrant flow reaching the United States,' helping to rekindle debates over immigration policy (Borjas 1999, 8). Conversely, Canadian policy makers were able to fashion a new policy paradigm premised on the notion that newcomers would be selected according to their ability to contribute to the country's economic needs. Their success in this regard has helped maintain a remarkable degree of acceptance for mass immigration in Canada, so much so that Canada's 'points system' has become a model for other countries formulating organized immigration policies (Shachar 2006).

In what follows I apply the analytical framework sketched above to explain the course of immigration policy paradigm change in Canada and the United States. As I will demonstrate, change was instigated by shifts in normative context that prompted policy stretching and unravelling. Political institutions shaped the course of paradigm change, such that outcomes in the two cases differed in important respects.

Dismantling White Canada, 1947–67

Stretching: 1947–52

Prime Minister William Lyon Mackenzie King presented the first important statement on Canada's post-war immigration policy in a speech before Parliament on 1 May 1947. According to King, Canada was intent on structuring its immigrant admissions policies as it had in the past: 'Asiatic' and other non-white immigration would be avoided so as to preserve Canada's white-European identity (Canada 1947a, 2546–644).

Yet officials understood that the changed normative conditions made such an approach problematic. Canada's membership in the UN carried with it an 'obligation to eliminate racial discrimination in its legislation,' by 'promoting and encouraging human rights and ... fundamental freedoms for all without distinction as to race, sex, language or religion.' Furthermore, Canada's positions in the General Assembly regarding the competency of the UN to intervene in the domestic affairs of member states indicated that it favoured a 'wide interpretation' of the provisions of the UN Charter. Yet there was no serious consideration given to opening Canada to immigrants from 'non-traditional' (i.e., non-European) source regions. Thus, efforts were made to avoid or at least minimize charges of hypocrisy by 'revising [Canada's] immigration legislation so as to avoid the charge of racial discrimination [while] effectively limiting Asiatic immigration.'[2]

This strategy of paradigm stretching defined Canadian immigration policy making in the early post-war period. First- and second-order changes in instrument settings and choice were advanced while the overriding goals of the established immigration policy paradigm were maintained. Thus, while pressure from the Committee for the Repeal of the Chinese Immigration Act moved the government to strike the law in 1947, the range of admissible 'Asiatics' set out under a new regulation (P.C. 1930–2115) was restricted to the wives of Canadian citizens and their children under eighteen years of age; other immigrant groups could sponsor a much broader range of relatives after they secured legal residency. Similar efforts to staunch charges of discrimination against nationals from Canada's Commonwealth partners in south Asia led to the establishment of a symbolic quota system that allowed 150 Indians, 100 Pakistanis, and 50 Ceylonese access to Canada on a yearly basis (Canada 1955, 301). Immigrants from European countries did not face quotas of this kind.

The new 1952 Immigration Act's provisions on immigrant admissions were similarly rooted in the logic of the established policy paradigm. The Governor-in-Council was empowered to prohibit or limit the admission of persons by reason of their

1. Nationality, citizenship, occupation, class, or geographical area of origin.
2. Peculiar customs, habits, modes of life, or methods of holding property.
3. Unsuitability vis-à-vis climatic, social, industrial, educational, labour, health, or other conditions or requirements existing temporarily or otherwise, in Canada or in the area or country from or through which such persons came to Canada.
4. Probable inability to become readily assimilated or to assume the duties and responsibilities of Canadian citizenship, within a reasonable time after admission (Hawkins 1988, 102).

As in the past, immigration was to be closely regulated to ensure that Canada's 'national character' remained unchanged.

Unravelling: 1952–62

The lack of fit between Canada's pre-war immigration policy paradigm and the emerging post-war normative context was acutely obvious to Canada's diplomatic corps. While officials in the Department of Citizenship and Immigration continued to insist that 'immigration must not have the effect of altering the fundamental character of the population,'[3] invocations of official policy became increasingly difficult to maintain in light of developments in Canadian foreign policy. The post-war transformation of international relations led Canada to take increasingly liberal positions in the UN and the British Commonwealth. Decolonization in Africa and Asia had transformed power relations in both organizations, placing racial discrimination at the top of their agendas. By 1961 African, Asian, and Latin American members constituted two-thirds of the UN General Assembly and anti-racist resolutions were becoming sharper and more frequent (Freeman 1997, 19). As Canada's ability to play an independent role in world affairs depended on the preservation and functioning of both organizations, it could not be a neutral party in debates over racial justice.

South Africa's membership in the Commonwealth was a particularly thorny issue. Non-white member states came out strongly against apartheid, demanding that South Africa be expelled if it maintained its grossly illiberal system of racial segregation (Bothwell 2007, 143). Canada's prime minister, John Diefenbaker, responded to their demands by condemning the principle of racial discrimination at the 1961 Commonwealth Conference in London, effectively placing Canada on the side of reform (Blanchette 1977, 302–6; Freeman 1997, 25). Diefenbaker's position made the already difficult job of administering Canada's immigration policy abroad even trickier. Canadian consular officials understood that the prime minister's strong international stance against racism invited questions concerning Canada's maintenance of discriminatory admissions policies at home.[4] These questions were frequently posed by prospective immigrants in the British West Indies and other 'non-traditional' source regions.

Domestic critics, such as the Canadian Council of Churches, the Canadian Jewish Congress, the Negro Citizenship Association, and the Canadian Congress of Labour also challenged the government's continuing use of racial categories, questioning its commitment to anti-discrimination, civil rights, and liberal democratic principles. They highlighted the discrepancy between the government's progressive rhetoric and the reality of ongoing discrimination against 'Asiatics,' 'Negroes,' and individuals of 'mixed-race,' appealing to Canada's obligation to live up to its commitment to international human rights and the elimination of discrimination based on race, colour, or creed.[5]

The Canadian government reacted to these demands by making minor changes to policy while endeavouring to meet the objectives of King's 1947 statement. Thus, India's annual quota was increased from 150 to 300 persons, an annual quota of female domestic workers from the British West Indies was introduced, and previously rejected sponsorship applications for immigrants from China and other non-preferred countries were reconsidered by the minister of immigration (Corbett 1963, 173).

These attempts to co-opt critics' demands while avoiding more fundamental reforms compounded the government's problems. The doubling of India's annual immigration quota prompted Pakistan to demand that its quota also be doubled.[6] Given that rejecting Pakistan's demand would likely lead to accusations of discrimination, Canadian officials had little choice but to comply.[7] Similarly, the use of ministerial discretion to increase the number of approved sponsorship applications from China failed to satisfy domestic advocacy groups, who now challenged the very maintenance of a discriminatory double standard.[8] In short, the strategy of stretching Canada's immigration policy paradigm to fit a changed normative context had reached an impasse. It was becoming increasingly apparent that more fundamental changes would be required if Canada were to successfully respond to accusations of hypocrisy. Normal policy making had succumbed to extraordinary demands.[9]

Shifting: 1962–7

The Diefenbaker government's 1962 immigration regulations marked a decisive break with the past, in that they rejected the pre-war paradigm's emphasis on race and sought instead to found Canadian immigration policy on individuals' satisfaction of universal criteria based on education, skills, and training (Canada 1962, 10). In her memorandum to Cabinet, minister of citizenship and immigration, Ellen Fairclough, noted that the revised regulations' principal objective was 'the elimination of any valid grounds for arguing that [Canadian immigration policy] contain[s] any restrictions or controls based on racial, ethnic or color discrimination.'[10]

Whether the 1962 reform marked the beginning of paradigm shifting is debatable. The Diefenbaker government's decision to limit the sponsorship rights of non-Europeans suggests that the pre-war policy paradigm continued to shape policy makers' understanding of immigration policy, particularly as it related to flows of family members. Officials feared that granting full sponsorship rights to migrants from Asia and Africa would prompt a sharp increase in non-white immigration and create a negative backlash among white Canadians (Hawkins 1988, 131). Similar anxieties lay behind the decision to interpret the 1962 reforms passively; while the door was opened to well-qualified migrants from non-traditional sources, only immigrants from the United States and Europe were actively recruited.[11] In retrospect, the 1962 reform stood somewhere between normal policy making and third-order change.

This 'in-between' period created space for the development of new approaches to immigration that would serve as the foundations of a new policy paradigm. These novel programmatic ideas were developed over the course of the early 1960s and presented in relatively distilled form in the 1966 *White Paper on Immigration Policy*, commissioned by Liberal Prime Minister Lester B. Pearson. The *White Paper* offered a two-pronged strategy: first, Canada would accentuate its effort to recruit well-educated and highly skilled immigrants; second, remaining discrimination in the realm of sponsorship rights would be ended. Rather than discriminating according to national background, the *White Paper* proposed making sponsorship rights for all landed immigrants equal (Canada 1966). For the first time, all landed immigrants would enjoy the right to sponsor the same array of dependants and 'eligible relatives.'

While the *White Paper*'s call for the elimination of remaining discrimination in the immigration regulations was applauded, critics continued to question how criteria relating to education and skills could be applied without a clearly defined set of standards (Canada 1967, 407). The 'points system' – developed by a working group of senior bureaucrats under the guidance of the then deputy minister of manpower and immigration, Tom Kent – was advanced in response to such questions. According to the scheme, prospective immigrants would be assigned a score based on their age, education, training, occupational skill in demand, knowledge of English or French, relatives in Canada, arranged employment, and employment opportunities in the area of destination. A score based on a personal assessment made by an immigration officer in an interview would be included in the total. Applicants meeting the threshold set by the government (initially 50 assessment points) would be admitted as independent immigrants and would enjoy the right to sponsor dependants (spouses and minor children) as well as more distant 'nominated relatives.' Nominated relatives were also subject to the points system but would be evaluated on a narrower set of criteria. Although the broadening of sponsorship rights would lead to increases in sponsored flows, officials believed the points system could be used to control this movement by regulating the number of nominated relatives granted entry according to labour market conditions.[12]

The new regulations came into effect in October 1967. Other reforms introduced at this time secured the institutional prerequisites for an immigration regime open to qualified applicants regardless of their 'race.' Canadian policy makers thus succeeded in crafting a non-discriminatory immigration policy paradigm that opened Canada to large-scale immigration from Asia, Africa, the Middle East, and other 'non-traditional' sources, while also offering officials a means of regulating the sponsored stream and harnessing immigration for economic needs. Their ability to arrive at a solution that met these objectives was facilitated by Canada's institutional configuration. While the bureaucrats responsible for developing the new paradigm responded to criticisms of the 1966 White Paper made during the course of public consultations, they did so in a way that retained the government's objectives. The points system was thus the product of puzzling among a relatively narrow group of policy makers insulated from partisan political pressures. The ability to implement these changes via regulations rather than the passage of a new act also dampened opposition, enabling a smooth transition from Canada's discriminatory pre-war immigration policy paradigm to the universal system based on the 1967 points system.

Immigration Reform in the United States, 1945–65

Stretching: 1945–52

As was the case in Canada, changes in normative context in the post-war period challenged the core premises of the US established immigration policy paradigm. Even before the war ended, national security concerns prompted the Roosevelt administration to eliminate the Chinese

Exclusion Act in an effort to neutralize Japanese claims that the US bar on Chinese immigration made American positions on human rights hypocritical and empty (Ong Hing 1993, 110). At home, the Citizens' Committee to Repeal Chinese Exclusion also made the case that the laws stood in the way of America's fulfilling its wartime mission to defeat fascism. While the exclusion laws were repealed in December 1943, they were replaced with a symbolic quota authorizing the admission of only 105 Chinese immigrants annually. Similar quotas were established for India and the Philippines (Skrentny 2002, 39–44). Asian exclusion was thus repealed in name but not in spirit.

After the war, critics continued to argue that the outright exclusion of most non-white migrants and tight controls against southern and eastern Europeans stipulated under the national origins quotas made a mockery of American leaders' claims that their country was a beacon of liberty. Conscious of the United States's increasingly important role in stabilizing the post-war world, President Harry S. Truman agreed that racial discrimination was hampering America's efforts to counter the influence of its ideological rival, the Soviet Union in Europe and the newly independent states of the 'Third World.' Truman thus supported the abolition of the quota system and other racially discriminatory policies, arguing that failure to act aggressively would assist 'those with competing philosophies ... prove our democracy an empty fraud and our nation a consistent oppressor of underprivileged people' (cited in Tichenor 2002, 179).

While most American politicians agreed that America's immigration and naturalization policies required modification, they rejected Truman's calls for radical reforms, insisting instead that the goals of established policies were legitimate. In its 1950 report on immigration policy, the Senate Judiciary Committee's subcommittee rejected theories of 'Nordic superiority' while simultaneously reserving the United States's right to restrict immigration 'in such a manner as to best preserve the [country's] sociological and cultural balance' (cited in Bennett 1966, 129–30).

The subcommittee's report thus recommended that the established immigration policy paradigm be adjusted in response to a changed normative context. The spirit of the report was captured in the 1952 Immigration and Nationality Act, also known as the McCarran-Walter Act, after its sponsors, Senator Pat McCarran (D-NV) and the chair of the House Immigration Subcommittee, Representative Francis E. Walter (D-PA). While the 1952 law formally abolished racist criteria in immigration and naturalization policy, it maintained the fundamental features of the national origins quota system and thus granted preference to immigrants from northwestern Europe (King 2000, 240). The 'Asiatic Barred Zone' was eliminated, but only 2000 visas per year were allotted to individuals born within the so-called Asia-Pacific Triangle – a region spanning India, China, Japan, and the Pacific Islands. The law also blocked the admission of 'Asiatics' from countries outside the Asia-Pacific Triangle by stipulating that individuals 'of as much as one-half Asian blood born outside the Triangle be charged against the quota of his country of Asian-Pacific ancestry' (Bennett 1966, 131; Daniels 2004, 116). The lifting of barriers to naturalization for immigrants from Asia was deemed a symbolic concession of little consequence, as 'the vast majority of non-citizens entering the country [would continue to come] from Europe' (Tichenor 2002, 196).

The passage of the 1952 Immigration and Nationality Act highlighted the durability of the United States's established immigration policy paradigm. While America's new role as a global superpower made the negative repercussions of discriminatory policies clear, policy makers in Congress opted to limit their response to first- and second-order changes in the hope that this minimal response would defuse criticism while preserving the ethnic composition of the American nation.

Unravelling: 1952–8

Changing norms helped propel the realignment of domestic forces, as ethnic groups, organized labour, religious organizations, civil liberties groups, and the liberal wing of the Democratic Party formed an influential coalition dedicated to the pursuit of immigration policy reform (Joppke 2005a, 55). Critics of discriminatory immigration admissions policies, which included the National Association for the Advancement of Colored People, organized labour, and prominent senators such as Herbert Lehman (D-NY) and Hubert Humphrey (D-MN), argued that the maintenance of an immigration system based on national origins quotas gave the lie to the American commitment to fundamental liberal-democratic norms (King 2000, 237; Zolberg 2006, 314). President Truman went several steps further while campaigning for the Democratic Party's nominee in the 1952 presidential election, arguing that conservative Republicans' continuing support of the national origins quota system perpetuated 'a philosophy of racial superiority developed by the Nazis, which we thought we had destroyed when we defeated Nazi Germany and liberated Europe.'[13] Truman also argued that the Republicans' presidential nominee, Dwight Eisenhower, and his running mate, Richard Nixon, supported the McCarran-Walter Act,[14] leading Eisenhower to insist that he, too, rejected the principles underlying the national origins quotas. This marked a significant setback for restrictionists in Congress.

The discrediting of scientific racism in the post-war period played an important role in this regard (Tichenor 2002, 179–80). The Presidential Commission on Immigration and Naturalization, appointed by Truman in September 1952, challenged the 'scientific' bases of the quota acts. The commission's report, *Whom We Shall Welcome* (1953), concluded that 'the best scientific evidence available today is that there [are] no ... inborn differences of personality, character, intelligence, or cultural or social traits among races. The basic racist assumption of the national origins system is invalid.' The presidential commission's report was very much in line with similar pronouncements on race at the time, including UNESCO's influential 1951 statement on race and racial differences.

Organized labour joined the movement to scrap the national origins quota system in 1955 (Tichenor 2002, 203–4). Labour's shift reinforced the Democratic Party's support of immigration reform – a trend strengthened by northern Democrats' strong backing for the nascent civil rights movement. High-profile statements, such as Senator John F. Kennedy's *A Nation of Immigrants* and Hubert Humphrey's *The Stranger at Our Gate*, helped 'frame a pro-immigrant narrative ... that further eroded the early-twentieth-century "policy paradigm" legitimating quotas' (ibid. 2002, 205; Zolberg 2006, 297). Slow but steady progress in the area of domestic anti-discrimination legislation also 'undermined the legitimacy of the national origins system posted on America's door' (Zolberg 2006, 300).

Foreign policy considerations complemented domestic political pressures. President Eisenhower argued that the national origins quotas made it difficult for him to offer sanctuary to refugees 'fleeing Communism' and this, in turn, hampered American efforts in the Cold War. Eisenhower thus demanded and received special powers to override quota limits, enabling a quick response to the 1956 Hungarian refugee crisis (King 2000, 239; Markowitz 1973; Skrentny 2002, 47–8). Although restrictionists in Congress viewed these concessions as a necessary price to pay for maintaining the national origins quota system, each exception undermined the coherence and effectiveness of the established immigration policy paradigm. By the end of the 1950s most newcomers entered the United States as a result of special exemptions to the McCarran-Walter Act (Joppke 2005a, 54; Gerstle 2001). Incremental responses to domestic and international pressures drove the unravelling of the national origins quota system, opening space for the emergence of new ideas in line with the prevailing normative context.

Shifting: 1958–65

The Democrats' success in the 1958 mid-term elections and John F. Kennedy's victory in the 1960 presidential election increased momentum for immigration reform. The Democrats sought the support of ethnic voters in both campaigns and employed language that emphasized civil rights and respect for cultural pluralism (DeLaet 2000, 39). The prospects of paradigm change increased when Kennedy introduced and helped pass a bill that authorized the immigration of 18,000 foreign relatives outside the quota system (Zolberg 2006, 325). The 1961 act also granted quotas to the newly independent states of the Caribbean and gave non-quota status to many close relatives of American citizens who were on waiting lists in Italy, Greece, Portugal, and elsewhere (Bennett 1966, 135–6).

While liberal Democrats were ascendant in the early 1960s, immigration restrictionists still exercised a great deal of power in Congress. Conservative Republicans and southern Democrats held the chairmanships of important congressional committees, which allowed them to block initiatives and otherwise manipulate the legislative process. President Kennedy remained wary of provoking these 'committee barons' and waited for nearly two years before submitting his comprehensive immigration reform bill to Congress (Tichenor 2002, 209).

The legislation Kennedy introduced included sweeping changes, including the abolition of the national origins quota system, the elimination of the Asia-Pacific Triangle, and the granting of preferences to immigrants with work-related skills (Reimers 1982). The bill envisioned transferring individual countries' quotas to a world quota pool, of which 50 per cent would be reserved for persons with special skills and training. The other 50 per cent would be reserved for spouses and children under twenty-one and married sons and daughters of US citizens over the age of twenty-one. The proposal rejected any limits to immigration from the western hemisphere and made special allowances for the reception of refugees (Schwartz 1968, 114; Skrentny 2002, 50–1).

The Kennedy bill enjoyed the support of the American Immigration and Citizenship Committee, a group that included the American Civil Liberties Union, religious organizations, trade unions, ethnic associations, and groups campaigning on behalf of refugees (Togman 2002, 37). High-ranking administration officials, including Secretary of State Dean Rusk, also supported of the bill (Skrentny 2002, 50). Despite this broad support, restrictionists used their control of congressional committees to block the bill's progress through the legislative process. It remained mired in Congress until Kennedy's assassination in 1963.

President Lyndon Johnson sought to rescue the moribund bill after assuming office. Although Johnson had supported the McCarran-Walter Act in 1952, like Truman and Eisenhower before him, he now believed that its continuation of the national origins quota system was hindering America's foreign policy interests. Johnson drew on his considerable political skills and capital to surmount congressional resistance, making immigration reform a part of his broader civil rights agenda. Restrictionists in the House and Senate responded by resisting Johnson's demand for a non-discriminatory admissions system. The Democratic chair of the House Immigration Subcommittee rejected giving preference to immigrants with special skills and training and demanded that preferences be granted instead to family members of American citizens and permanent residents. His position was supported by Senate conservatives and other restrictionists, who believed that it would favour nationalities already in the United States – that is, white Europeans. In an effort to limit the entry of non-whites from the Caribbean and Central and South America, Congressional restrictionists also demanded a ceiling on immigration from the western hemisphere – a region that had previously been exempt from numerical limits and was set to remain so under both the Kennedy and the Johnson bills (Zolberg 2006, 332–3). Johnson opted to strike a deal with his opponents, concluding that the switch in preferences from skilled immigrants to family members and limitations on western hemisphere immigration was a necessary price to pay for the elimination of the national origins quota system (Kennedy 1966, 147).

The amended act provided for 170,000 visas for immigrants originating in the eastern hemisphere (with no country receiving more than 20,000 spots) and 120,000 visas for immigrants from the western hemisphere (with no country limits). Spouses, minor children, and parents of American citizens were exempted from the numerical limits. As a result of the compromise forged between Johnson and his congressional opponents, 74 per cent of yearly visa allotments were dedicated to family reunification, preference being granted to brothers and sisters of American citizens; only 20 per cent were reserved for immigrants with occupational skills. Refugees – defined as people fleeing persecution from communism or the Middle East and victims of natural disasters, as specified by the president – received 6 per cent of the yearly visa allotment (Zolberg 2006, 133).

Johnson signed the new Immigration Act on 3 October 1965, in an elaborate ceremony held at the base of the Statue of Liberty in New York Harbour. In his speech, Johnson noted that, although the bill he was signing was not revolutionary, it did 'repair a deep and painful flaw in the fabric of American justice. The days of unlimited immigration are past. But those who come will come because of what they are – not because of the land from which they sprung' (cited in Reimers 1982, 38).

Conclusion

President Johnson and his contemporaries grossly underestimated the impact of the 1965 Immigration Act. The abolition of strict controls on immigration from the Asia-Pacific Triangle allowed for an increase of Asian immigration from 1.5 million in 1970 to 13.1 million in 2000 (US Census Bureau 2004). Immigration from Central and South America, Africa, and the Middle East also increased sharply, transforming America's cities and making the United States a diverse, multicultural society. Similarly, Canada's demographic profile was transformed as a result of increasing migration from so-called non-traditional sources, made possible by the introduction of the points system in 1967. Whereas the vast majority of immigrants arriving in Canada up to the late 1960s came from Europe, by 1971, 36 per cent of total migration originated from the 'Third World'; by 1980 this figure had reached 81 per cent. By 2002 immigrants from mainland China represented the largest single group entering Canada and were followed by immigrants from India, Pakistan, and the Philippines (Citizenship and Immigration Canada 2003). Changes in Canada's immigration policy paradigm ensured that the vision of a predominantly white European Canada defended in Prime Minister Mackenzie King's 1947 speech to Parliament was effectively overturned.

This chapter has explored how shifts in broadly encompassing normative contexts challenged the taken for granted beliefs animating Canadian and American pre-World War II immigration policy paradigms. The discrediting of scientific racism and the concomitant rise of global human rights after the war cast paradigms that relied on notions of racial hierarchy in a new light. The resulting glare – magnified by domestic and international critics – hampered efforts in Canada and the United States to pursue domestic and foreign policy objectives in the post-war period. Changes in norms led to a reappraisal of interests, as racial discrimination took on a very different meaning after the war.

Paradigm change proceeded incrementally, as the deeply entrenched logic of established paradigms continued to inform policy making. Yet rather than serving as a tool of continuity and stability, normal policy making, marked by first- and second-order change, prompted the stretching and unravelling of established policy paradigms, diminishing their intellectual coherence and administrative efficacy and creating space for the introduction of new ideas and approaches. Acknowledging the normative validity of critics' demands gave rise to an iterative process of normative contestation, whereby the very foundations of pre-war immigration policy paradigms were challenged and ultimately overturned.

Differing domestic institutional contexts affected the pace and depth of third-order change and paradigm shift. The executive's need to strike compromises with restrictionist defenders of the national origins quota system in Congress meant that paradigm change in the United States was contested and not entirely coherent; while racially discriminatory admissions criteria were ultimately jettisoned, the preference granted to family members in the 1965 act echoed concerns animating the pre-war paradigm. Conversely, the more insulated environment in which Canadian policy makers operated facilitated their efforts to reform immigration policy, such that it effectively responded to charges of racial discrimination while also meeting Canadian interests in the areas of sponsored migration and labour market need. While Canadian policy makers were not completely free of constraints, political institutions offered no comparable source of leverage to opponents of reform. Thus, broadly similar processes of normatively driven immigration policy paradigm change followed distinctive, institutionally structured, political pathways, with consequences that continue to inform immigration politics in Canada and the United States.

NOTES

1 This chapter is a revised and shortened version of Triadafilopoulos (2010).
2 Asiatic Immigration into Canada. NA, RG 76, vol. 854, file 554–5, pt 1.
3 Confidential Letter from Director of Immigration, C.E.S. Smith, to Under-Secretary of State for External Affairs, G. McInnes, 17 January 1957. NA, RG 76, vol. 830, file 552–1–644, pt 2.
4 Telegraph from Canadian Trade Commissioner in Port-of-Spain to Department of External Affairs, Ottawa, 20 March 1961.
5 Immigration by Discrimination, *Black Worker*, March 1952. NA, RG 26, vol. 123, file 3–32- 24; NA, Box 266, RG 76, vol. 830, file 552–1–644, pt 2.
6 Memorandum to Cabinet: Immigration Agreements with Pakistan and Ceylon, 23 October 1958. NA, RG 76, vol. 948, file SF-C-1–1, pt. 2.
7 Ibid.
8 Memorandum to Cabinet: Immigration Policies and Procedures (Immigration from China and Japan), 8 August 1958. NA, RG 76, vol. 948, file SF-C-1–1, pt 2.
9 Illiberal policies in other issue areas proved quite durable. Alberta's Sexual Sterilization Act was not repealed until 1972, in large part because of the very limited nature of public criticism. See Grekul, Krahn, and Ondynak (2004).
10 Memorandum to Cabinet Re: Immigration Regulations, 16 October 1961. NA, RG 26, vol. 100, file 3–15–1, pt 8.
11 'Although our policy is not racially biased we do concentrate our main operations in those countries (Europe and the United States) which have traditionally given us most of our immigrants. While our immigration intake has since 1962 been becoming less European and more racially varied, we have proceeded with some caution in order to avoid a too-rapid change, which might result in adverse reaction by the Canadian public, which in turn could weaken the whole concept of a universal and non-discriminatory policy.' Memorandum from Assistant Deputy Minister to Deputy Minister, Department of Citizenship and Immigration, 21 January 1966. NA, RG 26, vol. 145, file 3–33–6; cited in Satzewich (1989, 84).
12 Memorandum from the Assistant Deputy Minister (Immigration) to the Deputy Minister on the Parliamentary Committee on Immigration, 19 February 1968, 6. NA, RG 76, vol. 966, file 5000–14–2, pt 14.
13 Truman Assails Eisenhower as Supporting Isolationists, *New York Times*, 18 October 1952.
14 Eisenhower Accepts 'Nazi' Racial Views, Truman Declares, *Washington Evening Star*, 17 October 1952.

REFERENCES

Bélanger, Alain, and Éric Caron Malenfant. 2005. Ethnocultural Diversity
    in Canada: Prospects for 2017. *Canadian Social Trends* (Winter). Statistics
    Canada – Catalogue No. 11–008.
Benhabib, Seyla. 2009. Claiming Rights Across Borders: International Human
    Rights and Democratic Sovereignty. *American Political Science Review* 103
    (4):691–704.
Bennett, Marion T. 1966. The Immigration and Nationality (McCarran-Walter)
    Act of 1952, as Amended to 1965. *Annals of the American Academy of Political
    and Social Science* 367 (1):127–36.
Blanchette, Arthur E. 1977. *Canadian Foreign Policy 1955–1965: Selected Speeches
    and Documents*. Toronto: McClelland and Stewart.
Borjas, George J. 1999. *Heaven's Door: Immigration and the American Economy*.
    Princeton: Princeton University Press.
Bothwell, Robert. 2007. *Alliance and Illusion: Canada and the World, 1945–1984*.
    Vancouver: UBC Press.
Cairns, Alan C. 1999. Empire, Globalization, and the Fall and Rise of
    Diversity. In *Citizenship, Diversity, and Pluralism: Canadian and Comparative
    Perspectives*, edited by A.C. Cairns et al. Montreal and Kingston:
    McGill-Queen's University Press.
Canada. 1952. An Act Respecting Immigration: Ottawa: Queen's Printer.
– House of Commons. 1947a. *Debates*.
– Ministry of Mines and Resources. 1947b. P.C. 1930–2115 Prohibiting the
    Landing of Any Immigrant of the Asiatic Race. *Canada Gazette* 81
    (16 Sept.): 90.
– Special Committee on Estimates. 1955. Minutes of Proceedings and
    Evidence, No. 11.
– House of Commons. 1962. *Debates*.
– Department of Manpower and Immigration. 1966. *White Paper on
    Immigration*. Ottawa: Queen's Printer.
– Special Joint Committee of the Senate and House of Commons on
    Immigration. 1967. Minutes of the Proceedings and Evidence, No. 9.
Capoccia, Giovanni, and Daniel Kelemen. 2007. The Study of Critical
    Junctures: Theory, Narrative, and Counterfactuals in Historical
    Institutionalism. *World Politics* 59:341–69.
Carens, Joseph H. 1987. Aliens and Citizens: The Case for Open Borders.
    Review of Politics 49 (2):251–73.
Castles, Stephen. 1995. How Nation-States Respond to Immigration and
    Ethnic Diversity. *New Community* 21 (3):293–308.

Citizenship and Immigration Canada. 2003. *The Monitor,* 1/2 (Spring). Accessed 2003. Available from http://www.cic.gc/english/monitor/ issue01/02-immigrants.html.

Commission on Immigration and Nationalization. 1953. *Whom We Shall Welcome*. Washington, DC: Government Printing Office.

Corbett, David 1963. Canada's Immigration Policy, 1957–1962. *International Journal* 18 (2):166–80.

Daniels, Roger. 2004. *Guarding the Golden Door: American Immigration Policy and Immigrants since 1882*. New York: Hill and Wang.

DeLaet, Debra L. 2000. *U.S. Immigration Policy in an Age of Rights*. Westport, CT: Praeger.

Dirks, Gerald. 1995. *Controversy and Complexity: Canadian Immigration Policy during the 1980s*. Montreal and Kingston: McGill-Queen's University Press.

Elliot, Michael A. 2007. Human Rights and the Triumph of the Individual in World Culture. *Cultural Sociology* 1 (3):343–63.

Finnemore, Martha. 1996. Norms, Culture, and World Politics: Insights from Sociology's Institutionalism. *International Organization* 50 (2):325–47.

Fredrickson, George M. 2002. *Racism: A Short History*. Princeton: Princeton University Press.

Freeman, Linda. 1997. *The Ambiguous Champion: Canada and South Africa in the Trudeau and Mulroney Years*. Toronto: University of Toronto Press.

Füredi, Frank. 1998. *The Silent War: Imperialism and the Changing Perception of Race*. New Brunswick: Rutgers University Press.

Gerstle, Gary. 2001. *American Crucible*. Princeton: Princeton University Press.

Grekul, Jana, Harvey Krahn, and Dave Odynak. 2004. Sterilizing the 'Feeble-minded': Eugenics in Alberta, Canada, 1929–1972. *Journal of Historical Sociology* 17 (4):358–84.

Hall, Peter A. 1993. Policy Paradigms, Social Learning, and the State: The Case of Economic Policymaking in Britain. *Comparative Politics* 25 (3):275–96.

Hansen, Randall, and Desmond King. 2001. Eugenic Ideas, Political Interests, and Policy Variance: Immigration and Sterilization Policy in Britain and the U.S. *World Politics* 53:237–63.

Hawkins, Freda. 1988. *Canada and Immigration: Public Policy and Public Concern*. 2nd ed. Montreal and Kingston: McGill-Queen's University Press.

Hay, Colin. 2002. *Political Analysis: A Critical Introduction*. New York: Palgrave.

Heclo, Hugh. 1974. *Modern Social Politics in Britain and Sweden*. New Haven: Yale University Press.

Hollifield, James F. 1992. *Immigrants, Markets, and States: The Political Economy of Postwar Europe*. Cambridge, MA: Harvard University Press.

Huttenback, Robert A. 1976. *Racism and Empire: White Settlers and Colored Immigrants in the British Self-Governing Colonies, 1830–1910.* Ithaca: Cornell University Press.

Joppke, Christian. 2005a. *Selecting by Origin: Ethnic Migration in the Liberal State.* Cambridge, MA: Harvard University Press.

– 2005b. Are 'Nondiscriminatory' Immigration Policies Reversible? Evidence from United States and Australia. *Comparative Political Studies* 38 (1):3–25.

Katzenstein, Peter J. 1996. Introduction: Alternative Perspectives on National Security. In *Cultural Norms and National Security,* edited by P.J. Katzenstein. Ithaca: Cornell University Press.

Kelley, Ninette, and Michael Trebilcock. 1998. *The Making of the Mosaic: A History of Canadian Immigration Policy.* Toronto: University of Toronto Press.

Kennedy, Edward M. 1966. The Immigration Act of 1965. *Annals of the American Academy of Political and Social Science* 367 (1):137–49.

King, Desmond. 2000. *Making Americans: Immigration, Race, and the Origins of Diverse Democracy.* Cambridge, MA: Harvard University Press.

Koenig, Matthias. 2008. Institutional Change in the World Polity: International Human Rights and the Construction of Collective Identities. *International Sociology* 23 (1):95–114.

Kymlicka, Will. 2007. *Multicultural Odysseys: Navigating the New International Politics of Diversity.* Oxford and New York: Oxford University Press.

Lake, Marilyn, and Henry Reynolds. 2008. *Drawing the Global Colour Line: White Men's Countries and the International Challenge of Racial Equality.* Cambridge: Cambridge University Press.

Lauren, Paul Gordon. 1996. *Power and Prejudice: The Politics and Diplomacy of Racial Discrimination.* Boulder, CO: Westview.

Lieberman, Robert C. 2002. Ideas, Institutions, and Political Order: Explaining Political Change. *American Political Science Review* 96 (4):697–712.

Markowitz, Arthur A. 1973. Humanitarianism versus Restrictionism: The United States and the Hungarian Refugees. *International Migration Review* 7 (1):46–59.

Mazower, Mark. 2008. Paved Intentions: Civilization and Imperialism. *World Affairs* 171 (2):72–85.

Messina, Anthony. 2007. *The Logics and Politics of Post-WWII Migration to Europe.* Cambridge: Cambridge University Press.

Meyer, John W., John Boli, George M. Thomas, and Francisco O. Ramirez. 1997. World Society and the Nation-State. *American Journal of Sociology* 103 (1):144–81

Ngai, Mae M. 1999. The Architecture of Race in American Immigration Law: A Reexamination of the Immigration Act of 1924. *Journal of American History* 86:67–92.

Ong Hing, Bill. 1993. *Making and Remaking Asian America Through Immigration Policy, 1850–1990.* Stanford: Stanford University Press.

Orren, Karen, and Stephen Skowronek. 2004. *The Search for American Political Development.* Cambridge and New York: Cambridge University Press.

Peng, Ito, and Joseph Wong. 2008. Institutions and Institutional Purpose: Continuity and Change in East Asian Social Policy. *Politics and Society* 36 (1):61–88.

Pierson, Paul. 1993. When Effect Becomes Cause: Policy Feedback and Political Change. *World Politics* 45 (4):595–628.

– 2000. Increasing Returns, Path Dependence, and the Study of Politics. *American Political Science Review* 94 (2):251–67.

Reimers, David M. 1982. Recent Immigration Policy: An Analysis. In *In the Gateway: U.S. Immigration Issues and Policies,* edited by B.R. Chiswick. Washington, DC: American Enterprise Institute for Public Policy Research.

Risse, Thomas. 1999. International Norms and Domestic Change: Arguing and Communicative Behavior in the Human Rights Arena. *Politics and Society* 27 (4):1–38.

– 2000. 'Let's Argue!' Communicative Action in World Politics. *International Organization* 54 (1):1–39.

– and Kathryn Sikkink. 1999. The Socialization of International Human Rights Norms into Domestic Practices: Introduction. In *In The Power of Human Rights: International Norms and Domestic Change,* edited by T. Risse, S.C. Ropp, and K. Sikkink. Cambridge: Cambridge University Press.

Roy, Patricia E. 1989. *A White Man's Province: British Columbia Politicians and Chinese and Japanese Immigrants, 1858–1914.* Vancouver: UBC Press.

Ryder, Bruce. 1991. Racism and the Constitution: The Constitutional Fate of British Columbia Anti-Asian Immigration Legislation, 1884–1909. *Osgoode Hall Law Journal* 29 (3): 619–76.

Satzewich, Vic. 1989. Racism and Canadian Immigration Policy: The Government's View of Caribbean Migration, 1962–1966. *Canadian Ethnic Studies* 21: 77–97.

Schuck, Peter. 1985. Immigration Law and the Problem of Community. In *Clamor at the Gates: The New American Immigration,* edited by N. Glazer. San Francisco: ICS Press.

Schwartz, Abba P. 1968. *The Open Society.* New York: William Morrow.

Shachar, Ayelet. 2006. The Race for Talent: Highly Skilled Migrants and Competitive Immigration Regimes. *New York University Law Review* 81:101–58.

Shrestha, Laura B. 2006. The Changing Demographic Profile of the United States: Congressional Research Service Report for Congress.

Skrentny, John D. 2002. *The Minority Rights Revolution.* Cambridge and New York: Cambridge University Press.

Thelen, Kathleen. 1999. Historical Institutionalism in Comparative Politics. *Annual Review of Political Science* 2:369–404.

– 2006. Institutions and Social Change: The Evolution of Vocational Training in Germany. In *Rethinking Political Institutions: The Art of the State,* edited by I. Shapiro, S. Skowronek, and D. Galvin. New York: New York University Press.

Tichenor, Daniel. 2002. *Dividing Lines: The Politics of Immigration Control in America.* Princeton: Princeton University Press.

Togman, Jeffrey. 2002. *The Ramparts of Nations: Institutions and Immigration Policies in France and the United States.* Westport, CT: Praeger.

Triadafilopoulos, Triadafilos. 2010. Global Norms, Domestic Institutions and the Transformation of Immigration Policy in Canada and the United States. *Review of International Studies* 36 (1): 169–93.

Triadafilopoulos, Triadafilos, and Karen Schönwälder. 2006. How the Federal Republic Became an Immigration Country: Norms, Politics and the Failure of West Germany's Guest Worker System. *German Politics and Society* 24 (3):1–19.

US Census Bureau. 2004. *Facts for Features.*

Walzer, Michael. 1981. The Distribution of Membership. In *Boundaries: National Autonomy and its Limits,* edited by P.G. Brown and H. Shue. Totowa, NJ: Rowman & Littlefield.

Zolberg, Aristide R. 1981. International Migrations in Political Perspective. In *Global Trends in Migration: Theory and Research on International Population Movements,* edited by M.M. Kritz, C.B. Keely, and S.M. Tomasi. New York: Center for Migration Studies.

– 1987. 'Wanted but Not Welcome: Alien Labor in Western Development.' In *Population in an Interacting World,* edited by W. Alonso. Cambridge, MA: Harvard University Press.

– 2006. *A Nation by Design: Immigration Policy in the Fashioning of America.* Cambridge, MA: Harvard University Press.

Canadian Refugee Policy:
Understanding the Role of International
Bureaucratic Networks in Domestic
Paradigm Change

J.A. SANDY IRVINE

On 13 June 2001 Bill C-11, the Immigration and Refugee Protection Act (IRPA), was approved by the Canadian House of Commons. This legislation, which replaced the 1978 Immigration Act, introduced important changes in Canada's refugee policy. For policy makers a central goal of the new legislation was the tightening of the Canadian refugee system. In the words of Elinor Caplan, minister of citizenship and immigration, 'By saying "No" more quickly to people who would abuse our rules, we are able to say "Yes" more often to the immigrants and refugees Canada will need to grow and prosper in the years ahead' (Citizenship and Immigration Canada 2001a). This emphasis on a tighter immigration system fits with deeper changes that were occurring in the paradigm that had framed Canadian decision makers' understanding of refugee policy during the 1990s. In particular, it reflected a shift from an emphasis on refugee protection to one of security and control.

The new thinking could be explained by shifts in the domestic policy environment that included new migration trends and an increase in specific 'events' that raised concerns of security and control. However, this chapter proposes that, at best, these domestic factors offer only a partial explanation of paradigm change. Instead, it is argued that the intensified transnational activities of domestic bureaucrats provide an important source of new ideas to which domestic decision makers appealed and through which changes in the domestic environment can be interpreted. Although changes in the Canadian paradigm mirror and trail the securitization of refugee policy across most industrialized states (Huysmans 2000; Adamson 2006), almost no consideration has been given to the role of international norms in explaining domestic paradigm change. Indeed, the accepted belief that Canadian foreign policy and refugee policy are guided by a set of distinctly Canadian values means that both paradigm change and its international sources have been overlooked.

Two specific questions about the relationship between transnational actors and paradigm change are addressed here. First, how do transnational actors alter key decision makers' thinking about domestic paradigms? Second, how are ideas transferred from the transnational into the domestic realm? In answering these questions this chapter argues that informal, private exchanges akin to Anne-Marie Slaughter's (2004) global government networks provide an important avenue through which decision makers are socialized into international norms. Global government networks (GGNs) create a community of bureaucrats across jurisdictions and contribute to the socialization of its members to prevailing norms of the group. In turn, participating bureaucrats are uniquely positioned in the domestic policy process, especially as policy experts, to spread new ideas and have them accepted in the domestic policy realm.

This chapter begins by providing a definition of paradigm and paradigm change and builds a framework for understanding how transnational actors facilitate the transfer of international norms into the domestic realm. Central to the framework are the potential role of GGNs in creating the conditions that facilitate the adoption of new ideas and the role played by members of these global networks as a conduit between international norms and domestic paradigm change. The second section examines the case of a change in the paradigm governing Canadian refugee policy. This section outlines the paradigm change that has taken place and argues that Canadian bureaucrats' activities in a developing GGN on international migration resulted in their socialization and, in turn, shaped domestic debates and ultimately the broader policy paradigm.

Transnational Actors and Domestic Paradigm Change

Paradigms are defined here as decision makers' taken for granted, collective understandings of the world in which they operate. Drawing on both the public policy (Hall 1993) and international relations constructivist literatures, the components that make up decision makers' paradigms include decision makers' normative understandings, including beliefs about state goals or interests; definitions of appropriate behaviour and understandings of identity; and cognitive understandings of the cause and effect relationships pertaining to the manner in which the world operates.[1]

Traditional explanations of policy learning provide initial insights into how paradigm change might occur. Broadly, decision makers learn as they acquire new information about their environment and the efficiency of particular responses to it (Haas 1991; see also Meseguer 2005, 74). In this explanation the process of learning is a purposeful act of decision makers who, driven by their interests, seek a better understanding of policy and its operation (Levy 1994, 283; Meseguer 2005). There are various sources of new information that might provoke such change, including decision makers' experience (Levy 1994; Stein 1994), policy feedback (Pierson 1993; Hall 1993; Levy 1994, 304–6; McNamara 1998), and the experience of others (Meseguer 2005, 72; Stone 1999, 55–6; Dolowitz and Marsh 2000; McNamara 1998). New information may arise as the environment itself changes, destabilizing existing understandings and motivating actors to find new ones. Alternatively, changes in the pressures on decision makers from within the policy environment, such as new political dynamics or institutional change, may provide motivation for altering thinking. The same processes may be an important source of paradigm change. As pressures and perceived anomalies accumulate to an unmanageable level, paradigm change may take place (Hall 1993).

What is absent in these approaches is a thorough consideration of the social processes that alter decision makers' paradigms above and beyond these other processes of learning. Even Peter Hall's 'social' learning explanation ascribes a limited role to social processes in accounting for change.[2] It fails to highlight sufficiently that what is important for paradigm change is not simply a better understanding of an environment, but rather the attribution of new meanings to the environment as a result of social interaction. In addition, more attention needs to be paid to the possibility that transnationalism opens the door to the influence of international social factors in effecting paradigm change.

This chapter builds on the latter insights to propose an explanation of paradigm change in Canadian refugee policy. It argues that the increased transnational activities of bureaucrats through networks of government officials provide a venue through which these bureaucrats could be socialized into an alternative paradigm. One conceptualization of these networks is Anne-Marie Slaughter's global government networks. Slaughter (2004) defines GGNs as the interstate coordination of government officials in 'quasi-autonomous' forums to address specific and often critical concerns.[3] The activities of government officials are understood to go beyond the traditional constraints of formal inter-state diplomacy, reflecting the increased frequency and quasi-official nature of bureaucrats' transnational activities (Hocking 2004) that occur with minimal oversight from their political masters.

This recognition of the increasingly broad and informal activities of bureaucrats suggests that more weight should be placed on their importance in transferring policy ideas than has traditionally been the case in the policy transfer literature (Stone 2004, 62–3; see also Weyland 2004, 16; Dolowitz and Marsh 2000, 17). Focusing on GGNs suggests their possibility as socialization forums. Indeed, Slaughter argues that these networks 'build trust and establish relationships among their participants that then create incentives to establish a good reputation and avoid a bad one' (2004, 162). Furthermore, they are recognized as providing 'professional socialization to members from less developed nations' (ibid.).[4] Through interaction, decision makers increasingly see themselves as part of a community of professional and technical experts that transcends national borders.[5] The outcomes of these processes are not dissimilar to those found in the European integration literature, where there is evidence that regular interaction of state bureaucrats in the European forum has contributed to the adoption and consolidation of supranational identities (Trondal 2001).

An important source of the potential for GGNs to enable socialization is their ability to generate feelings of community through interaction (Flockhart 2004). Processes of socialization assume the existence of a community (Johnston 2001, 494; Finnemore and Sikkink 1998, 891–2). Therefore, the construction of a common identity provides an important process through which socialization and the adoption of new paradigms can take place. Indeed, social incentives and persuasion – two key mechanisms of socialization (Johnston 2001) – are recognized as being more effective when an actor is a member of a community whose values and opinions it respects (Bernstein and Cashore 2000, 81–2). In the case of social incentives, membership itself is a goal. In the process of acquiring or consolidating membership, actors seek to demonstrate their commitment to key values and to behave in a manner that is consistent with the community. Social rewards such as recognition, praise, and acknowledgment of leadership in the community reinforce actors' identification with the group (Finnemore and Sikkink 1998). Alternatively, social criticism lessens the status of an actor's membership. These processes apply directly to government decision makers interacting at the international level who seek to maintain a good reputation and avoid a bad one (Slaughter 2004). The possibility of persuasion is also reinforced by membership in a community or aspirations to it. Alastair Johnston suggests that persuasion is more likely if the persuadee views the persuader as 'knowledgeable' and 'trustworthy,' the existence of a common identity being one of the most likely indicators of whether the persuadee will hold this image of the persuader (Johnston 2001, 498). Thus, the community built within GGNs is likely to increase the potential for persuasion. Even the setting of GGN meetings – behind closed doors, where open and honest dialogue between peers in a less politicized form can take place – provides ideal conditions for persuasion and broader socialization.[6]

Socialization of bureaucrats is only the first step in demonstrating how domestic paradigms are affected by processes of transnationalism. It is also important to consider how these new ideas are disseminated to a point where domestic paradigms are shifted. GGNs themselves are an important part of this explanation. They reflect Finnemore and Barnett's observation of bureaucrats in international organizations whose 'status as being both "an authority" and "in authority" ... positions them well both to generate new ideas and to have those ideas heard and respected' (2004, 162). Bureaucrats who have a central position in the policy-making process are in an important position to convey ideas into the domestic arena because they are 'in authority.' In part, participants in GGNs are the very decision makers whom we would expect to be prominent carriers of domestic policy paradigms. Therefore, part of the exercise of translating new thinking from the international to the domestic realm is already completed when these key actors are socialized at the international level, especially in policy areas where their influence is greater than that of other actors. Furthermore, their position of authority in the policy process makes bureaucrats an important source from which new ideas might be pushed. Indeed, they can act as well-placed domestic norm entrepreneurs (Finnemore and Sikkink 1998, 896–99).

The authority of transnationally active bureaucrats is supported by their perception as experts in the field. Policy areas defined by high levels of complexity or technical knowledge require bureaucrats with specialized expertise. These bureaucrats are relied on to produce and interpret data about their policy fields. Thus, they have a privileged position in attributing meaning to policy-relevant knowledge. GGNs are important in this process because they provide members with information – and new interpretations of information – that can be expected to have significant effects on the domestic paradigm. For instance, effective GGNs may produce collections of data used by decision makers to understand the broader international policy field. Broad surveys of migration trends can be expected to frame issues in ways that do not reflect the experience of any individual's particular jurisdiction, especially if they are the outlier. As a result, the use of this information and framing of issues is likely to skew decision makers' understandings, as knowledge reflects the experience of the whole rather than that of the individual. GGNs may also provide an important function in interpreting and attributing meaning to domestic events or trends in specific jurisdictions. Decision makers can be expected to take their domestic experiences to GGNs, which act as an international 'support-group' of decision makers who can empathize with the experiences of colleagues in other jurisdictions. As decision makers get issues 'off their chests' and 'talk things out,' they are likely to be affected by the reasoning of others. Thus, domestic experiences could be expected to be interpreted and given meaning in these forums.

The ability to produce and interpret information as it is transferred from the international to the domestic realm also raises important insights about how transnational actors affect paradigm change. The selection of new ideas by domestic actors depends upon the ability of these ideas to address the needs of the policy environment or to fit with broader norms that are present there (Hall 1989; Keck and Sikkink 1998; Florini 1996; Bernstein and Cashore 2000, 81, 83). However, understandings of these needs are not fixed. Instead, iterated interaction in the international realm allows bureaucrats to adjust incrementally their understandings of the domestic policy environment. It seems likely that through this process the needs of the policy environment that have been identified as being important to selecting new thinking are, in fact, being shaped. Thus, changes in the domestic realm do not simply cause uncertainty among decision makers, who then choose from a menu of available ideas, selecting the ones that are most appropriate. Instead, bureaucratic socialization allows centrally positioned decision makers – through the production of domestically relevant policy knowledge – to set the appetite of domestic actors. As a result, processes of transnationalism may result in issues' being framed as new domestic problems that raise uncertainty, new understandings of needs and new expectations of efficient and appropriate policy, and altered actors' understandings of their identities.

In summary, the interaction of bureaucrats in GGNs has the potential to alter domestic paradigms via a process of common identity building and socialization with colleagues from like-minded states. Furthermore, the central position of these bureaucrats – at the interface of international and domestic realms – makes their socialization relevant for the study of domestic paradigm change. Changes in the domestic environment provide important opportunities for thinking about policy. However, decision makers' interpretations of those changes and the broader policy environment are likely to be influenced by their participation in GGNs.

Understanding Paradigm Change:
The Case of Canadian Refugee Policy

This section focuses on the case of Canadian refugee policy from 1975 to the summer of 2001. The period, book-ended by two important developments in Canadian policy, began with preparation for and implementation of the 1978 Immigration Act, which overhauled Canada's post-World War II immigration policy. It ended with an intensive policy review, culminating in the replacement of the 1978 act with the Immigration and Refugee Protection Act (IRPA). Although the IRPA was modified in the aftermath of the events of 9/11 and was not implemented until 2002, a finalized version of the act had made it through Parliament prior to the summer recess of 2001. What is evident in the discussion of policy around these two developments is that the paradigm that framed Canadian refugee policy had, in fact, changed over this period.[7] However, what is unclear is why this change took place and the role played by internationalization and the global government networks.

Canadian Paradigm Change

Between the mid-1970s and the summer of 2001 a shift occurred in the policy paradigm framing Canadian decision makers' understanding of refugee policy. Broadly, this has been articulated as a shift from a focus on refugee protection to one on control and security (Crépeau and Nakache 2006; Aiken 2000, 2001). The paradigms that define these two periods can be characterized as two ideal types. In the first instance the protection paradigm fits within a broader understanding of Canada's liberal humanitarian tradition and distinct values in conducting its international affairs. The refugee protection paradigm is characterized by the prioritization of policies that provide protection for refugees and refugee claimants. Problems are defined as those policies that fail to offer adequate protection, with the state understood as being capable of and obliged to provide levels of fairness and opportunity to refugee claimants similar to those available to Canadian citizens. The goals of this paradigm are to prioritize the protection of refugees, barring specific threats to the state's ability to control its borders or to ensure national/ public security. Appropriate policy responses are those that increase access and protection for refugees in all areas of policy, including determination and pre-/post-determination processes. Policies are expected not only to meet but to exceed established international standards of protection and to offer a model for other, often recalcitrant, states.

In contrast, the security-control paradigm is organized around the central tenet that state sovereignty, national security and public safety are higher priorities than affording opportunities to refugee claimants. The goals of the security-control paradigm include limiting the flows of unauthorized migrants and preventing entry to those who pose a risk. Canada's international obligations are interpreted as limiting the sovereignty of the state and increasing efforts to meet obligations minimally or to navigate around them. Migrants and by extension refugee claimants are increasingly viewed as posing a threat, rather than being in need of protection. Given this understanding of the world, appropriate policies are those that prioritize security and control while limiting the loss of state sovereignty. The potential for refugees or refugee claimants to be adversely affected by these policies weighs less heavily in their selection. Policies such as interdiction, increased use and scope of security screening, narrowed determination systems and appeal processes, as well as greater deterrence and removals are viewed as being increasingly appropriate. Rather than being distinct, the control-security paradigm suggests that Canada is part of a community of like-minded states, whose other members present viable sources of new thinking for dealing with problems common to all members.

One member of Parliament has suggested that by the end of the 1990s there had been a 'whole climate change' in Canada's approach to refugee policy (interview). This change was seen in a redefinition of Canada's identity in the field of refugee policy. The public debates of the late 1990s downplayed Canada's liberal humanitarian traditions and the narratives that had been prominent in the debates of the 1980s.[8] Rather than being an international champion of a uniquely humanitarian system that went above and beyond its international commitments, the Canadian state was portrayed as a victim of increased migration flows.[9] Furthermore, decision makers viewed other states as 'like-minded,' faced with common problems and to whom Canada had an obligation in terms of pulling its weight in efforts to enhance collective control and security.[10] In contrast to the 1980s, when the quality of partner states' protection was questioned, these states were understood to offer legitimate solutions to Canada's problems in dealing with migration (Parliamentary Standing Committee on Citizenship and Immigration 1999a, 1615; interviews).[11] In numerous debates Canadian decision makers pointed positively to policies of other states whose measures had been deemed inappropriate under the protection paradigm.

Understandings of the problems being faced had also changed by the end of the 1990s. In the 1970s and 1980s decision makers' thinking about refugee policy was driven by concerns that the system should be exceedingly fair and offer the best protection possible for refugees.[12] The broad terms of debate saw political parties gaining credibility based on their ability to offer even better protection for refugees than their opponents. Security and control were discussed, but as matters of routine concern rather than as the dominant lens through which policy was to be approached. Similarly, refugees and migrants more generally were viewed as being in need rather than as threats to state sovereignty and control.[13] In contrast, by the end of the 1990s the primary concern of decision makers was the problem of controlling illegal migration and preserving public safety and national security.[14] Decision makers increasingly saw illegal migrants / refugee claimants as abusers of the system, and this view was amplified by the regular arrival of refugee claimants without identity documents.

Linked to changes in the definitions of the problem was a shift in Canadian decision makers' understanding of appropriate policy responses. Several policy options that had been considered in the 1980s but deemed inappropriate were considered again at the end of the 1990s. Objections to a Safe Third Country (STC) agreement and high seas interdiction at the end of the 1980s had been based on the belief that these policies countered key principles of Canada's approach to refugee protection. In contrast, in debates at the end of the 1990s the reasons for not pursuing such agreements were based not on principled arguments but on logistical concerns. In the case of high seas interdiction, decision makers pointed to the fact that Canada did not have the resources to engage in this practice, including the lack of an offshore territory where claims could be determined, as well as the potential of legal constraints (Parliamentary Standing Committee on Citizenship and Immigration 1999a). In contrast, there were only minor concerns raised about the safety of refugee claimants.[15] Instead, one official suggested that because a significant proportion of migrants were believed to be illegal, policies of high seas interdiction would be appropriate (interview). This argument was bolstered by references to the claims that similar practices in other states such as the US and Australia were legitimate (ibid.) and that Canada had recently supported such practices elsewhere (Aiken 1999).

Further evidence of a shift in paradigmatic thinking can be seen in the policies and practices related to refugees and refugee claimants. These policy changes demonstrate that shifts in discourse were more than rhetorical. Most indicative of the protection policy paradigm was the establishment of the Immigration and Refugee Board (IRB) at the end of the 1980s. Despite the significant increase in the numbers of refugee claimants and the potential for security concerns among them, Canadian decision makers enacted a highly liberal system that offered extensive protection to refugee claimants. In contrast, by the end of the 1990s policies that had been rejected in the late 1980s, including an STC agreement, were being pursued. Furthermore, Bill C-44 (1995) and legislative amendments to the 1978 act in 1997 represented a tightening of the system. By the end of the 1990s there was also significant evidence that the practice of Canadian refugee policy had changed to reflect a more security- and control-oriented focus. Budgets related to enforcement aspects of the Immigration Department were protected from cutbacks and even increased (ibid. 1999c, 1550),[16] while indicators of enforcement also increased.[17]

GGNs and Bureaucratic Socialization

Over the course of the 1990s Canadian bureaucrats became increasingly involved in a migration GGN that could be expected to socialize them and in turn help to explain domestic paradigm change. At its core this GGN represented a group of like-minded public servants drawn from a core group of liberal-democratic states in Western Europe, North America, Australia, and New Zealand. Members interacted in a number of ways, including regional consultative processes (RCPs), bilateral meetings, and even the fringes of formal international organizations such as the Executive Committee of the UN High Commissioner for Refugees (UNHCR). This network of decision makers also functioned outside international meetings. Related activities included personal communication between meetings as well as individual meetings and extended networking.[18] Decision makers, as members of a network, were plugged in to one another at a variety of informal and semi-structured points.

One of the most significant forums in which these networks operated was a set of regional consultative processes initially established in the mid-1980s (Solomon 2005, July, annex A). According to the International Organization for Migration (IOM), RCPs provided states with a process of networking for the 'informal exchange of views about their respective positions and priorities on migration' (IOM 2007a). These networks operated through regular meetings of ministers and senior bureaucrats with technical expertise in a variety of formats that included 'seminars, capacity building training and workshops and information campaigns' (ibid.). The possibility that decision makers' thinking was affected by this process has been recognized by the IOM. The authors of an IOM expert chapter on regional consultative processes state, 'Since 1994, profound changes have taken place in the understanding of and international collaboration on migration' as a result of these processes. In so far as 'some shared understandings have emerged on the nature and role of migration in today's mobile world ... States now appreciate their common challenges and shared as well as complementary objectives in migration' (Solomon 2005, July, 3). The IOM's webpage states that RCPs allow 'states to better understand others' perspectives' and 'build confidence in inter-state dialogue, information sharing, cooperation and exploration of collaborative approaches to migration issues' (IOM 2007a.) Colleen Thouez and Frédérique Channac (2006) directly address the issue of socialization, arguing that RCPs produce informal socialization through a process of imitation that results in the convergence of national migration policies. In short, these processes are recognized as having the potential to contribute to a convergence in participants' understandings. They could, in turn, contribute to paradigm change in Canadian refugee policy.

Canadian officials actively participated in a number of these RCPs from the mid-1980s on (IOM 2007b). One of the more significant RCPs was the Inter-Governmental Consultation on Asylum, Refugee and Migration Policies (IGC). Over the course of the 1990s the IGC was organized around a small membership of industrialized states focused on migration management.[19] Regular meetings of participants, at no level higher than that of senior bureaucrat, occurred on a variety of topics. These meetings were held in closed sessions and little public information detailing the nature of the discussions was made available. This format of small, personal, and private meetings provided a unique environment, where feelings of community could be built and socialization could occur.

Canadian decision makers acknowledged that forums such as those provided by RCPs were useful for the exchange of ideas, although they argued that specific policy prescriptions were rarely if ever developed (interviews).[20] Despite this qualification, it seems likely that Canadian decision makers' thinking was altered by these interactions and that Canadian domestic paradigms were affected. The evidence outlined below suggests that through their interaction in GGNs Canadian officials increasingly came to see themselves as part of this community of like-minded states and subsequently to adopt the community's standards, which prioritized security and control.

In explaining paradigm change, the importance of Canadian bureaucrats' increased involvement in a GGN is supported by evidence of a developing international norm in this GGN. This norm has been widely noted in the literature on international migration and is captured in discussions of a 'Wall around the West' (Andreas and Snyder 2000; Macklin 2001), 'Fortress Europe' (Bloch, Schuster, and Galvin 2000; Gallagher 2002), and 'Fortress North America' (Rudd and Furneaux 2002). There is evidence that the content and tone of the discussion that took place within the GGN reflected this norm and exposed Canadian decision makers to perspectives they might not have found at home. For instance, one official who attended IGC meetings suggested that discussions reflected an emphasis on security and control, which occurred because the majority of other participants came from departments – such as Home Affairs or Ministries of the Interior – that placed greater organizational emphasis on policing, security, and public order. In contrast, immigration and refugee matters in Canada were contained in a separate department focused largely on the facilitation of migration (interviews). It is significant to note that the adoption of this norm in other jurisdictions preceded Canada's paradigm change. Thus, the timing of the development of the norm and the suggestion that it was prevalent in the framing of the GGN's thinking implies that it was an important potential source of new ideas consistent with the direction of change in Canadian policy.[21]

It is also evident that participation in this GGN resulted in bureaucratic socialization, owing to a sense of community among participants. On a personal level, regular meetings allowed Canadian officials to build strong relationships with their international colleagues. Officials suggested that they looked forward to meeting with their counterparts, enjoyed their time together, and often socialized outside formal meetings (interviews). Furthermore, Canadian participants came to hold their international partners in high esteem, describing them as 'good,' 'clever,' 'intelligent,' and 'honest' (ibid.). Most significant, they expressed the fact that they felt they could trust these officials (ibid.).

The development of trust was also an important indicator of the sense of community. Officials felt that, behind closed doors and without their political masters, they could talk honestly and that what was said would not become part of the domestic policy debate. Canadian officials suggested that the meetings provided a 'frank talk-shop' where they could shut the doors and 'clear their heads' (interviews). This also indicated a sense of 'we' versus 'them' mentality and a division between those who could participate and those who should not. Inside were experts who could be trusted to maintain confidentiality and who would responsibly weigh all policy options in a balanced manner. They were individuals who understood the complexities of managing migration and could be trusted to produce pragmatic and reasonable solutions to the problems that industrialized states faced.[22] On the outside were those who could not be trusted and would impede progress by politicizing and shutting down unpopular avenues of debate. To varying degrees outsiders included elected officials, journalists, advocacy groups, and members of the broader public.[23]

This sense of community created the conditions under which socialization could take place. Officials came to respect the opinions of their colleagues and were prepared to be persuaded by them. For example, in answer to the question 'Did you learn anything in the[se] meetings?' an official responded: 'Well it's hard to say ... whether you imported something directly from something that came up at the meeting but you can't help but be influenced by the proceedings because, you know, other people who come are very highly qualified, well experienced and thoughtful' (interview). Another official said: 'You get the advantage of trading on the experiences of people who know a lot more than we do' (ibid.). The fact that the thinking of the critical mass of the participants reflected the security-control norms could have moved Canadian officials towards a parallel domestic norm.

The influence of social incentives resulting from the development of this community was also evident in this case. Among international colleagues, despite public rebuttals by Canadian officials, there was an understanding that the Canadian system was weak and open to abuse (interviews).[24] In these closed-door settings and among those whom they respected, this poor reputation mattered to Canadian decision makers. At times, Canadian decision makers, especially those responsible for enforcement, felt 'inferior' when they met with American counterparts (ibid.). Another official felt that in these meetings Canadians needed to show 'good face' in order to alter international colleagues' perceptions (ibid.). The acceptance of the community's criticism translated into efforts to counter a poor reputation and contributed to the adoption of a more security-control-oriented framing of Canada's refugee policy. For instance, officials emphasized Canada's international leadership in policies that demonstrated their commitment to the values held by the community. Decision makers pointed to Canada as being the first to introduce the idea of overseas interdiction officers in 1992; as leading in the use of 1(F) provisions of the 1951 convention on inadmissibility; and by modelling responses to the problems of war criminals (ibid.).

A definitive demonstration of decision makers' socialization in a GGN for migration is difficult to achieve. However, there is considerable evidence to suggest that this socialization took place. The timing of Canadian officials' increased participation in global forums closely precedes the period of paradigm change. Furthermore, the evidence that officials developed a sense of camaraderie in this GGN suggests an important condition for socialization. Finally, there is also evidence that if Canadian decision makers were going to adopt new ideas from these foreign colleagues, those ideas were likely to reflect the security-control norm.

Environmental Pressures, International Ideas,
and Domestic Paradigm Change

If it is likely that Canadian officials active in the migration GGN were socialized into a security-control-oriented norm, it is nonetheless not clear that such socialization helps explain domestic paradigm change. Traditional explanations of policy change look to changes in the domestic policy environment as factors that provoked new thinking. Indeed, officials consistently pointed to the fact that it was the new realities of attempting to manage international migration in all liberal-democratic states that provoked the need for a new approach to policy (interviews). This point was made by the minister of immigration, Lucienne Robillard, who argued in 1999 that Canada required a new policy because, 'since the introduction of the *Immigration Act* in 1978, the world has changed immensely' (Citizenship and Immigration Canada 1999). However, it is not clear that the changes in the Canadian policy environment were significant enough to alter the refugee paradigm. This section outlines some of the most significant environmental changes that were identified by policy makers as the catalyst for new thinking. It then argues that these were not significant enough to provoke paradigm change. Finally, it suggests that new interpretations of the policy environment – originating with Canadian officials active in GGNs – contributed to paradigm change.

Alternative explanations of paradigm change in the Canadian case include changes in the policy environment, the rise of policy anomalies, and policy failures. Policy makers suggested that one of the most significant changes in the policy environment was the sharp spike in the number of migrants making refugee claims in Canada, beginning in the late 1980s. Refugee flows were understood to be increasingly mixed, consisting of both legitimate refugees and illegal migrants. The perception of a rise in the abuse of the system made decision makers increasingly sceptical of the legitimate status of large numbers of migrants. Furthermore, the rise of 'mixed flows' corresponded to increased concerns about the ability to identify who these migrants were, including whether they were criminals or threats to public safety and national security.[25]

Changes in policy makers' understanding of their environment were also furthered by specific migration events that reinforced fears about these flows. Publicized instances of war criminals and members of criminal gangs entering Canada through the refugee stream were identified as contributing to the pressure on decision makers to see these mixed flows as representing a threat to public safety. There were also high-profile cases where the leniency of the Canadian system was drawn into question. For instance, in the spring and summer of 1994 two high-profile murders in Toronto – one of a patron of the Just Desserts Café and the other of Todd Baylis, a Toronto police officer – were allegedly perpetrated by immigrants. In both cases the alleged murderers had faced deportation, owing to lengthy criminal records, but had avoided this fate because of what was broadly interpreted as a failure of the system: either through the leniency of the IRB or the failure of the department to track and remove known criminals. In 1999 two other significant events raised the issues of security and control. The first was the July-August arrival of four boatloads of Chinese migrants off the coast of British Columbia. The second was the December 1999 arrest of Ahmed

Ressam as he crossed the British Columbia-Washington border with the intention of bombing the Los Angeles International Airport.[26] These events were used to further substantiate a sense of growing abuse of the system, which the Canadian state could not manage.

These trends and events were also used to point to the failure of existing policy and the paradigm that framed it. Decision makers suggested that the policies that had been enacted in an earlier period were no longer efficient or appropriate for addressing current circumstances (Auditor General 1997, 25.27; interviews). Indeed, there was a strong belief among decision makers that these policies had, in fact, contributed to the problems. For instance, an overly fair refugee determination system, too many opportunities to appeal decisions, and long delays in processing claims all were identified as making the Canadian system more susceptible to abuse (interviews). Not the least of these concerns was the feeling among decision makers that the application of the Charter of Rights and Freedoms to refugee claimants impeded their ability to effectively deal with the problems faced by the system (Auditor General 1997, 25.15, 25.16; Parliamentary Standing Committee on Citizenship and Immigration 1999b).

Migration trends and events combined to provide a possible explanation of paradigm change. The accumulation of new pressures and the inability of existing policy to respond effectively appear to have contributed to decision makers' beliefs that a new approach was required. However, it is not evident that they had to draw this conclusion. First, there are indicators that suggested that – while problems still existed – the system was becoming increasingly effective in managing migration flows.[27] Secondly, it is not clear that many of the problems that decision makers pointed to over the course of the 1990s were significantly different than those found under the protection paradigm.[28] Therefore, if the protection paradigm existed under similar pressures why was change required? Similarly, the pressures on the Canadian system, given its relative geographic isolation, were not as great as those experienced by countries in Europe or by the United States, where illegal migration flows were significantly greater. Thus, Canadian policy makers did not face the same motivations for paradigm change as their counterparts in other countries. Indeed, some observed that they could not be certain that their negative interpretations of the policy environment could be substantiated.[29] Therefore, it is not clear why decision makers chose to interpret the policy environment of the 1990s in a way that culminated in paradigm change.

In seeking an explanation for why decision makers ultimately inter-preted the context as requiring a new paradigm, it is important to focus on the role of new ideas advanced by bureaucrats active in a migra-tion GGN. First and foremost, the organization and culture of Canada's Department of Citizenship and Immigration, as well as its importance in the policy-making process, provided the necessary conditions under which new ideas from the international realm could be spread and adopted. The senior leadership of the department was small and, as a result, policy development involved many of these individuals (inter-view). New ideas, introduced by a few transnationally active officials, were likely to circulate among the organization fairly effectively and to be engaged by much of the senior leadership.[30] This possibility was furthered by officials' tendency to rely on internal expertise to address new problems (ibid.).

Department officials also played an important role in the broader policy-making process, suggesting that at times they were 'in author-ity.' While authority ultimately resided with political leaders, bureau-crats in the field of Canadian refugee policy have been identified as central actors, often isolated from broader societal and political pres-sures (Hardcastle et al. 1994; Simmons and Keohane 1992). This isola-tion was furthered by the complex and technical nature of the policy field, which limited exposure to pressures from outside the depart-ment. Department officials also exercised significant influence over the minister of immigration (interviews).[31] Thus, once ideas gained ground in the department, its members were well placed to spread them to other actors in the decision-making process.

Central to their ability to disseminate new ideas was the authority bureaucrats enjoyed in the area of migration policy. Bureaucrats briefed MPs fully at the beginning of parliamentary sessions and in technical briefings (see, e.g., Parliamentary Standing Committee on Citizenship and Immigration 2001a). They were also regularly called on by MPs for clarification and were consulted extensively about subjects being pre-pared for standing committee reports or on specific legislation. In these meetings bureaucrats focused on explaining policies, practices, and their effects. Although department officials avoided engaging in politi-cal debates that explicitly judged policy, they did influence debates in less obvious ways. Officials made choices about which issues to address in their presentations and which information to present to the com-mittee. They also made decisions about how to frame their contribu-tions. These choices reflected their understanding of the problems as well as their understanding of possible and desirable policy responses. Although members of the standing committee were often critical of department officials' testimony, their ability to engage at the level of officials' expertise and their reliance on them to produce information in the first place suggests that they had an important role in injecting ideas into the policy debate.

The central role of department officials as authorities in migration policies meant that the influences upon them – in particular their social-ization in a GGN for migration – directly affected the broader domestic policy paradigm. Evidence suggests that it was not changes in the policy environment alone that provoked paradigm change. Rather, it was the use of information and interpretation of information developed through GGNs that challenged the existing paradigm and motivated its change.

Describing the IGC, one official stated: 'It was a meeting of like-minded people, basically you just wanted the experience of relating your problems and airing them and finding out what other people thought of them and were there any other approaches out there that were working' (interview). Furthermore, in the eyes of another GGN participant, 'what it did more than anything else [was to] prepare them better to deal with the issues domestically when those issues became current' (ibid.).

Canadian decision makers used broader information produced by the GGN on migration in their policy making. Data produced for this network – which were not publicly available – were regarded as some of the most trustworthy and useful information (interview). It is also likely that this information and specific discussions of the Canadian experience influenced bureaucrats' understanding of the problems Canada faced. For instance, the migratory pressures faced by Canada were interpreted in light of the broader experience of western lib-eral democracies. This larger context altered the understandings of Canada's domestic problems – often suggesting they were much more severe than actual experiences might indicate. For example, the levels of illegal migration found in Europe – which were much higher than those experienced by Canada – were connected directly to the prob-lems that Canada faced.

Bureaucrats used such information to influence the thinking of the broader policy community, as illustrated by the comments of a depart-mental official made before the standing committee in 1997: 'we share a common problem, and a problem that moves through Europe will often move to North America. So we're dealing with the same problem, and often the same person. So it's in all our interests to intercept this smuggling at any point along the route' (Parliamentary Standing Committee on Citizenship and Immigration 1997b, 1555; see also ibid. 2001b). Significantly, this framing of the issue was picked up by members of the broader policy community.[32] Similarly, in 1999 officials compared the four boats of Chinese migrants in 1999 with the twenty-eight boats that had arrived in Australia in a four-month period and twenty boats that had been intercepted by the US over the preceding eighteen months (comments by CIC official, ibid. 1999a; 2000, introduction). While it was acknowledged that Canada's problems were not as severe as those in other jurisdictions, the context in which these examples were raised presented them as a potential future reality for Canada. In this manner the understandings produced by officials' interaction in GGNs and their use in domestic policy debates suggest that transnationalism played a role in destabilizing the domestic paradigm. In short, it was not the development of trends and events on their own but how they were interpreted in light of the influence of transnational socialization.

Changes in the policy environment over the course of the 1990s did have the potential to raise concerns about issues of security and control. However, it is not clear that these changes were significant enough to explain paradigm change. Rather, it was the transnationalization of the policy environment – through the activities of Canadian officials in GGNs – that shaped the interpretation of this environment. In particular, the interaction allowed officials and the broader policy community to see problems and solutions that had not existed before. Thus, it was these new interpretations, originating through transnational socialization, that accounted for paradigm change.

Drawing Conclusions

This chapter has argued that the paradigm governing Canadian refugee policy changed during the 1990s and that the socialization of Canadian bureaucrats in a migration GGN helps account for the change. Explanations of paradigm change are incomplete without consideration of the role of bureaucratic socialization via transnational networks, a process that requires greater attention in further research. The Canadian case points to two interesting insights about the linkages between transnational actors and policy paradigm change that invite further study.

First, GGNs are a fruitful avenue for further study. The increased activities of domestic officials in these networks reflect an important reality of transnationalism that merits greater consideration. Furthermore, this chapter suggests that such networks have important implications for the domestic policy process. At their root they allow for the building of a sense of community among transnationally active bureaucrats, which facilitates the spread of ideas through the process of socialization. In addition, transnationally active bureaucrats' central position in the policy-making process and as policy experts gives them a unique opportunity to be conduits through which new thinking might be transferred into the domestic realm.

Second, the process through which new ideas are transferred into the domestic realm includes a consideration of changes in the domestic environment. However, that environment is not exclusively interpreted through domestic experiences. This chapter demonstrates that key domestic officials interpret the domestic environment in light of ideational commitments obtained in the international realm. In part this suggests that transnationalism can provoke paradigm change where it otherwise might not have occurred. Further, there is a need to refine arguments in the literature that suggest that the domestic environment dictates which ideas from the international realm will be accepted. It is important to consider that transnational actors, by offering alternative understandings of the domestic environment that reinforce and increase the demand for those very international ideas and solutions, can accelerate the process of paradigm change.

ACKNOWLEDGMENTS

An earlier version of parts of this chapter was presented at the International Studies Association 2007. I would like to thank Christopher G. Anderson, Jennifer L. Bailly, Peter Hall, Nancy Kokaz, Ito Peng, Grace Skogstad, and participants at the Internationalization and Policy Paradigm Change Workshop, Toronto, 11 April 2008, for their assistance in helping me to clarify my argument. I would also like to thank two anonymous reviewers for their helpful comments on this chapter.

NOTES

1 The inclusion of identity represents an important modification of the public policy approach (Surel 2000, 496, 500). It incorporates the constructivist literature's focus on the importance of identity in shaping state policy

(Johnston 1995; Bukovansky 1997; Loriaux 1999) and as a component of complex learning (Wendt 1999, 170) or intersubjective and collective knowledge (Adler 1997, 327).

2 For Hall, the rise of new information sparks changes in paradigms by challenging existing interpretations. However, the selection of new paradigms is determined by political competition, not social interaction (Checkel 2001; Flockhart 2004, 366).

3 GGNs are similar to Emanuel Adler's concept of seminar diplomacy, where decision makers meet in 'a plethora of face-to-face interactions on a large variety of technical, practical and normative subjects'(Adler 1997. 121) in a form of 'talk-shop' (Adler and Barnett 1998, 420). This component of international diplomacy, although occurring within a formal institutional setting, denotes informality and a limit to official government oversight at lower levels of diplomatic exchange. Furthermore, seminar diplomacy resembles GGNs even more where technical issues are discussed by expert bureaucrats from specific departments rather than career diplomats.

4 According to Adler, an outcome of seminar diplomacy is to teach 'would-be members of the community the principles on which the community should be based' and 'to socially construct shared values and mutual responsiveness in a given region and the transnational identity of a region.' (1998, 139, 138–9).

5 GGNs focus on complex and highly technical policy areas – including international migration – in which the decision maker is often seen as a professional and expert. In this way, the effects of GGN activities are similar to epistemic communities with the important difference that GGNs operate from within the state apparatus (Haas 1992; Adler and Haas 1992). These networks can be expected to develop common normative and principled beliefs, shared causal understandings, and notions of validity and a common policy enterprise as well as act as a vehicle for the spread of policy ideas across jurisdictions (ibid.).

6 For a consideration of the types of environments in which socialization might occur see Johnston (2001, 507); Adler and Barnett (1998, 44).

7 This research has used a variety of sources to capture these understandings of paradigms at the time of each development. The sources include analysis of primary government documents, contemporary editorial opinions, and the transcripts of parliamentary standing committee meetings from 1976 to 1982, 1998 to 2001, and during other key debates throughout this period. These sources were complemented by nineteen interviews with senior decision makers from across the period under investigation. The interviewees included standing committee MPs as well as senior bureaucrats in the departments responsible for refugee policy. These interviews

provide important and direct access to the thinking of policy makers. They allow for a better understanding of how policy makers understood refugee policy and provide a unique perspective on the development of their thinking over this period. In analysing these sources a method of triangulation was used that allows stronger conclusions to be drawn about the content of a given paradigm – and therefore shifts between paradigms – by checking that these interpretations are consistent across a variety of sources.

8 For instance, in the 1980s regular reference was made to Canada's strong history in assisting refugees. This included reference to cases such as the Hungarian, Czechoslovakian, and Indo-Chinese movements. By the 1990s these humanitarian aspects of Canada's policy were downplayed, replaced by milder claims such as being a 'welcoming' country for those in need (see, e.g., Elinor Caplan's comments as immigration minister: Parliamentary Standing Committee on Citizenship and Immigration 1999c, 1540). Indeed, anecdotes in the standing committee at the end of the 1990s were marked by examples of abuse of the system (see, e.g., ibid.,1620, 1635).

9 Lloyd Axworthy's comments to the standing committee in 1982 are indicative of the attitudes of decision makers in the 1980s. At that time he stated that he was determined that Canada would go beyond its international obligations to 'the higher traditional standards of fairness and justice' (Parliamentary Standing Committee on Labour, Manpower and Immigration 1982, 2010).

10 See, for instance, Special Senate Committee on Security and Intelligence 1999, chap. 2; Trempe, Davis, and Kunin 1997; Parliamentary Standing Committee on Citizenship and Immigration 1999a. These views were also confirmed in interviews.

11 For an indication of the attitude in the 1980s see comments by opposition MP Sergio Marchi: Parliamentary Standing Committee on Labour, Employment and Immigration 1987, 1000.

12 Consider, for instance, the principle of 'benefit of the doubt.' This principle holds that, when evidence cannot be found to either confirm or discredit an asylum seeker's claim, the benefit of the doubt is to be given to the claimant and refugee status granted (see Axworthy's comments: Parliamentary Standing Committee on Labour, Manpower and Immigration 1982, 2010; see also comments by the Immigration and Refugee Board chair, Gordon Fairweather: Parliamentary Standing Committee on Labour, Employment and Immigration 1989, 0940–55). By the end of the 1990s public expressions of this concept were rarely pushed. Indeed, one departmental official suggested that, if the system were being

set up at that time, it was unlikely that a minister would push for such a principle (interview).

13 Several debates, while recognizing illegal migration as a problem, emphasized concerns about the protection of illegal migration from abuse by consultants, employers, and even the state itself (see, e.g., comments by Minister Axworthy, Parliamentary Standing Committee on Labour, Manpower and Immigration 1981, 2030–5; see also ibid. 1977b, 1645; 1977a, 2100). Similar attitudes were expressed in editorial opinion (*Globe and Mail* 1981).

14 Most interviewees cited control as the number one problem facing the Canadian refugee system at the end of the 1990s (interviews). Alternatively, the first five meetings of the standing committee in the autumn of 1999 were dominated by discussions of security and control. Similarly, concerns were central to the discussion of the first meeting of the standing committee in a new session of Parliament on 21 October 1997.

15 For instance, in important debates there was an absence of significant criticism of proposed policies based on either migrants' safety or the potential that these migrants might have legitimate refugee claims (Parliamentary Standing Committeeon Citizenship and Immigration 1999a; see also comments by Liberal MP Andrew Telegdi: ibid., 1999d, 1020).

16 Funding under the category 'Managing access to Canada,' which included spending on control and security aspects of the immigration program, grew substantially from $81.1 million in 1998–9 to $123.5 million in 1999–2000 and $150.8 million in 2000–1 (Citizenship and Immigration Canada 2001a, 51).

17 For instance, the number of Minister's Permits, the device through which allowances can be made for those normally prevented from entry to Canada, dropped significantly from 1992, when 16,000 permits were granted, to 4,509 in 1997 and 3,989 in 2000 (Crépeau 1998; Citizenship and Immigration Canada 2001b). There was also an expansion of the number and function of Canada's Migration Integrity Officers responsible for interdiction overseas (Citizenship and Immigration Canada 2001c; Bossin 2001, 55–6; Dench 2001, 35). Within Canada, subsequent ministers at the end of the 1990s highlighted significant increases in the removal of failed refugee claimants (Crépeau 1998; Parliamentary Standing Committee on Citizenship and Immigration 1999c, 1715).

18 They included telephone calls and emails (interviews).

19 The IGC originally was formed in 1985 with forty-five members. In the early 1990s it comprised a much more focused group of fifteen industrialized states. It can be expected that those remaining constituted a more closely knit group of like-minded states.

20 Interestingly, the Australian government counters this position by claim-
    ing that the IGC was a forum to 'develop innovative policy approaches'
    (Australian Department of Immigration and Multicultural Affairs 2003).
21 Indeed, this is further supported by the fact that the timing of Canada's
    increased participation within the GGN – at the beginning of the
    1990s – closely preceded shifts in the Canadian paradigm.
22 One official suggested that 'the people on the outside assume that this
    business isn't complex ... and what you discover the more you get into
    [it] the more you realise that it takes a long time in this business to start ...
    to intuit the business ... it takes a long time to start getting that sense of
    what the issues are about' (interview).
23 The importance of this 'inside' group has been expressed in a number of
    ways. For instance, the IGC was established partially out of frustration
    with the public and often symbolic forum of the UNHCR. In this justifica-
    tion there was recognition for the need for pragmatic discussions among
    policy makers in a non-public forum. Similarly, one bureaucrat suggested
    that in bilateral cooperation between Canada and the United States there
    was an understanding of the domestic political constraints that might
    impede the progress that had been made at the level of bureaucratic coop-
    eration. Reference was also made to the desire to avoid 'another fight' with
    NGOs (interviews)
24 For instance, Canadian officials were privately criticized by European
    partners for adding gender-based persecution to the definition of refugees
    (Shenstone 1997, 48). Alternatively, Canadian officials acknowledged being
    applauded by their colleagues from other states for their leadership on
    overseas immigration control officers (interview), reinforcing Canada's
    participation in an international norm of security and control.
25 For a sense of the problems faced by decision makers see comments made
    by Paul Thibault, executive director of the IRB, at the Standing Committee
    on Citizenship and Immigration (Parliamentary Standing Committeeon
    Citizenship and Immigration 1997a, 1551).
26 The Ressam case pointed to a number of failures of the Canadian refu-
    gee system. Ressam had entered Canada on a false passport and made a
    refugee claim in 1994. Upon failing to attend his refugee hearing, he was
    ordered to be deported. He remained in Canada for several years and then
    left, travelling to Afghanistan. He subsequently returned to Canada, enter-
    ing again under a false identity and passport (CBC 2005).
27 For instance, the number of actual refugee claimants levelled off at an
    average of 23,422 between 1993 and 1998, significantly lower than the 1992
    level of 35,145 (Citizenship and Immigration Canada 2005, 62–3). Similarly,

on several markers, the effectiveness of the IRB to process claims improved over the latter part of the 1990s (IRB 1999,15; 2000, 8; 2001, 5; Auditor General 2001, chap. 12).

28 For instance, decision makers in the 1970s believed that there were up to 200,000 illegal migrants living in Canada (Robinson 1983, 23–4). Events comparable to those that occurred at the end of the 1990s also occurred during the protection paradigm. These include the arrival of two boats of migrants in the summers of 1986 and 1987, which prompted an 'emergency' recall of Parliament. There were also concerns that some of these migrants presented security concerns (Donovan 1987; Jones 1987).

29 For instance, in attempting to understand the level of abuse in the system, one official stated, 'I don't want to understate the importance of this. There is no objective measure. We had no idea of whether the right number was 5 per cent, 20 per cent, or 60 per cent. There was just no way of knowing' (interview). Another official suggested that 'welfare abuse [by migrants] is more of a myth than a reality. People who want to live off the dole usually don't migrate, they usually stay where they [are] and eke out an existence on what is available to them. Migrants, generally speaking, are a premium group of people and refugees, the real refugees among the migrants, are really a premium on the premium' (interview).

30 Canadian participants in GGNs included bureaucrats at the levels of deputy minister, assistant deputy minister, and director general. These bureaucrats participated in GGNs when discussions reflected their areas of domestic responsibilities.

31 Citizenship and Immigration Ministers Sergio Marchi (1994–6) and Elinor Caplan (1999–2002), in particular, were noted as having shifted their thinking in the direction of greater concern for security and control, partly as a result of the influence of the department (interviews). Other third-party observers have also noted the influence of the department. For instance, a leading academic discussing the Safe Third Country Agreement argued that the bureaucrats played a central role, leading the government in what amounted to a 'bureaucratic project' (James Hathaway, Parliamentary Standing Committee on Citizenship and Immigration 1996, 1055).

32 For example, in 1999 a Conservative MP suggested that Canada faced the same large number of migrants that Europe did. Commenting on the 500,000 migrants who had entered Europe in 1998, he suggested that 'a lot of those claimants will probably skip over Europe and head directly to us,' making Canada a final destination (ibid. 1999a, 1630).

REFERENCES

Adamson, Fiona B. 2006. Crossing Borders: International Migration and
    National Security. *International Security* 31 (1):165–99.
Adler, Emanuel. 1997. Seizing the Middle Ground: Constructivism in World
    Politics. *European Journal of International Relations* 3:319–63.
– 1998. Seeds of Peaceful Change: The OSCE's Security Community-Building
    Model. In *Security Communities,* edited by E. Adler and M. Barnett.
    Cambridge: Cambridge University Press.
– and Michael Barnett. 1998. Part I Introduction and Theoretical Overview.
    In *Security Communities,* edited by E. Adler and M. Barnett. Cambridge:
    Cambridge University Press.
– and Peter M. Haas. 1992. Conclusion: Epistemic Communities, World
    Order, and the Creation of a Reflective Research Program. *International
    Organization* 46 (1):367–90.
Aiken, Sharryn J. 1999. New Directions for Refugee Determination and
    Protection in Canada. *Refuge* 18 (1):12–17.
– 2000. Manufacturing 'Terrorists': Refugees, National Security, and
    Canadian Law. *Refuge* 19 (3):54–73.
– 2001. Manufacturing 'Terrorists': Refugees, National Security, and
    Canadian Law: Part 2. *Refuge* 19 (4):116–33.
Andreas, Peter, and Timothy Snyder, eds. 2000. *The Wall Around the West: State
    Borders and Immigration Controls in North America and Europe.* Lanham, MD:
    Rowman & Littlefield.
Auditor General of Canada. 1997. Chapter 25: Citizenship and Immigration
    Canada and Immigration and Refugee Board. The Processing of Refugee
    Claims. In *1997 December Report of the Auditor General.* Ottawa: Minister of
    Public Works and Government Services Canada.
– 2001. Chapter 12: Follow-up of Recommendations in Previous Reports.
    In *2001 December Report of the Auditor General.* Ottawa: Minister of Public
    Works and Government Services Canada.
Australian Department of Immigration and Multicultural Affairs. 2003.
    Annual Report, 2002–03.
Barnett, Michael, and Martha Finnemore. 2004. *Rules for the World:
    International Organizations in Global Politics.* Ithaca: Cornell University Press.
Bernstein, Steven, and Benjamin Cashore. 2000. Globalization, Four
    Paths of Internationalization and Domestic Policy Change: The Case of
    EcoForestry in British Columbia, Canada. *Canadian Journal of Political Science*
    33 (1):67–99.

Bloch, Alice, Liza Schuster, and Treasa Galvin. 2000. Editorial Introduction. *Journal of Refugee Studies* 13 (1):1–10.

Bossin, Michael. 2001. Limited Access to Refugee Determination and Protection. *Refuge* 19 (4):55–61.

Bukovansky, Mlada. 1997. American Identity and Neutral Rights from Independence to the War of 1812. *International Organization* 51 (2):209–43.

Canadian Broadcasting Corporation (CBC). 2005. *Indepth Osama Bin Ladin Ahmed Ressam: The Would-Be Millennium Bomber.* Broadcast 27 July. Available from http://www.cbc.ca/news/background/osamabinladen/ ressam_timeline.html.

Checkel, Jeffery T. 2001. Why Comply? Social Learning and European Identity Change. *International Organization* 55 (3):553–88.

Citizenship and Immigration Canada. 1999. News Release 99–01. Minister Lucienne Robillard announces new direction for Immigration and Refugee Protection Legislation and Policy.

– 2001a. News Release. Immigration and Refugee Protection Act Introduced.

– 2001b. Bill C-11, Immigration and Refugee Protection Act: What Is New in the proposed Immigration and Refugee Protection Act.

– 2001c. Review of the Immigration Control Officer Network – Final Report.

– 2001d. News Release. Strengthening Immigration Measures to Counter Terrorism. 12 October.

– 2005. Facts and Figures. Immigration Overview. Permanent and Temporary Residents, 2004.

Crépeau, François. 1998. International Cooperation on Interdiction of Asylum-Seekers: A Global Perspective. In *Canadian Council for Refugees, Interdicting Refugees.*

– and Delphine Nakache. 2006. Controlling Irregular Migration in Canada: Reconciling Security Concern with Human Rights Protection. *IRPP Choices* 12 (1).

Dench, Janet. 2001. Controlling the Borders: C-31 and Interdiction. *Refuge* 19 (4):34–40.

Dolowitz, David P., and David Marsh. 2000. Learning from Abroad: The Role of Policy Transfer in Contemporary Policy-Making. *Governance: An International Journal of Policy and Administration* 13 (1):5–23.

Donovan, Kevin. 1987. 7 Detained Refugees Said They'd Kill if Asked, Mounties Testified at Hearing. *The Toronto Star,* 24 July.

Finnemore, Martha, and Kathryn Sikkink. 1998. International Norm Dynamics and Political Change. *International Organization* 52 (4):887–917.

Flockhart, Trine. 2004. 'Masters and Novices': Socialization and Social Learning through the NATO Parliamentary Assembly. *International Relations* 18 (3):89–118.

Florini, Anne. 1996. The Evolution of International Norms. *International Studies Quarterly* 40:363–91.

Gallagher, Stephen. 2002. Towards a Common European Asylum System: Fortress Europe Redesigns the Ramparts. *International Journal* 58 (3):375–94.

Globe and Mail. 1981. Editorial: They Are Not Refugees. 4 December.

Haas, Ernst B. 1991. Collective Learning: Some Theoretical Speculations. In *Learning in U.S. and Soviet Foreign Policy*, edited by G.W. Breslauer and P.E. Tetlock. Boulder, CO: Westview Press.

Haas, Peter M. 1992. Introduction: Epistemic Communities and International Policy Coordination. *International Organizations* 46 (1):1–35.

Hall, Peter A. 1989. Conclusion: The Politics of Keynesian Ideas. In *The Political Power of Economic Ideas: Keynesianism across Nations*, edited by P.A. Hall. Princeton: Princeton University Press.

– 1993. Policy Paradigms, Social Learning, and the State: The Case of Economic Policymaking in Britain. *Comparative Politics* 25 (3):275–96

Hardcastle, Leonie, Andrew Parkin, Alan Simmons, and Nobuaki Suyama. 1994. The Making of Immigration and Refugee Policy: Politicians, Bureaucrats and Citizens. In *Immigration and Refugee Policy: Australia and Canada Compared*, edited by H. Adelman, A. Borowski, M. Burstein, and L. Foster. Vol. 1. Toronto: University of Toronto Press.

Hocking, Brian. 1994. Adaptation and the Foreign Policy Bureaucracy: The Experience of Federal States. *Diplomacy and Statecraft* 5 (1):47–72.

– 2004. Privatizing Diplomacy? *International Studies Perspective* 5(2):147–52

Huysmans, Jeff. 2000. The European Union and the Securitization of Migration. *Journal of Common Market Studies* 38 (5):751–77.

Immigration and Refugee Board (IRB). 1999. Immigration and Refugee Board: Performance Report: Period Ending March 31, 1999.

– 2000. Immigration and Refugee Board: Performance Report: Period Ending March 31, 2000.

– 2001. Immigration and Refugee Board: Performance Report: 2000–2001.

International Organization for Migration (IOM). 2007a. *Regional Consultative Processes: Contributions of RCPs.* Accessed 10 February 2007. Available from http://www.iom.int/jahia/Jahia/cache/offonce/pid/679.

– 2007b. *What is the IGC?* Accessed 23 February 2007. Available from http://www.iom.int/jahia/webdav/site/myjahiasite/shared/shared/mainsite/microsites/rcps/IGC_Flyer.pdf.

Interviews with senior bureaucrats and members of Parliament. Conducted September–December 2005; August–September 2006.

Johnston, Alastair Iain. 1995. *Cultural Realism: Strategic Culture and Grand Strategy in Chinese History.* Princeton: Princeton University Press.

– 2001. Treating International Institutions as Social Environments. *International Studies Quarterly* 45 (4):487–515.

Jones, Deborah. 1987. Migrants Still Detained in Halifax May Get News on Release Today. *Globe and Mail,* 7 August.

Keck, Margaret E., and Kathryn Sikkink. 1998. *Activists Beyond Borders: Transnational Advocacy Networks in International Politics.* Ithaca: Cornell University Press.

Levy, Jack S. 1994. Learning and Foreign Policy: Sweeping a Conceptual Minefield. *International Organization* 48 (2):279–312.

Loriaux, Michael. 1999. The French Developmental State as Myth and Moral Ambition. In *The Developmental State,* edited by M. Woo-Cumings. Ithaca: Cornell University Press.

Macklin, Audrey. 2001. New Directions for Refugee Policy: Of Curtains, Doors and Locks. *Refuge* 19 (4):1–4.

McNamara, Kathleen R. 1998. *The Currency of Ideas: Monetary Politics in the European Union.* Ithaca: Cornell University Press.

Meseguer, Covadonga. 2005. Policy Learning, Policy Diffusion, and the Making of a New Order. *ANNALS of the American Academy of Political and Social Science* 598 (1):67–82.

Parliamentary Standing Committee on Citizenship and Immigration. 1996. Minutes of Proceedings and Evidence. Meeting 3, 19 March 19.

– 1997a. Minutes of Proceedings and Evidence. Meeting 3, 23 October.

– 1997b. Minutes of Proceedings and Evidence. Meeting 5, 27 November.

– 1999a. Minutes of Proceedings and Evidence. Meeting 2, 3 November.

– 1999b. Minutes of Proceedings and Evidence. Meeting 4, 17 November.

– 1999c. Minutes of Proceedings and Evidence. Meeting 5, 24 November.

– 1999d. Minutes of Proceedings and Evidence. Meeting 6, 25 November.

– 2000. *Refugee Protection and Border Security: Striking a Balance.*

– 2001a. Minutes of Proceedings and Evidence Meeting 3, 13 March.

– 2001b. Minutes of Proceedings and Evidence Meeting 9, 5 April.

Parliamentary Standing Committee on Labour, Employment and Immigration. 1987. Minutes of Proceedings and Evidence. Meeting 34, 7 May.

– 1989. Minutes of Proceedings and Evidence. Meeting 2, 11 May.

Parliamentary Standing Committee on Labour, Manpower and Immigration. 1977a. Minutes of Proceedings and Evidence. Meeting 19, 6 May.

– 1977b. Minutes of Proceedings and Evidence. Meeting 30, 2 June.

- 1981. Minutes of Proceedings and Evidence. Meeting 5, 21 May.
- 1982. Minutes of Proceedings and Evidence. Meeting 22, 1 April.
Pierson, Paul. 1993. When Effects Become Causes: Policy Feedback and Political Change. *World Politics* 45 (4):595–628.
Robinson, W.G. 1983. Illegal Migrants in Canada. Report to the Honourable Lloyd Axworthy, Minister of Employment and Immigration.
Rudd, David, and Nicholas Furneaux. 2002. *Fortress North America? What 'Continental Security' Means for Canada.* Toronto: Canadian Institute of Strategic Studies.
Shenstone, Michael. 1997. *World Population Growth and Movement: Towards the 21st Century.* Ottawa: Department of Foreign Affairs and International Trade.
Simmons, Alan B., and Kieran Keohane. 1992. Canadian Immigration Policy: State Strategies and the Quest for Legitimacy. *Canadian Review of Sociology and Anthropology* 29 (4):421–52.
Slaughter, Anne-Marie. 2004. Disaggregating Sovereignty: Towards Public Accountability of Global Government Networks. *Government and Opposition* 39 (2):159–90.
Solomon, Michele Klein. 2005. *International Migration Management through Inter-State Consultation Mechanisms:* United Nations Expert Group Meeting on International Migration and Development. New York: Population Division, Department of Economic and Social Affairs, United Nations Secretariat.
Special Senate Committee on Security and Intelligence. 1999. *Report of the Special Senate Committee on Security and Intelligence.* Ottawa: Minister of Public Works and Government Services Canada
Stein, Janice Gross. 1994. Political Learning by Doing: Gorbachev as Uncommitted Thinker and Motivated Learner. *International Organization* 48 (2):155–83.
Stone, Diane. 1999. Learning Lessons and Policy Transfer across Time, Space and Disciplines. *Politics* 19 (1):51–9.
- 2004. Transfer Agents and Global Networks in the 'Transnationalization' of Policy. *Journal of European Public Policy* 11 (3):545–66.
Surel, Yves. 2000. The Role of Cognitive and Normative Frames in Policy-Making. *Journal of European Public Policy* 7 (4):495–512.
Thouez, Colleen, and Frédérique Channac. 2006. Shaping International Migration Policy: The Role of Regional Consultative Processes. *West European Politics* 29 (2):370–87.
Trempe, Robert, Susan Davis, and Roslyn Kunin. 1997. Not Just Numbers: A Framework for Future Immigration: Legislative Review Advisory Group. Ottawa: Minister of Public Works and Government Services Canada.

Trondal, Jarle. 2001. Is There a Social Constructivist-Institutionalist Divide? Unpacking Social Mechanisms Affecting Representational Roles amongst EU Decision-Makers. *Journal of European Public Policy* 8 (1):1–23.

Wendt, Alexander. 1999. *Social Theory of International Politics.* Cambridge: Cambridge University Press.

Weyland, Kurt, ed. 2004. *Learning from Foreign Models in Latin American Policy Reform.* Washington DC: Woodrow Wilson Center Press.

8 Institutional 'Stickiness' and Ideational Resistance to Paradigm Change: Canada and Early Childhood Education and Care (ECEC) Policy

LINDA A. WHITE

When do ideas become so convincing they overcome past policy practices? This chapter examines the phenomenon of alternative paradigm construction in the case of early childhood education and care (ECEC). Government spending on childcare and pre-primary education programs as a percentage of GDP has increased significantly over the past decade in most OECD countries (OECD 2006, 2011). In most countries, overall ECEC provision rates have grown (ibid.); more children are in non-parental childcare and pre-primary programs in the early 2000s than in the late 1980s. Despite this broad pattern of convergence, there is also divergence. The expansion of ECEC programs and services for young children is uneven across welfare states. Some governments remain reluctant to invest public resources in ECEC programs. Some spend a greater percentage of GDP on childcare programs and others on ECE programs. Some governments target ECEC services and others make them universally available, leading to higher overall provision rates. While some governments contract service delivery to private actors (for-profit and not-for-profit service providers), others deliver the services through public agencies such as schools and municipalities (see tables 8.1–8.4).

Whether such expansion in funding and supply is indicative of paradigm change – reflecting a change in governments' overall goals, policy instruments used to obtain those goals, and the precise settings of those instruments (Hall 1993) – is still subject to debate. Nevertheless, something is happening, particularly in liberal welfare states, to spur policy changes. The first part of this chapter examines the origins of new ECEC ideas and documents the process of alternative paradigm construction that is under way, mainly at the international level among transnational

Table 8.1

Typology of childcare and early childhood education services in selected OECD countries (Liberal ECEC regimes)

	Centre-based care		Family day care		Pre-school		Compulsory school	
Public*								
Private**								
Age	0	1	2	3	4	5	6	7
Australia	Accredited centres and family day care available part time (20 hours) or full time (up to 50 hours)				Reception/pre-school classes, with primary school (full time, out-of-school-hours care also provided)		Compulsory schooling	
Canada	Centre-based and family day care				Junior kindergarten Ontario	Kindergarten/ maternelles in Quebec	Compulsory schooling	
New Zealand	Childcare centres and some home-based services (family day care)		Community-based kindergarten, playcentres			Compulsory schooling		
UK	Nurseries, child minders, and playgroups			Playgroups and nurseries part time	Reception class, with primary school	Compulsory schooling		
USA	Childcare centres and family day care			Educational programs, including Head Start, prek			Compulsory schooling	

* Provision is largely publicly funded and managed (more than 50 per cent of enrolments are in publicly operated facilities).
** Provision is largely managed by private stakeholders (both for-profit and not-for-profit providers) and is publicly and privately financed.

Source: OECD (2011). Notes apply to tables 8.1–8.4.

Table 8.2
Typology of childcare and early childhood education services in selected OECD countries (Liberal mimicking ECEC regimes)

	Centre-based care		Family day care		Pre-school		Compulsory school	
Public								
Private								
Age	0	1	2	3	4	5	6	7
Austria	Tagesmutter (family day care) and Krippen (centres), part time (25 hrs)			Kindergarten (part time, 25 hrs). Out of school care provision under development			Compulsory schooling	
Czech Republic	Crèche (centres), full time			Materska skola (state kindergarten)				
Ireland	Regulated family day care and nurseries (centres)				Early Start and infant school (pre-school) with primary school		Compulsory schooling	
Japan	Centre-based care / Family day care			Kindergartens			Compulsory schooling	
Netherlands	Gastouderopvang (family day care), Kinderopvang (centres) and playgroups				Group 1, with primary school	Compulsory schooling (group 2 onwards)		
Poland	Nurseries			Pre-school/Nursery schools				Compulsory schooling
Portugal	Crèche familiare (family day care) and centres			Jardins de infancia (pre-school)			Compulsory schooling	
Switzerland	Crèche, Krippen, varies across cantons (centres)			Pre-school, mandatory in some cantons			Compulsory schooling	

Table 8.3

Typology of childcare and early childhood education services in selected OECD countries (continental ECEC regimes)

	Centre-based care		Family day care	Pre-school			Compulsory school	
Public								
Private								
Age	0	1	2	3	4	5	6	7
Belgium	Kinderdagverblif (centres) and family day care; crèches, and gardiennes encadarées (family day care) care			Kleuterschool, part time or full time, with out-of-school-hours care; école maternelle, part time or full time, with out-of-school-hours care			Compulsory schooling	
France	Crèche (centres) and Assistant maternelles (family day care), full time			École maternelle (pre-school)			Compulsory schooling	
Germany	Krippen (centres)			Kindergarten (pre-school)			Compulsory schooling	
Greece	Vrefonipiaki stahmi (crèche for children < 2.5 and nursery school for > 2.5			Nipiagogeia (kindergarten)			Compulsory schooling	
Hungary	Bolcsode (crèche), ft (40 hrs)			Ovoda (kindergarten)		Compulsory schooling		
Italy	Asili nidi (crèches) pt (20 hrs) and full time (< 50 hrs)			Scuola dell-infanzia (pre-school)			Compulsory schooling	
Korea	Child care centres			Kindergartens / Hakwon (pre-school)			Compulsory schooling	
Luxembourg	Crèche (centres) and Tagesmutter (family day care)			Enseignement pre-scholaire (pre-school)			Compulsory schooling	
Mexico	Educación inicial (centres)				Compulsory educación prescholar (pre-school)	Compulsory schooling		
Slovakia	Nursery schools			Kindergarten			Compulsory schooling	
Spain	Educación Pre-scolar (centres)			Education infantile (pre-school) with primary school			Compulsory schooling	

Table 8.4
Typology of child care and early childhood education services in selected OECD countries (Nordic ECEC regimes)

	Centre-based care		Family day care		Pre-school		Compulsory school	
Public								
Private								
Age	0	1	2	3	4	5	6	7
Denmark	Dagpleje (family day care) and Vuggestuer (crèches) full time (> 32 hrs)			Bornehaver (kindergarten) full time (> 32 hrs)				Compulsory schooling
Denmark	Adlersintegrer (age-integrated facility) full time (> 32 hrs)						Borne-haver (> 32 hrs)	
Finland	Perhepaivahoito (family day care) and Paivakoti (municipal early child development centres), full time (< 50 hrs)						Esiopetus (pre-school)	Compulsory schooling
Iceland	Day-care centres and 'day mothers' (family day care)			Pre-school			Compulsory schooling	
Norway	Barnehage, including rural familiebarnhager, full time (40 hrs)						Compulsory schooling	
Sweden	Forskola (pre-school), full time (30 hrs), some Familiedaghem (family day care) particularly in rural areas						Forskoleklass (pre-school), part time	Compulsory schooling

actors and international organizations. This chapter argues that transformations in ECEC policies signal the emergence of a variety of new ideas about desirable ECEC policies (White 2011), but those variations across liberal welfare states – Australia, Canada, New Zealand, United Kingdom, and the United States – in ECEC provision and funding indicate that the emergence of a new ECEC paradigm in these jurisdictions is not yet complete (White 2010).

The second part of the chapter examines the curious outlier that is Canada. While other liberal welfare states are increasing significantly their ECEC investment in some manner, Canada, other than Quebec,[1] has remained stubbornly resistant. In seeking explanations for English Canadian resistance to the new alternative paradigm, the chapter highlights the institutional and ideational barriers encountered by political actors supportive of new ECEC ideas. Federalism poses an institutional constraint when either order of government is unconvinced of the need for new policies, given that provincial governments retain substantive jurisdiction over education and social policy, but the federal government maintains more fiscal levers (Friendly and White 2008). Ideational barriers include a lack of scientific and economic consensus on the necessity of ECEC programs to address demographic, labour market, and educational challenges. As well, traditional norms regarding women's roles in the family remain powerfully persuasive politically and help explain societal resistance to non-parental forms of care for young children. The chapter thus highlights both the potential for paradigmatic change as well as the points of resistance in ECEC policy.

The next two sections document the observed changes in ECEC policy provision in recent decades and the explanatory factors driving the introduction of new policy ideas. The section following documents the ideational changes that have occurred in Canada and the institutional and ideological factors preventing these new ideas from being institutionalized.

ECEC Policy Development

Until the 1960s, when women began to enter the labour market in increasing numbers, formal childcare services were scarce, other than for children from disadvantaged backgrounds and often were used to encourage the employment of women on public assistance (Lewis 1992; Gauthier 1996; O'Connor, Orloff, and Shaver 1999). Furthermore, Barnett (1993, 520) notes that it was rare for pre-school children to attend formal educational programs or even to be cared for outside the home for more than a few hours per day.

By the late 1960s and early 1970s, however, a number of countries had begun to pass childcare legislation (Gauthier 1996, 108) and establish or expand public funding for childcare and early childhood education services such as kindergartens. As Turgeon (2009, chap. 2) and others (e.g., Morgan 2006) argue, the increase in women's labour market participation, particularly that of mothers, combined with changes in family structure – that is, the increase in single parenthood and divorce – created a 'crisis of care' that led to growing pressure for the state and market to provide social care services. Those changes experienced in the labour market and the economy at large challenged many of the assumptions upon which the post-war welfare state was built (Turgeon 2009, chap. 2), such as the sustainability of the male breadwinner / female caregiver model in light of an aging population and plunging fertility rates[2] in a number of European and East Asian countries that required economies to expand their labour pool (Daly 2007) and increasing numbers of single-parent families living in poverty (Gornick and Meyers 2003).

Still, by the end of the 1980s very few states had large numbers of children ages zero to three in formal childcare settings, and liberal welfare states had limited ECE programs for children ages three to compulsory school age, although quite a few continental European countries had extensively developed ECE services, including many non-Nordic countries such as Belgium, France, and Italy. These programs were often offered on a part-time basis (e.g., Germany), but some were full time (e.g., Belgium, France; see Gornick and Meyers 2003, 230–1). Starting in the late 1980s, European countries increasingly provided childcare and ECE programs, increasingly on a full-time basis (OECD 2006, 80–1). The OECD (ibid., 104) also notes that countries with comparatively low public expenditure on children's services in the past, such as Ireland, Portugal, the Netherlands, and the United Kingdom, have increased spending.

Measuring Paradigm Change in ECEC Provision

Comparative research on ECEC provision often analyses broad cross-national data such as overall patterns of childcare and ECE provision (e.g., Daly and Rake 2003) in order to determine the extent of cross-national policy change, general shifts in societal norms regarding work and family, and the respective roles of states, markets, and families in providing care. Jensen (2009), for example, explores the extent of ECEC norm change using two quantitative measures: percentage change in public expenditure on childcare and ECE services over time; and the extent to which a country's curriculum tradition emphasizes school readiness rather than social pedagogical tradition (discussed further below). But tracking the scope and nature of ECEC policy change is not easily done by looking at broad policy indicators, such as levels of public spending as a percentage of GDP, overall provision rates, or a country's traditional policy emphasis. For example, a country's total spending on ECEC may be low compared with other policy areas, but that figure may mask significant new investment or significant shifts in instrument choice. As well, overall levels of provision (i.e., the percentage of children who are using services) reveal little about the kinds of services in place, the mandate (educational or otherwise) of those services, and so on. Finally, coding countries' traditional curriculum emphases may not capture the quite radical shifts in both thinking and resultant policies witnessed recently in a number of countries.

Measuring the extent to which the scope and substance of these policy changes are indicative of paradigm change thus requires looking beyond broad policy indicators, such as levels of public spending as a percentage of GDP, overall provision rates, or changes in administrative authority. As Kamerman (2000) argues, we have to look at a number of other indicators that draw our attention to the beliefs about the appropriate roles of states, markets, and families in program provision, including ownership and agent responsible for delivery, funding strategies and targets, age group served, quality and effectiveness indicators, and accountability measures useful to maintaining quality and other policy goals. On the basis of these and other indicators, the changes witnessed in liberal welfare states especially are much less extensive than the broader policy indicators reveal (Friendly, Turgeon, and White 2010) but are still significant enough to warrant social scientific investigation.

Tables 8.1–8.4 identify some distinguishable patterns in ECEC provision. As of the mid-2000s variation can be seen, first, in norms regarding the appropriate age at which children should be attending school on a compulsory basis (ranging from age five in Hungary, Mexico, the Netherlands, New Zealand, and the UK, to age six in most other liberal and conservative welfare states, as well as Finland and Iceland, and to age seven in the rest of the Nordic welfare states and Poland); and second, the extent to which the state should be responsible for educating, socializing, and funding care for children prior to their entry into compulsory school. Governments in liberal welfare states still tend to conceive of public services for children ages zero to four as 'care' rather than 'education,' to be delivered mainly through markets.

Yet it is in the liberal welfare states where some of the greatest growth in public *funding* (though not necessarily public delivery) is occurring, particularly in ECE provision. The UK and USA stand out as current leaders among the liberal welfare states in terms of state expenditure on ECEC programs and Quebec stands out as a leader on childcare spending (OECD 2005, 2011). Surprisingly, given government spending in other social policy areas, the 'Rest of Canada' stands out as a laggard. The proportionately higher spending on ECE programs, especially in the UK and USA, compared with other liberal welfare states does not seem congruous with these countries' spending on primary and secondary education, which appears typical of other liberal welfare regimes.

What Accounts for Changing ECEC Provision?

The literature on policy paradigm change has identified necessary conditions for an alternative paradigm to replace an existing one. Scholars have signalled the role of crisis and perception of failure of the existing paradigm (Hall 1993; Walsh 2000; Wilson 2000); the existence of an alternative paradigm that is politically, economically, and administratively viable (Hall 1989); and a shift in the locus of authority or governing coalition to put in power supporters of the alternative paradigm (Hall 1993). The shift from Keynesianism to Monetarism, for example, occurred as a result of a perceived failure of the old paradigm as well as the perceived viability – politically, economically, and administratively – of the alternative (Hall 1989), often as a result of a shifting governing coalition or a new venue that emerges (Walsh 2000).

Since paradigm change is an intensely political process, the strategies of political actors are hugely important to its outcome (Davis et al. 2005). Some scholars also highlight the role of discourses – systems of communication linked by an underlying logic (Ferree and Merrill 2000, 455) – and strategic frames (i.e., persuasive devices) in shaping the content of policy responses (Surel 2000; Payne 2001). Schmidt (2008) notes that discourses and frames have to be tailored to the political-institutional context in order to be successful. Recent research also investigates the influence of learning processes, especially policy emulation of powerful players (Weyland 2006; Simmons, Dobbin, and Garrett 2008). Internationalization of domestic policy making via a policy role for international organizations and transnational policy actors can also shift the locus of policy making and provide more sources of policy ideas (Mahon and McBride 2008; Orenstein 2008). Finally, Pierson (2000) notes the importance of timing and particular sequencing of events as important factors affecting the persuasiveness of policy ideas.

The ideational literature thus suggests the importance of a number of interrelated factors that can help goad policy change (e.g., Haas, 2008). In what follows, I identify the importance of four interrelated factors influencing ECEC policy change.

Perception of a Crisis to Disrupt Standard Operating Procedures

The policy paradigm literature points to the role of exogenous shocks and other 'elements of rupture' (Surel 2000, 503) that can lead to policy change, such as economic globalization. One important factor prompting public investment in ECEC services appears to have been a change in the way countries approach the issue of economic productivity. As Jenson and Saint-Martin (2003, 93) argue, 'All countries are currently engaged in redesigning their welfare architecture and citizenship regimes'[3] to reflect a *social investment* model of welfare state program delivery out of concern that, under globalization, states will not be able to compete without a highly skilled workforce. This social investment model entails investing in human capital development policies that will ensure that all adults are productive participants in a competitive and globalized economy.

The belief in the need to be competitive in a globalized world of free-flowing capital ties in with human capital development arguments that labour markets need to be flexible and adaptable. That knowledgeable and adaptable workforce is necessary because, as Esping-Andersen argues, 'the only real asset that most advanced nations hold is the quality and skills of their people'; thus, industrialized economies depend more and more on being able to 'mobilize the productive potential of those who today are children' (2002, 28). If schools fail to create that workforce, then a government needs to adopt strategies and policies to make sure its workforce adapts – for example, through job retraining. But research has pointed out that 'remedial policies once people have reached adulthood are unlikely to be effective unless these adults started out with sufficient cognitive and social skills. A social investment strategy directed at children must [therefore] be a center-piece of any policy for social inclusion' (Esping-Andersen 2002, 30).

Given the belief in the importance of having a highly skilled and highly educated workforce in order to compete in an increasingly glo-balized economy, how countries perform on cross-national educational assessments has become increasingly important in swaying policy opin-ion. Since the introduction of the US Department of Education's Trends in International Mathematics and Science Study (TIMSS), especially since 2000, when the OECD introduced its Programme for International Student Assessment (PISA), cross-national benchmarking in educa-tional performance has been possible. The results of those assessments reveal that Canada's and Australia's performances are consistently above average, indeed, near the top of the international rankings, whereas the USA's performance is consistently at or below average on both PISA and TIMSS. The results for New Zealand and the UK vary. In the 1999 TIMSS results (which record figures for England), New Zealand and England performed similarly to the USA (i.e., at an average level) on mathematics achievement of eighth-graders, but while New Zealand and the USA performed similarly on science achievement (at an aver-age level), England performed at an above average level and similarly to Australia and Canada (IES 2008). On PISA assessments (which rec-ord figures for the entire UK), however, New Zealand performed con-sistently well at an above average level, similar to results from Australia and Canada, whereas the UK performed poorly (although not as poorly as the USA, which ranked at or below average among the participating countries; see table 8.5).

Countries that perform relatively poorly on these international rank-ings, such as the UK and USA, are likely to be more willing to invest public funding in early childhood education as a means to improve student test scores. And certainly some of the greatest increases in ECE programs are occurring in the UK and USA. New Zealand's investment in free ECE services for all families seems to disprove that hypothesis. However, New Zealand 's dissatisfaction with its extremely poor per-formance on the 1995 TIMSS assessment (Statistics New Zealand 1998, 30–1) may have prompted its government to invest in ECE.

Congruence of New Ideas with Dominant Paradigms

Surel (2000, 508) notes: 'Far from making a clean slate with the past, a new societal paradigm must in effect be composed of previous cognitive

Table 8.5
PISA country rankings (top 25)

Country	Reading literacy mean scores, PISA 2000*	Country	Mathematics mean scores, PISA 2006	Country	Science mean scores, PISA 2006
Finland	546	Chinese Taipei	549	Finland	563
Canada	534	Finland	548	HK-China	542
New Zealand	529	Hong Kong -China	547	Canada	534
Australia	528	Korea	547	Chinese Taipei	532
Ireland	527	Netherlands	531	Estonia	531
Korea	525	Switzerland	530	Japan	531
United Kingdom	523	Canada	527	New Zealand	530
Japan	522	Macao-China	525	Australia	527
Sweden	516	Liechtenstein	525	Netherlands	525
Austria	507	Japan	523	Liechtenstein	522
Belgium	507	New Zealand	522	Korea	522
Iceland	507	Belgium	520	Slovenia	519
Norway	505	Australia	520	Germany	516
France	505	Estonia	515	United Kingdom	515
USA	504	Denmark	513	Czech Republic	513
Denmark	497	Czech Republic	510	Switzerland	512
Switzerland	494	Iceland	506	Macao-China	511
Spain	493	Austria	505	Austria	511
Czech Republic	492	Slovenia	504	Belgium	510
Italy	487	Germany	504	Ireland	508
Germany	484	Sweden	502	Hungary	504
Liechtenstein	483	Ireland	501	Sweden	503
Hungary	480	France	496	Poland	498
Poland	479	UK...	495	Denmark	496
Greece	474	USA (35th)	474	USA (29th)	489

* PISA 2000 scores are used because PISA 2003 does not include the UK and PISA 2006 does not include the USA.
Sources: OECD PISA (2001, 2007).

and normative structures' To Jenson (2004, 2006) and others (e.g., Jenson and Saint-Martin 2003), the ideas documented above – which focus on social investment – are part and parcel of a neoliberal paradigm that flows logically from liberal ideas that came before. Rather than designing policies and programs to support the traditional male breadwinner / female caregiver and the long-term unemployed, these new policies encourage all adults to participate actively in the labour market. Governments increasingly pay attention to and eliminate the factors that prevent adult labour market participation (such as care-giving responsibilities, illiteracy and poor training, and poverty). Childcare services thus provide an important means of ensuring parents' full-time labour market participation, reducing social exclusion and labour shortages.

In addition, Dobrowolsky and Jenson (2004; see also Jenson 2004) argue that children, rather than adult wage-earners, have become the logical and legitimate subjects of a social investment strategy. Children are the core of this social investment strategy from both a population health and human capital development perspective. By investing in ECEC services, governments not only provide the means to allow parents to participate in the labour market as well as balance work and family life and stave off poverty and social exclusion, but also prepare all children for the future so that they themselves can be productive adults (Jenson 2006, 36–7). As Esping-Andersen et al. (2002, 20) articulate the argument: 'The quality of childhood matters ever more for subsequent life chances' because 'it is in childhood that citizens acquire most of the capital that they, later, will activate in the pursuit of a good life.'

Privileged Body of Knowledge Embodied in Experts
Using Appropriate Policy Frames

Not only is the content of ideas important, but so too are the carriers. Haas (1989, 384n20) and other constructivist scholars stress the important role of an epistemic community: a 'community of experts sharing a belief in a common set of cause-and-effect relationships as well as common values to which policies governing these relationships will be applied.' The scientific grounding of some policy areas privileges the voices of experts such as economists, developmental psychologists, doctors, even neuroscientists, as opposed to traditional policy actors such as childcare advocates and feminist advocacy groups. Haas (2004, 575) argues that these experts' professions carry esteem 'and thus command the greatest social legitimacy and deference when providing policy advice.' The weight of scientific or economic authority, the perceived degree of autonomy and independence of political experts, and the fit of proposed solutions with human capital development concerns, make ideas carried by an epistemic community more persuasive in overcoming traditional resistance to these programs, particularly in liberal welfare states without a strong tradition of support for public ECEC programs.

Institutionalization of Knowledge and Expertise
in Authoritative Offices

Agency-centred analyses of the mainly US-based ECE policy expansion assert that policy change is largely the result of *advocates,* namely, well-endowed lobbyists and skilled 'framers' of the policy debates that exist outside government but who are successfully using their organizational resources to persuade policy makers to act (e.g., Fuller 2007; Imig 2006; Imig and Meyer 2007; Kirp 2007). Other recent research on the US-experience suggests, however, that organized interests and policy entrepreneurs may not have as great an ability to sway policy makers as other researchers believe; there may be no connection between scientific consensus as to 'best practices' and the policies that emerge within a jurisdiction; and governments may play a stronger role in determining the scope and nature of pre-kindergarten policies than research suggests (e.g., Haskins 2005; Phillips and McCartney 2005; Bushouse 2007). Furthermore, Haas (2004, 572) notes that 'we shouldn't assume that all organizations are rational and will automatically recognize and adopt what prove to be the appropriate policy responses.' As Haas argues from analysis of climate change policy, 'science is seldom directly converted to policy. The path from truth to power is a circuitous route at best' (571).

'Usable' knowledge must thus find some way through the hallways of power. Key is that the knowledge is seen as 'accurate and politically tractable for its users' (ibid., 574). It must be credible, that is, believed to be true; believed to be legitimate and 'developed through a process that minimizes the potential for bias'; and salient, that is, presented in a timely manner. In addition, 'It must be capable of mobilizing sufficient political support to produce agreement,' 'capable of generating solutions that can be implemented,' and 'capable of generating solutions that are instrumental towards solving the problems for which they were designed' (575). It is also important that the knowledge be institutionalized in decision-making bodies such as relevant bureaucracies (Walsh 2000, 487).

Canadian ECEC Policy Development

This section observes the policy changes that have occurred, particularly in the 1993–2004 period under the federal Liberal governments of

Prime Ministers Jean Chrétien and Paul Martin. It finds that new ideas about the importance of early childhood education and care to human capital development have been influential in Canada as in other liberal welfare states, prompting the Martin government, in particular, to press for a national 'early learning and child care' or ELCC system, even in the face of federal opposition and some provincial government resistance. Those efforts were supported by a broader policy community in Canada advocating in support of these ideas and were reinforced by a domestic and transnational epistemic communities that have been influential because of the weight of scientific authority they carry. But, as documented below, these ideas also encountered resistance, thus slowing their adoption in Canada.

Federal involvement in childcare support began with the introduction of the federal Canada Assistance Plan (CAP) in 1966. It provided provinces and territories with cost-shared funds to support the cost of childcare for eligible low-income families. Federal conditions determined eligibility, which applied to both service providers and parent users. Although governments at the time conceptualized childcare purely as part of employment support for low-income families, not as an early learning program, the Royal Commission on the Status of Women in Canada recommended in 1970 that a national childcare program should be conceived of more broadly than simply part of social assistance as set up under CAP, and should 'be designed for all families who need it and wish to use it' (Canada 1970, 270).

The Canadian federal government began to talk seriously about federal funding for a national childcare program in the 1980s. Before its defeat in 1984 the Liberal government under Pierre Trudeau appointed the ministerial-level Task Force on Child Care (1986). The new Conservative government, led by Brian Mulroney, established a Special Parliamentary Committee on childcare, and then tabled the Canada Child Care Act (Canada 1988). The legislation died when Prime Minister Mulroney called the 1988 federal election, and the Conservative government did not revisit childcare policy again after its re-election. In 1993 the federal Liberal Party under Jean Chrétien campaigned on plans to spend $720 million on childcare over three years and to create up to 50,000 new regulated spaces per year for three years, but two caveats were added to its election platform promise: spaces would be created only in a year following a year of 3 per cent economic growth; and the program would be introduced only with the agreement of the provinces (Liberal Party of Canada 1993, 38–40). As a result of slow economic growth, that election promise was not fulfilled. Instead, after the 1995 Quebec referendum, the federal government pledged in its 1996 throne speech that it would 'not use its spending power to create new shared-cost programs in areas of exclusive provincial jurisdiction without the consent of a majority of the provinces.' It also stated that 'any new program will be designed so that non-participating provinces will be compensated, provided they establish equivalent or comparable initiatives' (Canada 1996, 4).

By the end of the 1990s the federal government appeared to be getting out of the business of funding national social service delivery, although it agreed in 1997 to the introduction of the National Child Benefit income supplement program. Surprisingly, then, in 2000 the Chrétien government negotiated the Federal-Provincial-Territorial Early Childhood Agreement (ECDA). Signed by all provinces except Quebec in September 2000, it provided federal transfer funds in the amount of $2.2 billion over five years, beginning in 2001–2 to help provincial and territorial governments improve and expand early childhood development programs and services in four priority areas: healthy pregnancy, birth, and infancy; parenting and family supports; early childhood development, learning, and care; and community supports (CICS 2000). Then, in an effort to direct monies more explicitly to childcare programs, in March 2003 the Federal Human Resources Minister Jane Stewart reached an agreement with provincial and territorial ministers responsible for social services (except Quebec), called the Multilateral Framework on Early Learning and Child Care Agreement (MFA). The federal government agreed to provide $900 million over five years, beginning in 2003, to support provincial and territorial government investments in early learning and childcare (ibid., 2003).

Before its defeat in December 2005, the federal Liberal government under Paul Martin negotiated with the provinces to spend an additional $5 billion over five years to build a national ELCC system. Prime Minister Martin was honouring a Liberal pledge in the 2004 election campaign (Liberal Party of Canada 2004, 29). As Friendly and White (2008, 189) argue, 'Getting agreement from the provinces to spend the $5 billion on building a national early learning and child care system became one of the defining issues of the Martin minority government.' The federal-provincial agreements that were signed were cancelled by the Conservative minority government elected in January 2006.

Explaining ECEC Policy Change in Canada

Had the Martin Liberal government returned to office in January 2006, existing intergovernmental ECEC agreements would have been maintained and more would likely have followed. A paradigm change in ECEC in Canada then might have occurred in time. However, it is worth asking why the federal Liberal government invested so much political capital in achieving these agreements when, in the end, they were vote losers; the federal Conservative party ran a successful campaign on 'universal childcare,' which essentially involved the creation of a family allowance of $100 per month per child under age six (Friendly and White 2008). The answer to this question lies with the prime minister himself.[4]

One could argue that Paul Martin was already predisposed to ECEC because of his interest in human capital development, including 'education, training, and research and development' (Delacourt 2003, 76). Martin was one of the authors of the 1993 Liberal election platform (*Red Book*), which contained a 'qualified reference to early childhood learning' and the explicit childcare promise (Liberal Party of Canada 1993, 38–40). One individual interviewed by the author of this chapter stated that it was Chrétien, not Martin, who requested that the growth conditions regarding childcare expansion be included because of budgetary concerns, given how poorly the economy was performing. In his 1996 budget speech, amid the further cuts to federal budgets and one year after the dismantling of CAP, Martin delivered what one individual interviewed by the author of this chapter referred to as 'the education speech': as part of the strategy for 'investing in our future,' Martin announced programs to support students, including raising the limits on tuition credits and Registered Education Savings Plan contributions and broadening eligibility for the federal Child Care Expense Deduction (CCED) to include students and single parents (Martin 1996, 19). Prior to taking over the Liberal leadership in December 2003 Martin held a series of policy roundtables (about twelve to fifteen) covering various policy areas, one of which was ECEC policy. Thus, by the time Martin became party leader, 'he was primed' to embrace a national policy, not of 'daycare' but as he clarified, 'early learning and child care.'[5] The question is, what did the priming?

International Organizations

Evidence suggests that international organizations (IOs) and other internationalization phenomena such as economic globalization played a role in shaping the beliefs of key political actors, including Martin. I focus attention on the OECD because, while a number of IOs have increasingly paid attention to ECEC issues, the OECD has established the largest research program and has been most visible in the industrialized countries in promoting these policies (see, e.g., OECD 2001, 2006, as well as the OECD's country notes and background reports on twenty countries).

Mahon (2006, 173–4, 179) observes that 'the OECD operates as in important source of transnational policy knowledge construction and dissemination,' especially at times when 'states are involved in a process of 'unlearning' old policies ... and learning new ones' While the vision of a successful ECEC strategy offered in the 2001 *Starting Strong Report* and the specific recommendations outlined in the 2006 *Starting Strong II Report* were not radical to some OECD countries, to many others, including Canada, that vision and those recommendations offered are radical, to say the least. Most liberal welfare states, for example, are far away from having established 'a universal approach to access' as well as 'substantial public investment in services and infrastructure' as the reports championed.

To illustrate how contrary the Starting Strong project was to traditional policy approaches in liberal welfare states in particular, we can examine why Canada failed to participate in the initial round of country reviews.[6] When the OECD embarked on its country reviews in the late 1990s, it deliberately adopted the language of 'early childhood education and care' as opposed to the language of 'child care,' which OECD reports and other studies had until then used (e.g., OECD 1990; European Commission Childcare Network 1990). Childcare, however, did not accurately capture the range of formal services that existed in many OECD countries for children under the age of compulsory school, nor did it fully capture the educational thrust behind its research agenda. When the Education Directorate of the OECD contacted country governments to ask them to be part of the review, government officials from Human Resources and Development Canada (HRDC) declined. They pointed out that education was a provincial responsibility. Then, when members of the Canadian delegation to the OECD's 2001 Early Childhood Education and Care: International Policy Issues Conference in Stockholm were successful in persuading the federal government to participate in the second round of reviews, HRDC had difficulty in persuading provincial governments to allow a federal government study in an area of provincial jurisdiction. In the end, only four provinces hosted site visits by the OECD review team: British Columbia, Manitoba, Prince Edward Island, and Saskatchewan (OECD 2004).

Thus, one of the significant impacts of the OECD project in Canada may have been to help link early childhood education and childcare in the minds of Canadian federal and provincial policy officials and to draw attention to the need to link childcare and education services administratively (although federalism concerns prevent those linkages from being made across levels of government). As Porter and Webb (2007) argue, through its knowledge production function, the OECD is also engaged in norm creation.

The other useful part of the OECD exercise was highlighting cross-national policy trends, the implication being that there are leaders and laggards. The power of the OECD thus lies in its peer review function (Pagani 2002). As Pagani argues, 'Peer pressure does not take the form of legally binding acts, as sanctions and other enforcement mechanisms. Instead, it is a means of soft persuasion which can become an important driving force to stimulate the State to change, achieve goals and meet standards' (6). OECD officials interact with country officials during the process of peer review, which can influence those officials' thinking. Peer review can also lead to 'peer pressure,' where the level of public scrutiny exercised during the process and after completion, along with the rankings that are often generated among countries, and domestic media attention and public opinion shifts can pressure change (5).

The OECD study was the first to highlight discrepancies in ECEC provision between liberal welfare states and those of continental Europe. Its two OECD studies with country background reports and country notes allowed policy researchers and advocacy organizations to highlight Canada's comparatively poor performance (e.g., Friendly et al. 2007). In countries where governments tend to be much more willing to borrow policy ideas from other jurisdictions, including IOs, shaming can resonate among domestic policy officials and be picked up by advocacy groups and the media. Indeed, while both Canada and the USA were chastised in the OECD (2001) report as laggards, the Canadian media gave this description much greater play than did the American media.[7] However, as Pagani (2002, 12–13) argues, for peer review and peer pressure to be effective, there must be 'convergence among the participating countries on the standards or criteria against which to evaluate performance,' and there must be mutual trust and credibility in the examiners chosen to conduct the review. One Canadian journalist questioned the credentials of those who conducted Canada's review. Margaret Wente (2004) claimed that the country note was written by 'two of Canada's leading daycare lobbyists.' Although the statement was incorrect, it undermined the credibility of the international team of examiners.[8] One individual interviewed by the author of this chapter also reported that the final version of the OECD country note required 'some negotiation and massage'; the first version of the country note was much harsher, especially with regard to ECEC services for aboriginal peoples in Canada, but it was reworked because federal and provincial governments were in the midst of negotiating policy changes.[9] All of these factors may have contributed to a lessening of peer pressure.

Domestic Epistemic Community

Although the OECD's work appears to have helped shape the domestic policy debate, a great deal of policy work had been done much earlier in Canada to persuade policy makers to act, at least at the federal government level. The OECD's country report on Canada was published in October 2004, but it had been completed a few years earlier and had circulated in Ottawa for a long time prior to its publication. It had been brought to Martin's attention by a member of his staff, who had been a former special adviser to the secretary general of the OECD, as well as by a member of his cabinet. An individual interviewed by the author described the OECD report as 'one of the "proof points" to describing the need' in Canada for a national program, but a domestic epistemic community operating within the centralized, executive-dominated Westminster parliamentary system has been very effective in transmitting ideas to the highest levels of political office in Canada. It has achieved greater (though so far fleeting) policy success than the pre-kindergarten network in the decentralized and fragmented decision-making environment of the USA (Fuller 2007; Kirp 2007).

A number of individuals interviewed for this project emphasized that the scientific underpinnings of arguments as well as the grounding of the ideas in human capital development concerns was 'very important, especially at the early stages' in persuading policy makers to act. Some interviewees emphasized that certain credible actors championing scientific ideas were also key to 'countering the ideologues of the world.' One interviewee claimed that much of the credit for Prime Minister Martin's conversion to ECEC champion was accomplished by Dr Fraser Mustard, founding president of the Canadian Institute for Advanced Research (CIAR, subsequently changed to CIFAR) and 'friends of Fraser Mustard.' Other interviewees highlighted the importance of leaders connected to the business community. Members of the domestic epistemic community included politicians such as Liberal MP John Godfrey, elected in 1993 and chair of the House of Commons Subcommittee on Children and Youth at Risk for much of the Chrétien government years (and one of the 'friends of Fraser Mustard').

The work of CIFAR appears to have been especially influential. Godfrey argues that his own 'conversion' occurred when he was a journalist and editor at the *Financial Post* and came across Mustard's work. CIFAR was established in 1982 to create an international multidisciplinary network of scholars working on complex problems of scientific, economic and social significance. One of its earliest projects was a population health program, which ran from 1987 to 2003 and explored social determinants of health. CIFAR's human development program, which ran from 1993 to 2003, stemmed directly from the population health program to look at social factors that affect not just health but also development, including child development. Some of the leading population health and child development researchers in the country were affiliated with CIFAR's projects. All became 'friends of Fraser Mustard' and academic champions of the need for early child development programs.

In addition to his role in CIFAR's research work, Dr Mustard has been personally influential as the co-chair with Margaret McCain of the Government of Ontario's Early Years study (McCain and Mustard 1999; see also the follow-up report, McCain, Mustard, and Shanker 2007). Mustard also co-authored a report with Frances Picherack (2002) for the Government of British Columbia on the state of early child development in the province. Leading members of the business and financial community, including Charles Coffey (executive vice-president, government and community affairs, RBC Financial Group; Coffey 2003) and David Dodge (former deputy minister of the federal Department of Finance and then governor of the Bank of Canada), credit Mustard's CIFAR work as 'instrumental in expanding the frontiers of our knowledge in this area' (Dodge 2003, 4). Coffey was also co-chair with Margaret McCain of the Commission on Early Learning and Child Care for the City of Toronto (Coffey and McCain 2002).

John Godfrey was a principal architect of change within the federal Parliament. As an MP, Godfrey served as chair of the National Children's Agenda Caucus Committee, chair of the National Liberal Caucus Social Policy Committee, and chair of the House of Commons Standing Subcommittee on Children and Youth at Risk, among other positions. Before being elected in 1993, Godfrey played a small role in writing the 1993 Liberal *Red Book,* whose major authors included Martin, as well as current CIFAR president and CEO Chaviva M. Hošek, Eddie Goldenberg, and Terrie O'Leary, who later went on to serve as Canada's representative to the World Bank and to promote the country's interests in education (Delacourt 2003, 79, 74, 76, 126). Peter Nicholson (former senior policy adviser in the Government of Canada, MLA and Liberal finance critic in Nova Scotia, and then senior vice-president of the Bank of Nova Scotia) and Lester Thurow (MIT economist) also weighed in on the platform at the fall 1991 Liberal conference in Alymer, Quebec (ibid., 74). The election of the Liberals in 1993 led to the importing of those ideas regarding productivity and human capital development to the highest levels of government.

Godfrey and Nicholson, the latter who became the federal Liberals' 'resident brain' and served as the Clifford Clark Visiting Fellow in the Finance Department in 1994–5 (Delacourt 2003, 86) introduced Martin to Fraser Mustard (Nicholson also served as a director and member of the research council of CIFAR). Nicholson then became special adviser to the secretary-general of the Organization for Economic Co-operation and Development (OECD) in 2002–3. When Martin became prime minister, Nicholson returned to Canada to become Martin's deputy chief of staff for policy. Nicholson and Godfrey brought the OECD report to Martin's attention.

People in Prime Minister Chrétien's policy shop were also sympathetic to the idea of early child development – after all, the Chrétien Liberals had introduced the Canada Prenatal Nutrition Program in 1994, implemented the Community Action Program for Children (CAPC) in 1994, and established Aboriginal Head Start in 1995 (Doherty 2007) – but were cautious about major monetary commitments. The evidence presented by the domestic epistemic community of the importance of ECD for human capital development and social equity as well as the benefits for parental labour market participation thus played a big role in convincing the federal government to act, first through the instrument of the ECD agreement and then, under the championing of Jane Stewart, the MFA on childcare. Universal early childhood education and care programs were front and centre in the broader policy discussion on early childhood development in the National Liberal Caucus Social Policy Committee.

One interviewee stated that the human capital development and women's labour market equality rationales resonated most strongly among senior policy makers as justification for a national ELCC program, although different people had different reasons for supporting the policies and programs. The interviewee confirmed, though, that a national system of early learning and childcare was not conceived of simply as an anti-poverty measure or solely a part of human capital development but rather as something broader. In fact, other actors in Ottawa such as Senator Landon Pearson, appointed by the Chrétien government to the Senate in 1994 and who worked with Godfrey on the National Children's Agenda Caucus Committee, championed ECEC as part of a broader children's rights agenda based on Canada's ratification of the UN Convention on the Rights of the Child. The election in 1997 of Claudette Bradshaw, who in 1974 founded the Moncton Headstart Early Family Intervention Centres and who became minister of labour and minister responsible for homelessness in the second Chrétien term, also added to the parliamentary 'bench strength' on these issues. As one interviewee stated, it was useful to present the scientific research when critics tried to reduce ECEC to babysitting.

Evidence that these ideas resonated among both federal and provincial officials lies in the fact that Social Development Canada Minister Ken Dryden managed to execute a series of bilateral agreements with all provinces, including Quebec, to spend an additional $5 billion over five years (beyond the $900 million already committed through the MFA) to build a national system of early learning and childcare based on the QUAD principles: Quality, Universality, Accessibility, and Developmental[ly-focused] programs. In the earlier MFA agreement signed in 2003, all provinces (except Quebec) had agreed to spend federal funds on regulated programs only and had agreed to report annually to Canadians on 'descriptive and expenditure information' using QUAD-based indicators of availability, affordability and quality (CICS 2003). In each of the Agreements-in-Principle (AIPs) signed in 2005 the provinces agreed to provide a general outline along lines similar to those of the MFA (Mahon 2006) as to how the funds were to be used and to develop a more specific action plan for the five-year phase, after which the provincial and federal government would sign a funding agreement. However, when the federal Liberal government fell at the end of 2005 on a non-confidence motion, only two provinces, Manitoba and Ontario, had finished the process; Quebec and the federal government had already signed a five-year funding agreement without an AIP because Quebec's ELCC program was already much more advanced, and seven AIPs were in various stages of progress (Friendly and White 2008). The subsequent loss by the Liberals of the 2006 election highlights the lack of institutionalization these alternative policy ideas.

Constraints on Policy Paradigm Change

Institutional Stickiness

Federalism clearly plays a major role in slowing the pace of paradigmatic change in Canada, a constraint that unitary liberal welfare states such as New Zealand and the United Kingdom do not face. The federal Liberal government is constrained, for example, by jurisdictional issues surrounding federal funding for explicitly educational programs. Whereas the federal government had some role in childcare financing after the introduction of the Canadian Assistance Plan in 1966 (cancelled in 1996) and it has provided some funding for higher education, it has never spent money on children 'who have crossed the threshold to primary and secondary school.' In fact, one interviewee confirmed that the federal government used the language of 'early learning and child care' rather than the OECD standard of 'early childhood education and care' because it was sensitive to the fact that the provinces have exclusive authority over primary and secondary education, and, unlike other social policy areas, primary and secondary education remains a jurisdictionally watertight compartment. 'Learning' is considered a broader term, which can encompass non-school-based educational programs.

In fact, many provinces were very reluctant to agree to the OECD's country review of Canada's ECEC programs, questioning whether the Government of Canada could participate in research in an area of provincial jurisdiction. In the end, only four provinces participated in the OECD country review: British Columbia, Manitoba, Prince Edward Island, and Saskatchewan (OECD 2004). In the absence of a national crisis in educational performance, it is likely that these ECE jurisdictional battles will continue.

Within provincial governments, some reforms of the administrative apparatus to deliver these programs have occurred. Although some provinces are merging responsibility for childcare and education, it still largely rests with two different ministries, usually the Ministry of Education for kindergarten and either a Ministry of Health and Community and Social Services or Children's Services for childcare (Friendly et al. 2007, 195–7).

Political Resistance

The 2006 election revealed that the Liberal government had not had sufficient time to reframe national ELCC policy discourse in order to institutionalize (and insulate) the bilateral agreements. Instead, the 2006 federal election campaign sparked a maelstrom of public debate and newspaper commentary regarding the desirability of non-parental care (see Friendly and White 2008), and the Conservative leader, Stephen Harper, promised to cancel the recently negotiated childcare agreements and to introduce his own 'universal childcare' program (which resembled, in fact, a federal family allowance). The federal Liberals pledged to make the ELCC agreements permanent in the 2006 election campaign (Liberal Party of Canada 2006), while the Conservatives pledged to end the bilateral ELCC agreements after one year and to introduce, instead, a $1,200 taxable allowance for each child under age six (Conservative Party of Canada 2006, 31). The Conservatives followed through on both promises once they assumed office in February 2006. The popularity of the universal childcare benefit made opposition parties hesitant to attack it in the 2008 federal election. The vagaries of the election cycle thus brought a halt to reforms in Canada, whereas the Blair government in the UK had three terms and the Howard government in Australia four terms in office to secure their respective policy reforms.

Lack of a Scientific Consensus as to the Necessity of ECEC Programs

As discussed in earlier sections of this chapter, concerns about creating a skilled workforce are leading many countries to embrace at least the rhetoric of 'social investment' in ECEC services. There have been some profound public funding increases in early learning in some liberal welfare states, particularly the UK and USA, which perform badly on cross-national educational assessments. In contrast, continental European and East Asian welfare states, facing demographic challenges and related labour market shortages, are increasingly turning to childcare programs to encourage both women's labour market participation and higher birth rates (e.g., Gauthier 1996; Peng 2002).

In Canada (and to some extent Australia) 'PISA complacency' as opposed to 'PISA shock' could explain why there is less domestic outcry for early childhood education programs than elsewhere (Martens, Rusconi, and Leuze 2007). As Coulombe (2007) argues, Canada does well not just in terms of overall performance results in cross-national educational assessments but also in terms of other measures such as educational equality of opportunity. That is, the gap between the performance of students from families with high socio-economic status versus low socio-economic status was smaller in Canada on the 2003 PISA than in other industrialized countries. This outcome indicates that 'the Canadian school system does a relatively good job of improving the skills of students with a low socio-economic background and, therefore, of reducing socio-economic disparities' (Coulombe 2007, 59, citing Bussière et al. 2004). In addition, the percentage of students ranked as 'poor' performers on the 2003 PISA was lower in Canada than in every other country save Finland. These outcomes suggest that 'Canada might well have one of the best public education systems in the world for primary and secondary schooling' (Coulombe 2007, 59).

In the absence of a perceived crisis, it may be hard to mobilize policy opinion in support of significant ECEC investment. In fact, half of the six judges on the Canadian-based Institute for Research on Public Policy's (IRPP) Canadian Priorities Agenda recommended against the adoption of a national early childhood development program because there was not enough evidence 'to justify adopting a national template at this time' (Tuohy 2007, 527). Evidence that extremely vulnerable populations are not as prevalent in Canada (other than in aboriginal communities) as in the United States weakens arguments for universal programs.[10] Indeed, it might not be a coincidence that the two provinces with the best scores on international tests – Alberta and Quebec – are also the provinces who demonstrated most resistance to national initiatives.

There is one small irony in the way that governments in Canada deliver ECEC services. Unlike governments in Australia, the UK, and the USA, which have expanded supply of ECEC services in recent years by investing heavily in the ECEC market, governments in Canada retain some antipathy to the wholesale embracing of markets. Despite its relatively low levels of ECEC funding and provision, Canada stands out as an outlier among liberal welfare states for two reasons. First, most (but not all) provincial governments have accepted that if childcare services are to be delivered by the private sector, the governance structure should be predominantly not-for-profit, rather than for-profit (see Friendly et al. 2007 for statistics). Second, most provincial governments have (so far) accepted that, if early childhood education services such as kindergarten are going to be delivered, they should be provided through public schools.[11] Thus, while Canada ranks lowest in the percentage of four-year-olds with access to publicly funded ECE services, it stands out as the only country[12] where those ECE services are predominantly delivered through public schools by trained teachers. This means that any expansion of those services will prove expensive and challenging to implement (Prentice 2006).

Conclusion

This chapter has investigated the causal factors behind ECEC policy changes as well as the points of resistance in Canada. It has argued that alternative policy ideas are emerging that challenge 'taken-for-granted beliefs about what are possible and desirable public policies' (introduction to this text) in the area of early childhood education and care. Certain policy actors are playing key roles in shifting thinking on childhood, the nature of learning, and the kinds of programs necessary for successful child and adult lives. International organizations, while not their creators, popularize the ideas that are bubbling up from the domestic (and increasingly transnational) epistemic communities (White 2004). The scientific underpinnings of those policy ideas are crucial in persuading policy makers to act. Furthermore, international organizations and epistemic communities, as authoritative actors, provide the authoritative evidence that these policies are needed for a host of reasons, including human capital development, social development, and gender equality. It is not yet clear whether these new ideas are evidence of the emergence of a new paradigm, but they certainly are contributing to some policy changes and, in particular, public financing of ECEC services in liberal welfare states.

This chapter has also examined the puzzle of explaining Canada as an outlier in the context of ECEC investment. It has argued that internationalized ideas have encountered barriers in the form of institutional and ideational stickiness in Canada. Key political decision makers attempted to implement extensive ECEC investment in the 2000s, but provincial governments acted as veto players, as did federal opposition parties. Pockets of societal opposition to non-parental forms of care galvanized the federal Conservatives to reject federal-provincial-territorial plans for major ECEC investment, and the absence of an educational, employment, or demographic crisis created resistance in the federal and some provincial bureaucracies to further ECEC investment. Analysis of ECEC provision thus contributes to our theoretical and empirical understanding of the factors that contribute to growth, shrinkage, or stagnation of contemporary welfare states and to the literature on what makes a paradigm successful.

ACKNOWLEDGMENTS

Financial support for this research was provided by the Social Sciences and Humanities Research Council of Canada grant #72033728. The author gratefully acknowledges the helpful comments of Jane Jenson, Paul Kershaw, and Rianne Mahon on an earlier draft of this chapter.

NOTES

1 In 1997 the Quebec government began to phase in its publicly funded universal early learning and childcare program, beginning with expansion of kindergarten to full day for all five-year-olds. It then gradually implemented a five dollar per day parent fee for regulated childcare – raised to seven dollars per day in 2003 by a provincial Liberal government – and provided capital funding to encourage the expansion of childcare spaces in not-for-profit *centres de la petites enfances* – centre-based and family day care (Friendly et al. 2007, xviii).
2 Gauthier (1996, 2-3) argues that 'demographic changes have been a major driving force in bringing population and family issues to the political agenda and influencing the development of related policies,' although political ideology and country history has determined particular governments' reactions to those concerns.
3 Jenson and Saint-Martin (2003, 93) define a citizenship regime as 'the institutional arrangements, rules and understandings that guide and shape concurrent policy decisions and expenditures of states, problem definitions by states and citizens, and claims-making by citizens' and, in particular, the 'responsibility mix' between states, markets, and families regarding social reproduction and the boundaries of rights inclusion in a political community.
4 This section is based on confidential interviews with people connected to the federal Liberal government.
5 Prime Minister Paul Martin's exchange with Ottawa Bureau Chief John Geddes, in a year-end interview (macleans.ca, 17 Dec. 2004) was as follows: Geddes: 'Social Development Minister Ken Dryden is expected to deliver

big things on early childhood education in 2005. Why are you focusing on nationwide daycare rather than just helping parents, no matter how they choose to raise their young kids?'; Martin: 'First of all, this is not daycare, this is early learning and child care. We want to make sure that children are ready to excel as soon as they go to formal school, regardless of income.'

6 The following information is based on a presentation given on 15 August 2001 by one of the Canadian delegates to the OECD's Early Childhood Education and Care: International Policy Issues Conference held in Stockholm, 13-15 June 2001.

7 For documentation of the media reports and advocacy organization responses to the OECD (2004) country report, see CRRU's issue file. Available from http://www.childcarecanada.org/res/issues/oecdthematicre viewcanadareports.html. See, for example, Strang and Chang (1993, 250) on the US's non-participation in international standard setting on social welfare through the ILO and its refusal to sign the Kyoto Protocol.

8 The OECD's international team consisted of John Bennett from the OECD, Bea Buysse from Belgium, Païve Lindberg from Finland, and Helen Penn from the UK (OECD 2006, 438). The background report, in contrast, as in all countries, was written by three in-country experts (Doherty, Friendly, and Beach 2003) and was commissioned by the Government of Canada.

9 Pagani (2002, 13) states, 'The involvement of the reviewed State in the process and its ownership of the outcome of the peer review is the best guarantee that it will ultimately endorse the final report and implement its recommendations. However, the State's involvement should not go so far as to endanger the fairness and the objectivity of the review. For example, the State under review should not be permitted to veto the adoption of all or part of the final report.'

10 However, see Doherty (2007) on the problems of pinpointing vulnerable populations.

11 For information on the creation of full-day early learning in Ontario, see the Ministry of Education's website: http://www.edu.gov.on.ca/earlylearning/.

12 The state of Oklahoma similarly delivers its universal ECE program through public schools (Barnett et al. 2006).

REFERENCES

Barnett, Steven W. 1993. New Wine in Old Bottles: Increasing the Coherence of Early Childhood Care and Education Policy. *Early Childhood Research Quarterly* 8 (4):519–58.

Battle, Ken, and Sherri Torjman (in collaboration with the National Liberal Caucus Social Policy Committee). 2002. *Architecture for National Child Care.*

Ottawa: Caledon Institute of Social Policy. Available from http://www.ontla.on.ca/library/respository/mon/5000/10309539.pdf.

Bushouse, Brenda. 2007. Universal Preschool Policy Change in the Pioneer States. Paper read at the Annual Meeting of the American Political Science Association, 30 August–2 September, Chicago.

Bussière, Patrick, Fernando Cartwright, Tamara Knighton, and Todd Rogers. 2004. *Measuring Up: Canadian Results of the OECD PISA Study*. Cat. No. 81–590-XPE – No. 2. Ottawa: Statistics Canada.

Canada. 1970. Royal Commission on the Status of Women in Canada. *Report of the Royal Commission on the Status of Women*. Ottawa: Information Canada.

– 1986. Task Force on Child Care. *Report of the Task Force on Child Care* (Cooke Report). Ottawa: Status of Women Canada.

– 1988. House of Commons. Bill C-144. An Act to authorize payments by Canada toward the provision of childcare services, and to amend the Canada Assistance Plan in consequence thereof. Second Session, Thirty-Third Parliament. Ottawa: Minister of National Health and Welfare.

– 1996. House of Commons. Speech from the Throne to Open the Second Session, Thirty-Fifth Parliament of Canada. *Debates of the House of Commons of Canada*. 27 February.

CICS (Canadian Intergovernmental Conference Secretariat). 2000. *First Ministers' Meeting Communiqué on Early Childhood Development*. Ref. 800–038/005 (11 Sep.). Available from http://www.scics.gc.ca/cinfo00/800038005_e.html.

– 2003. Multilateral Framework on Early Learning and Child Care. Ref. 830–779/005 (13 March). Available at http://www.scics.gc.ca/cinfo03/830779005_e.html.

Coffey, Charles. 2003. *Never Too Early to Invest in Children: Early Childhood Education and Care Matters to Business! Report*. Toronto: Voices for Children.

– and Margaret McCain. 2002. *Commission on Early Learning and Childcare for the City of Toronto: Final Report*. Toronto: City of Toronto.

Conservative Party of Canada. 2006. *Stand Up for Canada*. Federal Election Platform. Ottawa: Conservative Party of Canada.

Coulombe, Serge 2007. Smart Human Capital Policy: An Alternative Perspective. In *A Canadian Priorities Agenda: Policy Choices to Improve Economic and Social Well-Being*, edited by J. Leonard, C. Ragan, and F. St-Hilaire. Montreal: Institute for Research on Public Policy.

Daly, Kevin. 2007. Gender Inequality, Growth and Global Ageing. Goldman Sachs Global Economics Paper No. 154. Available from http://www.ftd.de/wirtschaftswunder/resserver.php?blogId=10&resource=globalpaper154.pdf.

Daly, Mary, and Katherine Rake. 2003. *Gender and the Welfare State*. Cambridge: Polity Press.

Davis, Gerald F., Doug McAdam, W. Richard Scott, and Mayer N. Zald, eds. 2005. *Social Movements and Organization Theory*. New York: Cambridge University Press.

Delacourt, Susan. 2003. *Juggernaut: Paul Martin's Campaign for Chrétien's Crown*. Toronto: McClelland and Stewart.

Dobrowolsky, Alexandra, and Jane Jenson. 2004. Shifting Representations of Citizenship: Canadian Politics of 'Women' and 'Children.' *Social Politics* 11:154–80.

Dodge, David. 2003. Human Capital, Early Childhood Development, and Economic Growth: An Economist's Perspective. Speech at the 14th Annual Meeting of the Sparrow Lake Alliance, Bayview-Wildwood Resort, Ontario.

Doherty, Gillian. 2007. Ensuring the Best Start in Life: Targeting versus Universality in Early Childhood Development. *IRPP Choices* 13 (8).

Esping-Andersen, Gosta. 2002. A Child-Centred Social Investment Strategy. In Esping-Andersen et al., *Why We Need a New Welfare State*.

– Duncan Gaillie, Anton Hemerijck, and John Myles. 2002. *Why We Need a New Welfare State*. Oxford: Oxford University Press.

European Commission Childcare Network. 1990. *Childcare in the European Community, 1985–1990*. Brussels: The Commission.

Ferree, Myra Marx, and David A. Merrill. 2000. Hot Movements, Cold Cognition: Thinking about Social Movements in Gendered Frames. *Contemporary Sociology* 29:454–62.

Friendly, Martha, and Linda A. White. 2008. From Multilateralism to Bilateralism to Unilateralism in Three Short Years: Child Care in Canadian Federalism, 2003–2006. In *Canadian Federalism: Performance, Effectiveness and Legitimacy*. 2nd ed. Edited by G. Skogstad and H. Bakvis. Toronto: Oxford University Press.

Friendly, Martha, Jane Beach, Carolyn Ferns, and Michelle Turiano. 2007. *Early Childhood Education and Care in Canada, 2006*. Toronto: Childcare Resource and Research Unit.

Fuller, Bruce. 2007. *Standardized Childhood: The Political and Cultural Struggle over Early Education*. Stanford: Stanford University Press.

Gauthier, Anne Hélène. 1996. *The State and the Family: A Comparative Analysis of Family Policies in Industrialized Countries*. Oxford: Clarendon Press.

Gornick, Janet C., and Marcia K. Meyers. 2003. *Families that Work: Policies for Reconciling Parenthood and Employment*. New York: Russell Sage Foundation.

Haas, Peter. 1989. Do Regimes Matter? Epistemic Communities and Mediterranean Pollution Control. *International Organization* 43:377–403.

– 2004. When Does Power Listen to Truth? A Constructivist Approach to the Policy Process. *Journal of European Public Policy* 11:569–92.

– 2008. Trafficking in Ideas: Constructing International Environmental Governance. Paper read at the Munk Centre for International Studies, 4 April, University of Toronto.

Hall, Peter A. 1989. Conclusion: The Politics of Keynesian Ideas. In *The Political Power of Economic Ideas*, edited by P.A. Hall. Princeton: Princeton University Press.

– 1993. Policy Paradigms, Social Learning, and the State: The Case of Economic Policymaking in Britain. *Comparative Politics* 25:175–96.

Haskins, Ron. 2005. Child Development and Child-Care Policy: Modest Impacts. In *Developmental Psychology and Social Change*, edited by D.B. Pillemer and S.H. White. New York: Cambridge University Press.

IES (Institute of Education Sciences, US Department of Education). 2008. *TIMSS 1999 Results Highlights*. Available from http://nces.ed.gov/timss/results99_1.asp.

Imig, Doug. 2006. Building a Social Movement for America's Children. *Journal of Children and Poverty* 12 (1):21–37.

– and David S. Meyer. 2007. The Politics of Universal Pre-Kindergarten. Paper read at the Annual Meeting of the American Political Science Association, 30 August–2 September, Chicago.

Jensen, Carsten 2009. Institutions and the Politics of Childcare Services. *Journal of European Social Policy* 19 (1): 7–18.

Jenson, Jane. 2004. Changing the Paradigm: Family Responsibility or Investing in Children. *Canadian Journal of Sociology* 29 (2):169–92.

– 2006. The LEGO Paradigm and New Social Risks: Consequences for Children. In *Children, Changing Families and Welfare States*, edited by J. Lewis. Cheltenham, UK: Edward Elgar.

– and Denis Saint-Martin. 2003. New Routes to Social Cohesion? Citizenship and the Social Investment State. *Canadian Journal of Sociology* 28 (1):77–99

Kamerman, Sheila B. 2000. Early Childhood Education and Care: An Overview of Developments in OECD Countries. *International Journal of Educational Research* 33:7–29.

Kirp, David. 2007. *The Sandbox Investment: The Preschool Movement and Kids-First Politics*. Cambridge, MA: Harvard University Press.

Lewis, Jane. 1992. Gender and the Development of Welfare Regimes. *Journal of European Social Policy* 2:159–73.

Liberal Party of Canada. 1993. *Creating Opportunity: The Liberal Plan for Canada (Red Book)*. Ottawa: Liberal Party of Canada.

– 2004. *Moving Canada Forward: The Paul Martin Plan for Getting Things Done*. Ottawa: Liberal Party of Canada.

– 2006. *Securing Canada's Success*. Ottawa: Liberal Party of Canada.

Mahon, Rianne. 2006. Main Features of the Early Learning and Child Care
   Bilateral Agreements. Available from http://b2c2.org/pdfs/riannes-table.pdf.
– and Stephen McBride, eds. 2008. *The OECD and Transnational Governance.*
   Vancouver: UBC Press.
Martens, Kerstin, Alessandra Rusconi, and Kathrin Leuze, eds. 2007. *New
   Arenas of Education Governance: The Impact of International Organizations and
   Markets on Educational Policy Making.* New York: Palgrave Macmillan.
Martin, Paul. 1996. *Budget Speech (6 March).* Ottawa: Department of Finance.
McCain, Margaret, and Fraser Mustard. 1999. *Reversing the Real Brain Drain.
   Early Years Study Final Report.* Toronto: Children's Secretariat of Ontario.
McCain, Margaret, Fraser Mustard, and Stuart Shanker. 2007. *Early Years Study
   2: Putting Science into Action.* Toronto: Council for Early Child Development.
Morgan, Kimberly J. 2006. *Working Mothers and the Welfare State.* Stanford:
   Stanford University Press.
Mustard, Fraser, and Frances Picherack. 2002. *Early Childhood Development in
   BC: Enabling Communities.* Toronto: Founders Network.
National Institute for Early Education Research. 2006. *The State of Preschool:
   2006 State Preschool Yearbook.* Brunswick, NJ: NIEER, Rutgers University.
O'Connor, Julia S., Ann Shola Orloff, and Sheila Shaver. 1999. *States, Markets,
   Families: Gender, Liberalism and Social Policy in Australia, Canada, Great Britain
   and the United States.* New York: Cambridge University Press.
OECD (Organization for Economic Cooperation and Development). 1990.
   Employment Outlook July 1990. Paris: OECD.
– 2001. *Starting Strong: Early Childhood Education and Care.* Paris: OECD.
– 2004. *Early Childhood Education and Care Policy: Canada Country Note.*
   Paris: OECD.
– 2005. *Babies and Bosses: Reconciling Work and Family Life.* Vol. 4: *Canada,
   Finland, Sweden and the United Kingdom.* Paris: OECD.
– 2006. *Starting Strong II: Early Childhood Education and Care.* Paris: OECD.
– 2011. *Enrolment in Day-care and Pre-schools (PF 11).* OECD Family Database.
   Available from www.oecd.org/els/social/family/database.
OECD PISA. 2001. Knowledge and Skills for Life: First Results from the
   OECD Programme for International Student Assessment (PISA) 2000.
   Paris: OECD.
– 2007. *PISA 2006: Science Competencies for Tomorrow's World.* Vol 1: *Analysis.*
   Paris: OECD.
Orenstein, Mitchell A. 2008. *Privatizing Pensions: The Transnational Campaign
   for Social Security Reform.* Princeton: Princeton University Press.
Pagani, Fabrizio. 2002. Peer Review: A Tool for Co-operation and Change:
   An Analysis of an OECD Working Method. OECD General Secretariat,
   Directorate for Legal Affairs Working Paper SG/LEG (2002)1.

Payne, Rodger A. 2001. Persuasion, Frames and Norm Construction. *European Journal of International Relations* 7:37–61.

Peng, Ito. 2002. Social Care in Crisis: Gender, Demography, and Welfare State Restructuring in Japan. *Social Politics* 9 (3):411–43.

Phillips, Deborah, and Kathleen McCartney. 2005. The Disconnect between Research and Policy on Child Care. In *Developmental Psychology and Social Change: Research, History, and Policy*, edited by D.B. Pillemer and S.H. White. New York: Cambridge University Press.

Pierson, Paul. 2000. Not Just What but When: Timing and Sequence in Political Processes. *Studies in American Political Development* 14:72–92.

Porter, Tony, and Michael Webb. 2007. The Role of the OECD in the Orchestration of Global Knowledge Networks. Unpublished paper presented at the Annual Meeting of the Canadian Political Science Association, Saskatoon, Saskatchewan.

Prentice, Susan. 2006. Childcare, Co-production and the Third Sector in Canada. *Public Management Review* 8 (4):521–36.

Royal Commission on the Status of Women in Canada. 1970. *Report of the Royal Commission on the Status of Women*. Ottawa: Information Canada.

Schmidt, Vivien A. 2008. Discursive Institutionalism: The Explanatory Power of Ideas and Discourse. *Annual Review of Political Science* 11:303–26.

Simmons, Beth A., Frank Dobbin, and Geoffrey Garrett, eds. 2008. *The Global Diffusion of Markets and Democracy.* New York: Cambridge University Press.

Statistics New Zealand. 1998. New Zealand Now: Children. Wellington: Statistics New Zealand.

Strang, David, and Patricia M.Y. Chang. 1993. The International Labour Organization and the Welfare State: Institutional Effects on National Welfare Spending, 1960–1980. *International Organization* 47 (2):235–62.

Surel, Yves. 2000. The Role of Cognitive and Normative Frames in Policy-Making. *Journal of European Public Policy* 7 (4):495–512.

Tuohy, Carolyn Hughes. 2007. Policy Priorities for Canada: Making Choices. In *A Canadian Priorities Agenda: Policy Choices to Improve Economic and Social Well-Being*, edited by J. Leonard, C. Ragan, and F. St-Hilaire. Montreal: Institute for Research on Public Policy.

Turgeon, Luc. 2009. Tax, Time and Territory: The Development of Early Childhood Education and Child Care in Canada and Great Britain. Unpublished dissertation, Department of Political Science, University of Toronto.

Walsh, James I. 2000. When Do Ideas Matter? Explaining the Successes and Failures of Thatcherite Ideas. *Comparative Political Studies* 33 (483–516).

Wente, Margaret. 2004. The Horrors of Unregulated Daycare. *Globe and Mail*, 16 November, A19.

Weyland, Kurt. 2006. *Bounded Rationality and Policy Diffusion: Social Sector Reform in Latin America*. Princeton: Princeton University Press.

White, Linda A. 2004. Trends in Child Care / Early Childhood Education / Early Childhood Development Policy in Canada and the United States. *American Review of Canadian Studies* 34 (4):665–87.

– 2010. Must We All Be Paradigmatic? Social Investment Policies and Liberal Welfare States. Unpublished manuscript.

– 2011. The Internationalization of Early Childhood Education and Care (ECEC) Issues: Framing Gender Justice and Child Well-Being. *Governance: An International Journal of Policy, Administration and Institutions* 24 (2):285–309.

Wilson, Carter A. 2000. Policy Regimes and Policy Change. *Journal of Public Policy* 20 (3):247–74.

9 Conclusion

GRACE SKOGSTAD

Amid a proliferating literature on the importance of ideas to public policy development, this collection has focused on those constellations of ideas or policy paradigms that, in Peter Hall's (1993, 290, 279) terms, structure 'what can and should be done in a sphere of policy.' This focus has led the contributors to this book to map domestic policy paradigms and developments around them, including their continuity and transformation, in national macro-economic and social policies in western European countries (Schmidt, chapter 2), family policy in Germany (Kollman, chapter 5), immigration policies in the United States and Canada (Triadafilopoulos, chapter 6), refugee policy in Canada (Irvine, chapter 7), and early childhood education and care (ECEC) policies in Canada (White, chapter 8). There has also been a focus on the development of transnational paradigms in case studies of accounting standards and vehicle safety standards (Porter, chapter 3) and in risk regulation of genetically modified organisms in the EU (Skogstad, chapter 4).

These empirical studies enable some conclusions to be drawn about the questions at the fore of this collection. They are, first, which of the differing conceptualizations of policy paradigms / paradigm change are most satisfactory? Second, does transnationalism – where this term refers to norms and epistemes inscribed in dominant global frames and institutions, as well as to the endeavours of transnational political actors to construct and diffuse geographically epistemes, norms, and even paradigms – have an impact on domestic policy paradigm development? If so, do transnational ideas and actors always work in interaction with domestic institutional and other contextual factors so that the policy ideas of domestic actors are ultimately determinative of paradigm developments? And third, do we need to revise our theories of policy paradigms to take account of policy making in a transnational context?

The answers that emerge from this volume in response to the first question about how best to conceptualize policy paradigms and their processes of change are, first, policy paradigms vary in their coherence and commensurability; replacement paradigms may be something entirely new or they may be amalgams of ideas in earlier paradigms as well as new ideas. Second, changes in material circumstances are precipitating conditions for paradigm development/change, but whether these openings lead to paradigm change depends upon the capacity of strategic political actors to interpret them in a way that makes the case for change. Third, there is more than one pathway to paradigm change; it can be evolutionary and the result of cumulative changes over time, or it can be relatively quick, depending upon the institutional framework of policy making.

The answer provided to the second question is that transnational actors do make a difference to the construction, diffusion, and implementation of policy paradigms. They do so in all of the following ways: by directly building a consensus across parties on standards of behaviour, by de-legitimating some standards of appropriate behaviour and legitimating other standards, by constructing (new) authoritative knowledge about how best to understand the nature and causes of problems, and by socializing domestic actors to new understandings of their identity and new norms of behaviour. What gives transnational actors this influence are their resources – of expertise, moral standing, legal authority, and public support. At the same time, domestic institutional factors and the discursive strategies and political resources of domestic actors loom large in accounts of paradigm change.

As to the third question of whether we need to revamp our theories of policy paradigms to take into account the potential influence of transnationalism, the analyses here indicate that we do. Most obviously, we need to be alert to the possibility that new policy ideas/paradigms originate outside the domestic arena – in international organizations or as a result of agreement among private economic actors; that the balance of power between competing policy paradigm coalitions is affected by the ability of domestic actors to leverage the ideas and resources of transnational actors to their advantage; and, less obviously, that the content and stability of sectoral policy paradigms are affected by their congruence or incongruence, not only with domestic developments in other policy arenas and domestic 'meta' ideas, but also with global and regional 'meta' ideas, particularly those that are inscribed in treaties, international conventions, and formal institutions.

Conceptualizing Policy Paradigms and Their Development and Change

The Introduction to this book signalled a debate about the constituent features of policy paradigms that has implications for their resilience. Are policy paradigms best conceptualized as relatively internally coherent ideas that are 'taken for granted and unamenable to scrutiny' for a period of time, and incommensurable with the paradigms that replace them (Hall 1993, 279)? Or are they likely to be not wholly consistent, contested even while they hold sway, and shared to some degree with other paradigms, including those they replace (cf. Jobert 1989; Surel 2000; Sabatier and Jenkins-Smith 1993; Carstensen forthcoming)? The empirical analyses here provide evidence for both positions.

On the one hand, there are policy paradigms whose ideas are relatively coherent, readily distinguishable from their rivals, and incommensurable from them in fundamental respects. German family policy, Canadian and American immigration policies, and Canadian refugee policy all are good examples. Germany's traditional family paradigm protected and promoted the nuclear family made up of a married heterosexual couple and their biological children; its replacement recognizes other family forms, including same-sex unions, as a human right (chapter 5). Through to the post-World War II period, Canadian and American immigration paradigms were underwritten by scientific and normative ideas that relied on notions of racial hierarchy and white supremacy. Their replacement paradigm takes equality of peoples, regardless of race, as its starting point (chapter 6). Canada's refugee protection paradigm through to the late 1990s prioritized refugee protection and providing opportunities for refugee claimants similar to those available to Canadian citizens. By contrast, the security-control paradigm that has replaced it puts priorities of national security and public safety ahead of providing opportunities for refugee claimants and increasingly views the latter as a threat, rather than as needing protection (chapter 7).

On the other hand, some policy paradigms contain conflicting ideas and are at least partly commensurable with one another. Schmidt (chapter 2) argues that this is the case for social and economic policy paradigms in Europe. Porter (chapter 3) eschews the notion of 'paradigm'

as an ideational construct to advance an alternative conception of paradigms as 'assemblages': that is, as 'relatively autonomous and far-flung
humans, objects and networks to manage complex problems.' Using
this conceptualization and the examples of vehicle safety and accounting standards, Porter argues that new and old paradigms can share
common elements but differ insofar as these elements are reassembled
in the new paradigm in a distinct way. For example, the global accounting standard paradigm that has replaced different American and EU
standards incorporates both US and EU standards. At the same time,
Porter also argues that there are limits to the commensurability of policy
paradigms that are enmeshed in different physical settings. While both
standards for safe vehicles and accounting practices are entangled with
their material environment, the greater materiality of vehicle safety
standards – comprising the physical properties of the vehicle and the
physical environment in which vehicles are driven – has impeded the
emergence of a single paradigm to harmonize American and European
standards.

Besides vehicle safety and accounting standards, another example of
replacement paradigms including ideas of earlier, antecedent paradigms,
is the EU's GMO risk regulation paradigm. The idea in the 1990 EU GMO
paradigm – that GMOs are novel entities with unique risks – persists in
the reconstituted paradigm in the early twenty-first century, even while
additional ideas, including that GMO risks are scientifically ascertain-
able and that the consumer has a right to know, are found in the new
paradigm (chapter 4). A final example is German family policy. While its
goals have shifted – from promoting the nuclear family of a heterosexual
couple and their biological children to bestowing rights on loving, intimate family relationships, regardless of the couple's sexuality – the new
paradigm retains the 'marriage instrument' of its predecessor. Like the
traditional family paradigm, it recognizes civil relationships and bestows
rights and duties on monogamous couples.

A second debate, also signalled in the Introduction to this book, cen-
tred on the agents and precipitating conditions of paradigm change
and the relative importance of policy anomalies and paradigm failures,
crises, and other events as precipitating conditions for paradigm
change. It also addresses the relative importance of different social and
political actors – including transnational political actors – as agents of
paradigm construction, diffusion, and implementation.

Empirical analyses presented in this volume suggest that changing material and normative circumstances have the capacity to trigger

policy change, but whether they do so depends upon the capacity of strategic actors to interpret them in a way that persuades others that new ways of thinking are needed and/or desirable. Contextual changes acquire significance for policy paradigm development when political actors succeed in bringing 'new perceptions and new ways of thinking' (Béland and Cox 2010, 11) to them and/or can point to how they raise 'pressing problems' that extant ideas are unable to deal with (Carson, Burns, and Calvo 2009, 21). This finding is not dissimilar to Hall's argument that paradigm change is triggered by policy anomalies and policy failures. (Porter's conceptualization of policy paradigms as entanglements of ideational and material factors leads him to reject anomalies as an explanation of paradigm developments.) Social structural shifts – material and normative – are prominent in several accounts of paradigm change. The European same-sex union norm was given a hearing in Germany, Kollman argues, because the normative basis of the traditional family had begun to erode under evidence of higher divorce rates, increasing numbers of single-parent households, and a cultural shift towards greater tolerance of homosexuality (chapter 5). Canadian and American immigration paradigms through to the post-World War II period, argues Triadafilopoulos, were underwritten by a *transnational* normative context shaped by scientific racism, imperialism, and intense nationalism. These paradigms, he argues, were challenged by a series of 'transformative events and processes' that included the discrediting of assumptions about inborn racial differences in intelligence, character, personality, or cultural or social traits by scientific studies and the Nazi atrocities; a global human rights regime emerging; and decolonization. The 'friction' between the old paradigm and this altered context opened the door in both countries for a shift to a new paradigm in which restrictions of immigrants based on racial and ethnic criteria were no longer permissible (chapter 6).

Early childhood education and care (ECEC) policies represent another case of altered socio-economic conditions creating a context conducive to new policy paradigms. Economic globalization, with competitiveness pressures, states White, has heightened policy makers' belief in the need for flexible and adaptable labour markets. The diffusion of the ECEC paradigm across countries is a response to this contextual change and is supported by social scientific thinking that investment in early childhood education makes labour markets more flexible and competitive. The failure of the same paradigm to diffuse (in Canada under the Harper Conservative government) can be explained at least in part by the anomaly between its epistemic claims and Canada's experience of high educational achievement in the absence of ECEC programs (chapter 8).

The EU GMO risk regulation case also supports theorizing about how events in the broader normative and social context affect the legitimacy of an extant policy paradigm and its rivals, as well as its course of development. Two events were decisive. One was the crisis in the loss of authority and legitimacy of EU-level institutions to regulate GMOs, itself precipitated by events that included the BSE debacle and food safety crises. The other was external to the EU and entailed the US decision to use WTO rules to promote its own rival risk regulation paradigm. Resolving the legitimacy crisis, policy makers agreed, required stronger norms of transparency, accountability, and public participation in EU GMO risk regulation. Responding effectively to the US action, they concluded, required a stronger scientific basis for EU GMO risk regulation.

A final case of the impact of both changes in the material environment and altered norms is Canadian refugee policy. A sharp spike in the number of migrants making refugee claims, a perceived rise in abuse of the refugee system by criminals, and boatloads of Chinese migrants off Canada's west coast did require decision makers to rethink Canadian refugee policy, argues Irvine. Nonetheless, Canada's problems with refugees were relatively modest compared with those of European countries and the United States. Irvine argues that what was decisive in changing Canada's refugee paradigm to one that limited the flows of unauthorized migrants and their access was a shift in the norms of Canadian bureaucrats. Their willingness to interpret Canada's migratory pressures in light of the broader experience of western liberal democracies rendered anomalous the normative basis of Canada's refugee protection paradigm and promoted the shift to the security-control paradigm.

These cases provide compelling evidence in support of the proposition that structural and normative changes create an environment conducive to fundamental/paradigm change, but that what is ultimately consequential to paradigm development is the *interpretation* political actors give of events and structural changes and how such interpretations shape others' understandings of appropriate and effective public policies (Calder 2008; Chin and Stubbs 2011). Such interpretations need to be tailored to the specific institutional context of policy making, as Schmidt (chapter 2) argues, and they will normally include arguments that go beyond 'cognitive necessity' to include the 'normative legitimacy' of reform.

Transnationalism and Policy Paradigms

The case studies here affirm analyses elsewhere that the ideas of transnational political actors and those dominant in global and regional regimes affect domestic policy paradigm development. They do so in several ways.

First, transnational political actors directly shape policy paradigm development by acting as agents who build a consensus across parties on standards of behaviour. The example here is of private economic actors working through international organizations to create regional and global vehicle safety and accounting standards. Their incentive to develop harmonized paradigms has been driven by competitiveness concerns; discrepancies between a US-oriented policy paradigm and a European-oriented one have created unwanted costs for international business actors. As noted above, these efforts have been successful in accounting standards but less so in vehicle safety standards (chapter 3).

Second, transnational actors shape policy paradigm developments through their *knowledge-making and remaking activities* in the international arena. As theorists of policy paradigms have argued (Hall 1993; Carson, Burns, and Calvo 2009, 24), paradigm transition often revolves on the success of political actors in de-legitimating existing experts and their expertise/knowledge and legitimating other experts and expertise. Transnational knowledge makers and domestic ideational entrepreneurs often interact in this process. White argues that although many of the transformative ideas around ECEC in Canada had been 'bubbling up' from domestic policy actors, international organizations have 'popularized' these ideas, and provided the 'authoritative evidence' that policies based on these ideas are needed. OECD reports, in particular, says White, affected the thinking of officials in the Liberal government headed by Prime Minister Martin by drawing attention to the need to link childcare and education services administratively and, further, pointing out that Canada is a laggard in ECEC.

Knowledge-making activities are not the exclusive preserve of professionally trained experts and, as suggested above, civil society groups can play an active role in this process. In GMO risk regulation in the EU, transnational consumer and environmental advocacy groups, in conjunction with the European Parliament, have played such a role. Consistently and discursively, these actors have successfully constructed 'truth claims' about GMOs that have undermined the knowledge-making authority of national regulators and an EU-wide epistemic community of scientific experts. What has given the truth claims of non-governmental actors political force is their resonance with the European public, a factor that is consistent with Seabrooke's (2006) argument that the 'everyday legitimacy' of the public is highly consequential to transformative policy change. At the same time, the knowledge claims of other actors, most notably the United States and professionally trained scientists, have also shaped the EU GMO risk regulation paradigm. The US has been able to turn to an authoritative international institution, the World Trade Organization, to force the EU to incorporate elements of the US policy paradigm in its own GMO policies.

Third, transnational actors legitimate new international norms and create a normative context that has effects on policy paradigms when it undermines domestic decision makers' identity and their ability to realize their policy goals. Triadafilopoulos argues that opponents of racial discrimination in Canada and the United States 'took advantage' of the new normative context of human rights to argue the 'lack of fit' between these countries' liberal-democratic identity and their extant immigration policy paradigms. Vulnerable to charges of hypocrisy and seeking to avoid the costs of reputation loss, Canadian and American decision makers eventually reformed the racist immigration policies that were hampering their ability to pursue their domestic and foreign policy objectives (chapter 6).

Fourth, transnational actors can also teach domestic social and political actors new norms and new understandings of their identity that, in turn, shape paradigm development. Kollman argues that the German lesbian, gay, bisexual, and transgendered (LGBT) movement changed its core goal and identity under the dual influences of the transnational LGBT European movement and the soft norm it promoted, which the EU adopted for the legal recognition of same-sex relationships. The German LGBT redefined itself from a sexual liberation movement to a human rights movement, abandoning the rhetoric of sexual liberation to argue that all citizens, regardless of their sexual orientation, should have access to the same human rights. In Kollman's view, the new language and goals, amid the European norm, were crucial to the success of the German LGBT movement: 'The European norm gave the LGBT movement the language, goals, and framework necessary to find politi-cal allies in the German political establishment and to work with these allies to define a common political project' (chapter 5).

Irvine provides another example of the indispensible role of trans-national actors in socializing domestic political actors to new under-standings, without which paradigm change would not have occurred. He argues that an explanation of paradigm change in Canadian refu-gee policy in the 1990s would be 'incomplete' without considering the role of a transnational network of bureaucrats in socializing Canadian bureaucrats to an alternative understanding of refugees. Through their interaction with colleagues from like-minded states, Canadian officials built a 'common identity' and 'sense of community' that led them to a different understanding of Canada's refugee system (as inadequate and open to abuse). Having accepted this (new) definition of refugees as a problem, Canadian bureaucrats also accepted the solution proposed by their peers from other countries: policies that prioritized state security and refugee controls over refugee protection.

In engaging in these various activities and thereby affecting policy paradigm development, transnational actors who possess resources – of expertise, moral standing, legal authority, and public support – are more influential than those who lack these resources. International organizations delegated legal authority by their members, such as the EU and the WTO, are well placed to affect policy paradigm develop-ments. Both German family policy and EU GMO risk regulation are two good examples. In the first example, the EU's increasingly strin-gent anti-discrimination measures, argues Kollman, were requisite to convincing sceptical German policy makers and members of the pub-lic to accept the premise of the rights-based family policy paradigm. EU institutions also played a 'crucial role' in entrenching Germany's new family policy paradigm when the European Court of Justice (ECJ) upheld an EU directive stipulating that survivors in registered partner-ships receive the same pension benefits as married spouses. Germany's Constitutional Court accepted the ECJ decision to rule that withhold-ing the rights and benefits that accrue to married couples from same-sex registered partners violated the German Basic Law. In the second example, the EU's GMO risk regulation paradigm has been affected by the legal authority of both EU and WTO institutions. The EU's legal authority (over intra-EU environmental, food safety, and internal mar-ket regulation, as well as external trade policy) has both made it a cen-tral node for transnational advocacy group activity and required it to find a compromise across competing GMO risk regulation paradigms. In exercising its legal authority to uphold international trade agreements to which the EU and its member states are signatories, the WTO has eliminated the possibility that the EU GMO risk regulation would incorporate the precautionary principle as a long-term basis for GMO risk regulation.

Still, international organizations' exercise of their legal – and coercive – authority to decisively shape paradigm debates can be controversial, as GMO risk regulation indicates. Accordingly, the more legitimate role of international organizations in paradigm developments is likely to be in their 'soft-law' role of establishing benchmarks and guidelines of good performance. That role appears to be enhanced when it interacts with non-state civil society groups and/or epistemic communities (Stone 2003, 2004; Djelic and Sahlin-Andersson 2006; Mahon and McBride 2008). For example, like the Martin Liberal government in Canada, the OECD and the epistemic community that developed the ECEC paradigm and highlighted leaders and laggards on ECEC were successful by virtue of their 'soft persuasion' and 'priming' of governments,.

The capacity of global government networks to transform domestic policy, argues Irvine (chapter 7), does not come from their exercise of formally delegated state authority or from their linkages to civil society groups. Rather, the importance of international bureaucratic networks lies in their capacity to socialize officials who are in a central position in the domestic decision-making process and who thereby can act as 'conduits' for transferring new thinking from the international to the domestic arena.

The examples of vehicle safety and accounting standards indicate that international organizations with formal legal authority (the EU and the WTO) are not necessary actors in transnational policy paradigm developments. In these cases, the 'private authority' of economic actors (Cutler, Haufler, and Porter 1999) has catalysed change, but their actions have been coordinated in international organizations where public officials have often been present.

Notwithstanding arguments that transnational actors and ideas have made the difference in paradigm developments, a working premise of this book, as signalled in the Introduction, has been that it is what domestic political actors are able to make of transnational ideas that is ultimately decisive. Both the institutional framework and the cultural context of domestic policy making affect domestic political

actors capacity to deploy transnational actors in the service of paradigm change. As the chapters in this book affirm, institutional decision-
making rules and procedures have an impact on paradigm-shifting
efforts by determining who has access to decision-making bodies, the
resources and power of state and non-state actors, and their incentives
and opportunities to forge coalitions. A sharp distinction in terms of
institutional arenas that affect all of these – access, resources, coalition
incentives – can be made between institutional settings that entail single
veto players compared with those that consist of multiple veto players
(Tsebelis 1995). Another important distinction is between institutional
contexts that make it possible to shift debates and decisions to friend-
lier venues and those that do not (Baumgartner and Jones 1993).

   As theorized elsewhere (Risse-Kappen 1995; Orenstein 2008), single
veto player systems expedite paradigm change once the veto player
has been persuaded of the need for change. In the aftermath of World
War II, when both Canadian and American governments faced unstop-
pable pressure to reform their immigration paradigms, the concentra-
tion of decision-making authority in the Canadian executive, combined
with the relative insulation of Canadian policy makers from societal
pressures, made the transition in the domestic immigration policy
paradigm easier, quicker, and more complete in Canada than it was
in the American 'separation of powers' system of multiple veto players. Canada's single veto player system on refugee admission policies also expedited paradigmatic change in Canadian refugee policy
(chapter 6).

   However, single veto player systems do not appear to have any advantages for actors seeking paradigm change when those with a monopoly on decision making are not convinced of the need for change. As
Canadian ECEC policy demonstrates, single veto player systems can be
as 'institutionally sticky' as multiple veto player systems. In Canada's
federal system, provincial governments' exclusive authority over primary education requires the Government of Canada to obtain provincial agreement for ECEC policies. This institutional constraint initially
delayed the transition to an ECEC paradigm. Another institutional
feature – the executive-dominated parliamentary system – enabled the
Conservative Party that replaced the defeated Liberal government to ter-
minate paradigm-shifting federal-provincial agreements (chapter 8).

   By contrast, the EU cases confirm that multi-veto player systems provide domestic and transnational political actors bent on policy change
with an important strategic resource: the opportunity to shift policy

debates to more sympathetic venues of decision making (Keck and Sikkink 1998, 1999; Guiraudon 2000; Pralle 2003; Princen 2007). The European and German LBGT movements pursued venue shifting to good effect, eliciting support for their cause across different sites of authority (parliaments, courts, and executives). The legal authority of non-elected institutions – notably, domestic courts in the form of the German Federal Constitutional Court – was important in maintaining the family policy shift when Laender governments challenged the legality of the law recognizing same-sex unions (chapter 5).

Venue-shifting strategies also characterized the transnational advocacy groups that mobilized around EU GMO risk regulation policies. Venue shifting occurred not only across national states and the EU, but also from the EU to the WTO. Shifting responsibility to the WTO to determine the legality of EU GMO regulations proved an adroit strategy for the American-based pro-biotechnology coalition to influence the EU GMO risk regulation paradigm (chapter 4).

The three Canadian cases – ECEC, immigration policy, and refugee policy – provide an opportunity not only to contrast the impact of different decision-making rules and structures on paradigm developments within a single country, but also to reflect on the proposition that policy ideas diffuse across culturally similar states that share, for example, languages and social norms (Simmons and Elkins 2004; Weyland 2005). On the one hand, human rights norms in good standing in the international arena (or at least in liberal democracies) have diffused into Canadian immigration and refugee policies. On the other hand, Canada is an outlier in the group of liberal welfare states that have adopted the ECEC paradigm. Perhaps Canadians' beliefs about the appropriate role of each of families, states, and markets in providing early childcare and education need to change for Canadians to become more culturally similar to their liberal peers. Or perhaps the proposition that countries emulate and learn from their cultural cousins overstates the influence of shared cultural norms.

Theorizing Policy Paradigm Development in a Transnational Context

A third and final objective of this book has been to address the adequacy of conceptualizations of policy paradigms and theories of paradigm change in light of the emergence of transnational actors and their efforts to construct, legitimate, and diffuse policy ideas and policy paradigms cross-nationally. The summary of chapter findings that has been presented in the preceding section indicates, first, the need to expand our analyses beyond domestic borders to identify the sources of policy paradigms and their core ideas. Second, it also suggests that the dynamics and outcomes of paradigm contestation will be better understood if we take into account the ideas and resources of transnational actors.

And third, attentiveness to the transnational context of policy paradigm development directs greater attention to 'meta' ideas and policy-nested effects. Meta ideas are ideas, like the authority of science, that prevail across policy spheres (what Jobert and Muller 1987 refer to as a 'global référentiel'). Sectoral policy ideas are nested within meta ideas, even while they may be complementary to or in conflict with them in some respects. While domestic sectoral policies are certainly nested within dominant polity-wide ideas (ECEC policies, for example, in neoliberalism), international organizations sometimes institutionalize meta ideas. Carson, Burns, and Calvo (2009, 375) argue that policy paradigm development in the EU takes place within a context of 'first-order guiding principles' that are institutionalized in EU treaties, and that specify appropriate relationships between states, markets, and citizens in realizing economic integration goals but also constitutive principles for social, environmental, and health policy paradigms. Taking into account the transnational context means being alert to the influence of such guiding principles on sectoral policy paradigms.

At the same time, the case studies in this book have not suggested the need to revise our thinking that there are two possible different paths and processes of paradigm change. Sometimes paradigm change occurs in policy networks of either bureaucratic officials or private economic actors who are insulated from the partisan arena and the public. The respective examples here are accounting and vehicle safety standard setting, Canadian refugee policy, and, to a considerable degree, Canadian immigration policy. This insulated model, consistent with Schmidt's observation in chapter 2 that coordinative discourses may sometimes suffice, suggests that dynamics of learning and persuasion (including socialization) are at the fore. The closed policy networks that characterize vehicle safety and accounting standards coordination are also consistent with theorizing elsewhere that technical policy paradigms are the preserve of elites (Campbell 1998; Newman 2008). However, neither refugee nor immigration policy is technical in the same sense, and the wide latitude that Canadian appointed and elected officials have had in transforming these policies, so that they are more consistent with regional and global norms, owes much (as discussed further below) to the autonomy provided them by Canada's executive-dominated parliamentary government.

At other times, policy paradigm change entails a mixture of top-down and bottom-up interactions in which communicative discourses across a host of mobilized political actors become crucial (Schmidt, chapter 2). In this pathway, and consistent with Hall's (1993) theorizing, the outcomes of debates and political contestation across societal groups, epistemic elites, and political leaders are decisive. This model describes most instances of paradigm change described in this book: American immigration policy, EU GMO risk regulation, German family policy, and Canadian ECEC policy. Here, powering dynamics are fully evident as state and non-state actors used their positional advantages and political resources to promote, delay, and even reverse (in the case of Canada's Conservative government and ECEC) paradigm change.

The two models correspond with two paces of policy paradigm change. One, as illustrated by the Canadian refugee paradigm change, is relatively quick, even while change may follow attacks on the preceding paradigm for some time. The other is slower and is much as Hall (1993) described it. As in Canadian and American immigration policies, it entails decision makers' first attempting to salvage existing paradigms by 'stretching' them and trying to shore up them. These efforts only hasten the paradigm's 'unravelling' in terms of its intellectual coherence and administrative efficiency, and eventually the paradigm is abandoned. This process can be lengthy; in the case of Germany's family policy, paradigm change was achieved only after a ten-year period of legislative initiatives and judicial rulings in both Germany and the EU.

When paradigm change occurs over an extended period of time – as a sequence of reactions to earlier decisions/events – some junctures and events are nonetheless likely to be more important than others. While specific events, such as the election or defeat of politicians sympathetic to a new paradigm, are undoubtedly important and likely to have larger consequences than others, it is usually the combination of several factors that matters (Capano 2009, 27). Inevitably, then, there will be considerable contingency in the outcomes of paradigm contestation.

Compared with case studies that have examined the role of transnational actors, including international institutions, in processes of paradigm change in developing countries (cf. Hall 2003; Stone 2003; Orenstein 2008), the case studies here suggest a much stronger role for domestic civil society actors. At the same time, they affirm literature's main theme that transnational actors can and do make a difference to policy paradigm development. Yet much more research is clearly needed to uncover more fully how domestic and transnational ideational activity, institutions, and contexts interact to affect policy paradigm developments. One line of desirable research would be to explore more systematically how processes of paradigm development in the EU differ from those in liberal democracies such as Canada and the United States. North American and European liberal democracies share many cultural values, but they differ in other ways that theorizing would suggest is consequential for policy paradigm developments. Most obviously, all paradigm development in the EU takes place in a transnational context wherein the European Commission often acts as policy entrepreneur (cf. ibid.; Coleman and Tangermann 1999; Garzon 2006; Jabko 2006) and does so in a 'a networked polity' (Ansell 2000) of transnational networks of state and non-state political actors that is likely without parallel elsewhere. Comparative case studies across the Atlantic will help to determine just what difference these institutional differences make to paradigm development. In addition, we need more studies of the construction and implementation of transnational paradigms. There is ample reason to expect that clashes between national paradigms will provide incentives for the development of transnational paradigms. As they do, the constraints on transnational paradigms – posed, for example, by the material embeddedness of paradigms and contextually specific constructions of legitimate knowledge/ expertise – will become clearer, as will the competing pressures from a variety of transnational actors around their development.

REFERENCES

Ansell, Chris. 2000. The Networked Polity: Regional Development in Western Europe. *Governance* 13 (2):279–91.
Baumgartner, F.R., and B.D. Jones. 1993. *Agendas and Instability in American Politics*. Chicago and London: University of Chicago Press.
Béland, Daniel, and Robert Henry Cox. 2010. Introduction: Ideas and Politics. In *Ideas and Politics in Social Science Research* edited by D. Béland and R.H. Cox. New York: Oxford University Press.
Calder, Kent E. 2008. Critical Junctures and the Contours of Northeast Asian Regionalism. In *East Asian Multilateralism: Prospects for Regional Stability,* edited by Kent E. Calder and Frances Fukuyama. Baltimore: Johns Hopkins University Press.

– and Min Ye. 2004. Regionalism and Critical Junctures: Explaining the 'Organization Gap' in Northeast Asia. *Journal of East Asian Studies* 4 (2):191–226.

Campbell, John L. 1998. Institutional Analysis and the Role of Ideas in Political Economy. *Theory and Society* 27:377–409.

Capano, Giliberto. 2009. Understanding Policy Change as an Epistemological and Theoretical Problem. *Journal of Comparative Policy Analysis: Research and Practice* 11 (1):7–31.

Carson, Marcus, Tom R. Burns, and Dolores Calvo, eds. 2009. *Paradigms in Public Policy: Theory and Practice of Paradigm Shifts in the EU.* Frankfurt: Peter Lang.

Carstensen, Martin. Paradigm Man vs. the Bricoleur: Bricolage as an Alternative Vision of Agency in Ideational Change. *European Political Science Review,* 3 (1):147–67.

Chin, Gregory, and Richard Stubbs. 2011. China, Regional Institution-Building and the China-ASEAN Free Trade Area. *Review of International Political Economy,* forthcoming.

Coleman, William D., and Stefan Tangermann. 1999. The 1992 CAP Reform, the Uruguay Round and the Commission: Conceptualizing Linked Policy Games. *Journal of Common Market Studies* 37:385–405.

Cutler, A. Claire, Virginia Haufler, and Tony Porter, eds. 1999. *Private Authority and International Affairs.* Albany: SUNY Press.

Djelic, Marie-Laure, and Kerstin Sahlin-Andersson, eds. 2006. *Transnational Governance: Institutional Dynamics of Regulation.* New York: Cambridge University Press.

Dobbin, Frank, Beth Simmons, and Geoffrey Garrett. 2007. The Global Diffusion of Public Policies: Social Construction, Coercion, Competition or Learning? *Annual Review of Sociology* 33:449–72.

Garzon, Isabelle. 2006. *Reforming the Common Agricultural Policy: History of a Paradigm Change.* New York: Palgrave Macmillan.

Guiraudon, V. 2000. European Integration and Migration Policy: Vertical Policy-Making as Venue Shopping. *Journal of Common Market Studies* 38 (2):251–7.

Hall, Peter A. 1993. Policy Paradigms, Social Learning, and the State: The Case of Economic Policymaking in Britain. *Comparative Politics* 25:175–96.

Hall, Rodney Bruce. 2003. The Discursive Demolition of the Asian Development Model. *International Studies Quarterly* 47 (1):71–99.

Jabko, Nicholas. 2006. *Playing the Market: A Political Strategy for Uniting Europe, 1985–2005,* Ithaca: Cornell University Press.

Jobert, B. 1989. The Normative Frameworks of Public Policy. *Political Studies* 37:376–86.

– and P. Muller. 1987. *L'état en action*. Paris: Les Presses Universitaires de France.

Keck, M.E., and K. Sikkink. 1998. *Activists Beyond Borders: Advocacy Networks in International Politics*. Ithaca: Cornell University Press.

– 1999. Transnational Advocacy Networks in International and Regional Politics. *International Social Science Journal* 51 (159):89–101.

Mahon, Rianne, and Stephen McBride. 2008. *The OECD and Transnational Governance*. Vancouver: UBC Press.

Newman, A.L. 2008. Building Transnational Civil Liberties: Trans-governmental Entrepreneurs and the European Data Privacy Directive. *International Organization* 62 (1):103–30.

Orenstein, Mitchell A. 2008. *Privatizing Pensions: The Transnational Campaign for Social Security Reform*. Princeton: Princeton University Press.

Pralle, Sarah B. 2003. Venue Shopping, Political Strategy, and Policy Change: The Internationalization of Canadian Forest Advocacy. *Journal of Public Policy* 23 (3):233–60.

Princen, Sebastiaan. 2007. Advocacy Coalitions and the Internationalization of Public Health Policies. *Journal of Public Policy* 27 (1):13–33.

Risse-Kappen, Thomas. 1995. Bringing Transnational Relations Back In: Introduction. In *Bringing Transnational Relations Back In: Non-State Actors, Domestic Structures and International Institutions*, edited by T. Risse-Kappen. Cambridge: Cambridge University Press.

Sabatier, Paul A., and H.C. Jenkins-Smith. 1993. *Policy Change and Learning: An Advocacy Coalition Approach*. Boulder, CO: Westview Press.

Seabrooke, Leonard. 2006. *The Social Sources of Financial Power: Domestic Legitimacy and International Financial Orders*. Ithaca: Cornell University Press.

Simmons, Beth A., and Zachary Elkins. 2004. The Globalization of Liberalization: Policy Diffusion in the International Political Economy. *American Political Science Review* 98 (1):171–89.

Stone, Diane. 2003. The 'Knowledge Bank' and the Global Development Network. *Global Governance* 9:43–61.

– 2004. Transfer Agents and Global Networks in the 'Transnationalization' of Policy. *Journal of European Public Policy* 11 (3):545–66.

Surel, Yves. 2000. The Role of Cognitive and Normative Frames in Policy-Making. *Journal of European Public Policy* 7:495–512.

Tsebelis, George. 1995. Decision Making in Political Systems: Veto Players in Presidentialism, Parliamentarism, Multicameralism, and Multipartyism. *British Journal of Political Science* 25: 289–326.

Weyland, Kurt. 2005. Theories of Policy Diffusion: Lessons from Latin American Pension Reform. *World Politics* 57:262–95.

Contributors

J.A. Sandy Irvine holds a PhD from the University of Toronto and lectures in the Department of Political Science at McMaster University.

Kelly Kollman is a Senior Lecturer in Politics in the School of Social and Political Sciences at the University of Glasgow.

Tony Porter is a Professor of Political Science at McMaster University.

Vivien Schmidt is Jean Monet Professor of European Integration, Director of the Center for International Relations, and Professor of International Relations at Boston University.

Grace Skogstad is a Professor of Political Science at the University of Toronto.

Triadafilos (Phil) Triadafilopoulos is an Assistant Professor of Political Science at the University of Toronto.

Linda A. White is an Associate Professor of Political Science and Vice-Principal of Woodsworth College at the University of Toronto.

Studies in Comparative Political Economy and Public Policy

www.ingramcontent.com/pod-product-compliance
Lightning Source LLC
Chambersburg PA
CBHW032123020426
42334CB00016B/1048